1982 Supplement

CONSTITUTIONAL LAW

1982 Supplement

Kauper and Beytagh
CONSTITUTIONAL LAW:
Cases and Materials

Fifth Edition

Francis X. Beytagh
Dean and Professor of Law
University of Toledo

Little, Brown and Company   *Boston and Toronto*

Library of Congress Catalog Card No. 79-89120

ISBN 0-316-48355-9

FG

Published simultaneously in Canada
by Little, Brown & Company (Canada) Limited

PRINTED IN THE UNITED STATES OF AMERICA

Contents

Table of Cases

(Principal cases are in italics. In addition to new cases decided during the 1979-1980, 1980-1981, and 1981-1982 Terms, earlier cases cited and discussed at some length in the supplement are included.)

Preface

The Fifth Edition of this casebook was published in the spring of 1980 and has been in use during the past two academic years in a number of law schools across the country. The book is intended principally as a teaching tool, and it is satisfying to have the impression that it is serving that purpose effectively. Faculty and students alike seem to appreciate my attempt to perpetuate one of the book's distinctive characteristics — inclusion of fuller opinions than one finds in most such casebooks. Others have commented favorably on the transitional notes and the questions at the end of many of the principal cases. The material in the Notes is sometimes extensive, but is included to ensure thorough coverage of a matter that may be of particular interest to certain persons. Listings of secondary materials are obviously provided for reference purposes, and the Selected Bibliography and congressional statutes relating to civil rights (both included in the Appendix) have been viewed as adding strength to the book as a research vehicle. More generally, the book's straightforward yet flexible organization has been regarded as a distinct asset.

As the preface to the casebook indicates, its coverage extends through the end of the Court's 1978-1979 Term. Materials from the 1979-1980 and 1980-1981 Terms were contained in an earlier supplement. The current supplement includes not only those materials, in an edited form, but also contains opinions and related materials from the 1981-1982 Term. Thus, the 1982 Supplement is intended to update the book through the inclusion of materials from the past three Terms. New principal cases include Fullilove v. Klutznick (the minority contractor set-aside decision explicating and building on *Bakke* in the context of so-called reverse discrimination), Harris v. McRae (the abortion funding case presenting privacy together with equal protection issues arising in the wake of Roe v. Wade and its progeny), Richmond Newspapers, Inc. v. Virginia (the case involving the extent to which the First Amendment protects the access of the media to courtrooms during criminal trials), Lassiter v. Department of Social Services of Durham County (an important procedural due process decision dealing with the right of indigents to counsel in child custody cases), Rostker v. Goldberg (where the Court upheld the all-male draft registration requirement over an equal protection challenge), Haig v. Agee (the passport revocation decision presenting right to travel, free speech, and procedural due process questions in the national security context), and Valley Forge Christian College v. Americans United for Separation of Church and State (containing a comprehensive review and restatement of the Court's position on the standing issue). In addition, several new principal cases from the 1981-1982 Term have been included, as indicated in the Table of Contents. Other cases of some consequence are discussed in narrative form, with language from Court opinions included where it seems particularly pertinent. References to leading articles in legal journals published during the past three years, as well as to important federal statutory developments, have been included as well. Finally, errata are provided to the extent that they relate to the substance of the materials contained in the casebook. In order to accommodate cases decided toward the end of the 1981-1982 Term, it was necessary to provide for an addendum to the basic supplement.

I would like to express sincere thanks to several persons who assisted me in preparing this supplement. In particular, my research assistants, Frederick R. Troncone and Alan M. Schall, worked closely with me, and my secretaries, Susan K. Bail and Shirley A. Baker, assisted in typing the manuscript. Members of the Toledo and other law faculties have provided me with helpful comments and suggestions, some of which I have sought to incorporate in this supplement and others of which I hope to include in the next edition of the casebook. The assistance of the personnel of the Law Division of Little, Brown and Company is also appreciated. I am pleased to have received considerable commentary on the casebook from teachers and from students. It is our responsibility as legal educators to assist those who study law to gain as great an understanding as possible of the increasingly complex subjects to which they are exposed in our law schools. To the extent that casebooks such as the Fifth Edition, kept current by supplements like this one, facilitate that process, our efforts are worthwhile and the task of preparing such materials is a rewarding one.

Francis X. Beytagh

Toledo, Ohio
July 1982

Chapter One

The Federal Judiciary in Our Constitutional System

Page 6:

In line 13 of the first full paragraph in Marbury v. Madison change "31" to "3d."

Page 11:

In line 7 of the first paragraph of Note 2, change "no mention of" to "little reliance on."

Page 12. At the end of the second paragraph of Note 5 add:

Berger, The Scope of Judicial Review: An Ongoing Debate, 6 Hastings Const. L.Q. 527 (1979).

Page 13. At the end of Note 7 add:

Kaufman, The Essence of Judicial Independence, 80 Colum. L. Rev. 671 (1980).

Page 14. At the end of Note 9 add:

Ginsburg, Some Thoughts on Judicial Authority to Repair Unconstitutional Legislation, 28 Clev. St. L. Rev. 301 (1979); Prygoski, Supreme Court Review of Congressional Action in the Federalism Area, 18 Duq. L. Rev. 197 (1980).

Page 25:

In line 7 of the second full paragraph in Muskrat v. United States, change "actively" to "actually."

Page 32. At the end of Note 5 add:

Brilmayer, The Jurisprudence of Article III: Perspectives on the "Case or Controversy" Requirement, 93 Harv. L. Rev. 297 (1979).

Page 35. At the end of Note 1 add:

See Princeton University v. Schmid, — U.S. — , 102 S. Ct. 867, — L. Ed. 2d — (1982), where the Court held, in a per curiam decision, that it lacked an adequate jurisidictional ground to resolve the dispute presented. The Court reasoned that, because the University had revised the allegedly unconstitutional regulation which formed the basis of this suit, the entire question had become moot.

Page 41. After Note 4 add:

For consideration of the ripeness of claims involving Iranian assets in this country, effectively "unfrozen" incident to the agreement for release of American hostages, see Dames & Moore v. Regan, infra in this Supplement, addition to Casebook p.298, concluding that taking clause contentions were "not [yet] ripe for review."

Page 41. At the end of the first paragraph of Note 5 add:

See also Vitek v. Jones, 445 U.S. 480, 100 S. Ct. 1254, 63 L. Ed. 2d 552 (1980), especially the dissenting opinion of Justice Blackmun.

Page 42. At the end of Note 5 add:

For cases rejecting a mootness argument in the context of class actions, where appeals were taken from denials of class certification, see Deposit Guaranty National Bank v. Roper, 445 U.S. 326, 100 S. Ct 1166, 63 L. Ed. 2d 427 (1980), and United States Parole Commn. v. Geraghty, 445 U.S. 338, 100 S. Ct. 1202, 63 L. Ed. 2d 479 (1980), relying, *inter alia,* on *Sosna* and United Airlines, Inc. v. McDonald, 432 U.S. 385, 97 S. Ct. 2464, 53 L. Ed. 2d 423 (1977).

Page 54:

In the first line on the page change "states" to "stated."

Page 54. At the end of Note 1 add:

Cf. Fair Assessment in Real Estate Assn., Inc. v. McNary, — U.S. — , 102 S. Ct. 177, — L. Ed. 2d — (1981), where the Court held that principles of comity bar a taxpayer damage suit brought in federal court under 42 U.S.C. 1983 to redress the alleged unconstitutional administration of a state tax system.

Page 54. At the end of Note 3 add:

VALLEY FORGE CHRISTIAN COLLEGE v. AMERICANS UNITED FOR SEPARATION OF CHURCH AND STATE, — U.S. — , 102 S. Ct. 752, — L. Ed. 2d — (1982). Respondents brought suit challenging the Secretary of Education's conveyance of a former military hospital to a church-related college, acting pursuant to the Federal Property and Administrative Services Act of 1949, which provides a system for the disposal of governmental property that has outlived its usefulness and is declared "surplus." This property may be transferred to either private or public entities. However, the Act further provides that the Secretary may sell such property to non-profit, tax-exempt educational institutions for consideration that takes into account any benefit which may accrue to the United States from the transferee's use thereof. The Secretary determined the appraised value of the property here to be $577,500 but discounted the sale price to the college by 100 percent, due to the alleged public benefit which would inure to the United States. Thus, in essence, the college received the property without making any financial outlay. Respondents — Americans United and individual members who were federal taxpayers — based their challenge to the conveyance on the grounds that it violates the establishment clause of the First Amendment and would also deprive the organization's members of the proper use of their tax dollars. The district court dismissed the complaint, finding that the organization and its members lacked standing to sue as taxpayers under the facts presented. The court of appeals reversed, holding that, although the respondents lacked standing as taxpayers, they had standing merely as "citizens" claiming "injury in fact" to their shared individualized right to a government that "shall make no law respecting the establishment of religion."

Writing for the Court's majority in reversing the court of appeals and concluding that the district court correctly found standing to be lacking, Justice Rehnquist thoroughly canvassed and analyzed the Court's standing decisions, stating:

"Following the decision in *Frothingham*, the Court confirmed that the expenditure of public funds in an allegedly unconstitutional manner is not an injury sufficient to confer standing, even though the plaintiff contributes to the public coffers as a taxpayer, [citing *Doremus*]. Thus the Court reaffirmed that the 'case or controversy' aspect of standing is unsatisfied 'where a taxpayer seeks to employ a federal court as a forum in which to air his generalized grievances about the conduct of government or the allocation of power in the Federal System.'...

"Unlike the plaintiffs in *Flast*, respondents fail the first prong of the test for taxpayer standing. Their claim is deficient in two respects. First, the source of their complaint is not a congressional action, but a decision by HEW to transfer a parcel of federal property. *Flast* limited taxpayer standing to challenges directed 'only [at] exercises of congressional power.' ...

3

See Schlesinger v. Reservists Committee to Stop the War, 418 U.S. 208, 228 (1974) (denying standing because the taxpayer plaintiffs 'did not challenge an enactment under Art. I, §8, but rather the action of the Executive Branch').

"Second, and perhaps redundantly, the property transfer about which respondents complain was not an exercise of authority conferred by the taxing and spending clause of Art. I, §8. The authorizing legislation, the Federal Property and Administrative Services Act of 1949, was an evident exercise of Congress' power under the Property Clause, Art. IV, §3, cl. 2. . . .

"Any doubt that once might have existed concerning the rigor with which the *Flast* exception to the *Frothingham* principle ought to be applied should have been erased by this Court's recent decisions in United States v. Richardson, 418 U.S. 166 (1974), and Schlesinger v. Reservists Committee to Stop the War, 418 U.S. 208 (1974), [where standing was found to be lacking because the challenges in question did not relate to spending power measures].

"Respondents, therefore, are plainly without standing to sue as taxpayers. The Court of Appeals apparently reached the same conclusion. It remains to be seen whether respondents have alleged any other basis for standing to bring this suit.

"Although the Court of Appeals properly doubted respondents' ability to establish standing solely on the basis of their taxpayer status, it considered their allegations of taxpayer injury to be 'essentially an assumed role.' 619 F.2d, at 261. . . . In the court's view, respondents had established standing by virtue of an ' "injury in fact" to their shared individuated right to a government that "shall make no law respecting the establishment of religion." ' Ibid. The court distinguished this 'injury' from 'the question of "citizen standing" as such.' Id., at 262. Although citizens generally could not establish standing simply by claiming an interest in governmental observance of the Constitution, respondents had 'set forth instead a particular and concrete injury' to a 'personal constitutional right.' Id., at 265. . . .

"In finding that respondents had alleged something more than 'the generalized interest of all citizens in constitutional governance,' . . . the Court of Appeals relied on factual differences which we do not think amount to legal distinctions. The court decided that respondents' claim differed from those in *Schlesinger* and *Richardson*, which were predicated, respectively, on the Incompatibility and Accounts Clauses, because 'it is at the very least arguable that the Establishment Clause creates in each citizen a "personal constitutional right" to a government that does not establish religion.' 619 F.2d, at 265. . . . The court found it unnecessary to determine whether this 'arguable' proposition was correct, since it judged the mere allegation of a legal right sufficient to confer standing.

"This reasoning process merely disguises, we think with a rather thin veil, the inconsistency of the court's results with our decisions in *Schlesinger* and *Richardson*. The plaintiffs in those cases plainly asserted a 'personal right' to have the government act in accordance with their views of the Constitution; indeed, we see no barrier to the *assertion* of such claims with respect to any constitutional provision. But assertion of a right to a particular kind of government conduct, which the government has violated by acting differently, cannot alone satisfy the requirements of Art. III without draining those requirements of meaning.

"Nor can *Schlesinger* and *Richardson* be distinguished on the ground that the Incompatibility and Accounts Clauses are in some way less 'fundamental' than the Establishment Clause. Each establishes a norm of conduct which the federal government is bound to honor — to no greater or lesser extent than any other inscribed in the Constitution. To the extent the Court of Appeals relied on a view of standing under which the Art. III burdens diminish as the 'importance' of the claim on the merits increases, we reject that notion. The requirement of standing 'focuses on the party seeking to get his complaint before a federal court and not on the issues he wishes to have adjudicated.' Flast v. Cohen, supra, at 99. Moreover, we know of no principled basis on which to create a hierarchy of constitutional values or a complementary 'sliding scale' of standing which might permit respondents to invoke the judicial power of the United States. . . .

"The complaint in this case shares a common deficiency with those in *Schlesinger* and *Richardson*. Although they claim that the Constitution has been violated, they claim nothing else. They fail to identify any personal injury suffered by the plaintiffs *as a consequence* of the alleged constitutional error, other than the psychological consequence presumably produced by observation of conduct with which one disagrees. That is not an injury sufficient to confer standing under Art. III, even though the disagreement is phrased in constitutional terms. . . .

"In reaching this conclusion, we do not retreat from our earlier holdings that standing may be predicated on noneconomic injury. See, e.g., United States v. SCRAP, 412 U.S., at 686-688; Data Processing Service v. Camp, 397 U.S., at 153-154. We simply cannot see that respondents have alleged an *injury* of *any* kind, economic or otherwise, sufficient to confer standing. Respondents complain of a transfer of property located in Chester County, Pennsylvania. The named plaintiffs reside in Maryland and Virginia; their organizational headquarters are located in Washington, D.C. They learned of the transfer through a news release. Their claim that the government has violated the Establishment Clause does not provide a special license to roam the country in search of governmental wrongdoing and to reveal their discoveries in federal court. The federal courts were simply not constituted as ombudsmen of the general welfare.

"The Court of Appeals in this case ignored unambiguous limitations on taxpayer and citizen standing. It appears to have done so out of the conviction that enforcement of the Establishment Clause demands special exceptions from the requirement that a plaintiff allege ' "distinct and palpable injury to himself" ' . . . that is likely to be redressed if the requested relief is granted.' Gladstone, Realtors v. Village of Bellwood, 441 U.S., at 100 (quoting Warth v. Seldin, 422 U.S., at 501). The court [incorrectly] derived precedential comfort from Flast v. Cohen. . . .

"Implicit in the [court of appeals' analysis] is the philosophy that the business of the federal courts is correcting constitutional errors, and that 'cases and controversies' are at best merely convenient vehicles for doing so and at worst nuisances that may be dispensed with when they become obstacles to that transcendent endeavor. This philosophy has no place in our constitutional scheme. It does not become more palatable when the underlying merits concern the Establishment Clause. Respondents' claim of standing implicitly rests on the presumption that violations of the Establishment Clause typically will not cause injury sufficient to confer standing under the 'traditional' view of Art. III. But '[t]he assumption that if respondents have no standing to sue, no one would have standing, is not a reason to find standing,' [citing] *Schlesinger.* . . . This view would convert standing into a requirement that must be observed only when satisfied. Moreover, we are unwilling to assume that injured parties are nonexistent simply because they have not joined respondents in their suit. The law of averages is not a substitute for standing.

"Were we to accept respondents' claim of standing in this case, there would be no principled basis for confining our exception to litigants relying on the Establishment Clause. Ultimately, that exception derives from the idea that the judicial power requires nothing more for its invocation than important issues and able litigants. The existence of injured parties who might not wish to bring suit becomes irrelevant. Because we are unwilling to countenance such a departure from the limits on judicial power contained in Art. III, the judgment of the Court of Appeals is reversed."

Justice Brennan, joined by Justices Marshall and Blackmun, dissented, stating:

"The opinion of the Court is a stark example of this unfortunate trend of resolving cases at the 'threshold' while obscuring the nature of the underlying rights and interests at stake. The Court waxes eloquent on the blend of prudential and constitutional considerations that combine to create our misguided 'standing' jurisprudence. *But not one word is said about the Establishment Clause right that the plaintiff seeks to enforce.* And despite its pat recitation of our standing decisions, the opinion utterly fails, except by the sheerest form of *ipse dixit*, to explain why this case is unlike Flast v. Cohen, 392 U.S. 83 (1968), and is controlled instead by Frothingham v. Mellon, 262 U.S. 447 (1923).

"There is now much in the way of settled doctrine in our understanding of the injury-in-fact requirement of Article III. At the core is the irreducible minimum that persons seeking judicial relief from an Article III court have 'such a personal stake in the outcome of the controversy as to assure that concrete adverseness which sharpens the presentation of issues upon which the court so largely depends. . . .' Baker v. Carr, 369 U.S. 186, 204 (1962).

See Duke Power Co. v. Carolina Environmental Study Group, 438 U.S. 59, 72 (1978). Cases of this Court have identified the two essential components of this 'personal stake' requirement. Plaintiff must have suffered, or be threatened with, some 'distinct and palpable injury,' Warth v. Seldin, 422 U.S. 490, 501 (1975). In addition, there must be some casual connection between plaintiff's asserted injury and defendant's challenged action. Simon v. Eastern Ky. Welfare Rights Org., 426 U.S. 26, 41 (1976); Arlington Heights v. Metropolitan Housing Development Corp., 429 U.S. 252, 261 (1977). The Constitution requires an Article III court to ascertain that both requirements are met before proceeding to exercise its authority on behalf of any plaintiff, whether the form of relief requested is equitable or monetary.

"But the existence of Article III injury 'often turns on the nature and source of the claim asserted.' Warth v. Seldin, supra, at 500. Neither 'palpable injury' nor 'causation' is a term of unvarying meaning. There is much in the way of 'mutual understandings' and 'common law traditions' that necessarily guides the definitional inquiry. *In addition,* the Constitution, and by legislation the Congress, may impart a new, and on occasion unique, meaning to the terms 'injury' and 'causation' in particular statutory or constitutional contexts. The Court makes a fundamental mistake when it determines that a plaintiff has failed to satisfy the two-pronged 'injury-in-fact' test, or indeed any other test of 'standing,' without first determining whether the Constitution or a statute defines injury, and creates a cause of action for redress of that injury, in precisely the circumstance presented to the Court.

"It may of course happen that a person believing himself injured in some obscure manner by government action will be held to have no legal right under the constitutional or statutory provision upon which he relies, and will not be permitted to complain of the invasion of another person's 'rights.' It is quite another matter to employ the rhetoric of 'standing' to deprive a person, whose interest is clearly protected by the law, of the opportunity to prove that his own rights have been violated. It is in precisely that dissembling enterprise that the Court indulges today.

"The 'case and controversy' limitation of Article III overrides no other provision of the Constitution. To construe that Article to deny standing 'to the class for whose sake [a] constitutional protection is given,' ... simply turns the Constitution on its head. Article III was designed to provide a hospitable forum in which persons enjoying rights under the Constitution could assert those rights. How are we to discern whether a particular person is to be afforded a right of action in the courts? The Framers did not, of course, employ the modern vocabulary of standing. But this much is clear: The drafters of the Bill of Rights surely intended that the particular beneficiaries of their legacy should enjoy rights legally enforceable in courts of law. See West Virginia State Bd. of Educ. v. Barnette, 319 U.S. 624, 638 (1943). . . ."

Justice Brennan next discussed *Frothingham*, concluding that its general rule displays "sound judgment." However, he further explained that the *Frothingham* rule must necessarily give way to an appropriate establishment clause claim, reviewing some of the Court's important decisions based on that provision of the First Amendment. He continued:

"It is clear in the light of this history, that one of the primary purposes of the Establishment Clause was to prevent the use of tax monies for religious purposes. *The taxpayer was the direct and intended beneficiary of the prohibition on financial aid to religion.* This basic understanding of the meaning of the Establishment Clause explains why the Court in [Everson v. Board of Education, 330 U.S. 1 (1947)], while rejecting appellant's claim on the merits, perceived the issue presented there as it did. The appellant sued 'in his capacity as a district taxpayer,' 330 U.S., at 3, challenging the actions of the Board of Education in passing a resolution providing reimbursement to parents for the cost of transporting their children to parochial schools, and seeking to have that resolution 'set aside.' Appellant's Establishment Clause claim was precisely that the 'statute . . . forced inhabitants to pay taxes to help support and maintain' church schools. Id., at 5. It seems obvious that all the Justices who participated in *Everson* would have agreed with Justice Jackson's succinct statement of the question presented: 'Is it constitutional to tax this complainant to pay the cost of carrying pupils to Church schools of one specified denomination?' Id., at 21 (Jackson, J., dissenting). Given this view of the issues, could it fairly be doubted that this taxpayer alleged injury in precisely the form that the Establishment Clause sought to make actionable? . . .

The Justices who participated in *Flast* were not unaware of the Court's continued recognition of a federally cognizable 'case or controversy' when a *local* taxpayer seeks to challenge as unconstitutional the use of a *municipality's* funds — the propriety of which had, of course, gone unquestioned in *Everson*. The Court was aware as well of the rule stated in Doremus v. Board of Education, 342 U.S. 429 (1952), that the interest of a taxpayer, even one raising an Establishment Clause claim, was limited to the actions of a government involving the expenditure of funds. But in reaching its holding, it is also quite clear that the Court was responding, not only to *Everson's* continued acceptance of municipal taxpayer actions but also to *Everson's* exposition of the history and meaning of the Establishment Clause. . . .

"It is at once apparent that the test of standing formulated by the Court in *Flast* sought to reconcile the developing doctrine of taxpayer 'standing' with the Court's historical understanding that the Establishment Clause was intended to prohibit the Federal Government from using tax funds for the advancement of religion, and thus the constitutional imperative of taxpayer standing in certain cases brought pursuant to the Establishment Clause. The two-pronged 'nexus' test offered by the Court, despite its general language, is best understood as 'a determinant of standing of plaintiffs alleging only injury as taxpayers who challenge alleged violations of the Establishment and Free Exercise Clauses of the First Amendment,' and not as a general statement of standing principles. Schlesinger v. Reservists Committee to Stop the War, 418 U.S. 208, 238 (1974) (Brennan, J., dissenting); *Flast*, supra, at 102. The test explains what forms of governmental action may be attacked by someone alleging *only* taxpayer status, and, without ruling out the possibility that history might reveal another similarly founded provision, explains why an Establishment Clause claim is treated differently from any other assertion that the federal government has exceeded the bounds of the law in allocating its largesse. Thus, consistent with *Doremus, Flast* required, as the first prong of its test, that the taxpayer demonstrate a logical connection between his taxpayer status and the type of legislation attacked. . . . Appellants' challenge to a program of grants to educational institutions clearly satisfied this first requirement. . . . As the second prong, consistent with the prohibition of taxpayer claims of the kind advanced in *Frothingham*, appellants were required to show a connection between their status and the precise nature of the infringement alleged. . . . They had no difficulty meeting this requirement: the Court agreed that the Establishment Clause jealously protects taxpayers from diversion of their funds to the support of religion through the offices of the Federal Government. . . .

"Blind to history, the Court attempts to distinguish this case from *Flast* by wrenching snippets of language from our opinions, and by perfunctorily applying that language under color of the first prong of *Flast's* two-part nexus test. The tortuous distinctions thus produced are specious, at best: at worst, they are pernicious to our constitutional heritage. . . .

"More fundamentally, no clear division can be drawn in this context between actions of the legislative branch and those of the executive branch. To be sure, the First Amendment is phrased as a restriction on Congress' legislative authority; this is only natural since the Constitution assigns the authority to legislate and appropriate only to the Congress. But it is difficult to conceive of an expenditure for which the last governmental actor, either implementing directly the legislative will, or acting within the scope of legislatively delegated authority, is not an Executive Branch official. The First Amendment binds the Government as a whole, regardless of which branch is at work in a particular instance.

"The Court's second purported distinction between this case and *Flast* is equally unavailing. The majority finds it 'decisive' that the Federal Property and Administrative Services Act of 1949 'was an evident exercise of Congress' power under the Property Clause, Art. IV, §3, cl. 2,' while the government action in *Flast* was taken under the Art. I, §8. The Court relies on United States v. Richardson, 418 U.S. 166 (1974), and Schlesinger v. Reservists Committee to Stop the War, 418 U.S. 208 (1974), to support the distinction between the two clauses, noting that those cases involved alleged deviations from the requirements of Art. I, §9, cl. 7, and Art. I, §6, cl. 2, respectively. The standing defect in each case was *not*, however, the failure to allege a violation of the Spending Clause; rather, the taxpayers in those cases had not complained of the distribution of government largesse, and thus failed to meet the essential requirement of taxpayer standing recognized in *Doremus*.

"It can make no constitutional difference in the case before us whether the donation to the defendant here was in the form of a cash grant to build a facility, see Tilton v. Richardson, 403 U.S. 672 (1971), or in the nature of a gift of property including a facility already built. That this is a meaningless distinction is illustrated by *Tilton*. In that case, taxpayers were afforded standing to object to the fact that the Government had not received adequate assurance that if the property that it financed for use as an educational facility was later converted to religious uses, it would receive full value for the property, as the Constitution requires. The complaint here is precisely that, although the property at issue is actually being used for a sectarian purpose, the government has not received, nor demanded, full value payment. Whether undertaken pursuant to the Property Clause or the Spending Clause, the breach of the Establishment Clause, and the relationship of the taxpayer to that breach, is precisely the same.

"Plainly hostile to the Framers' understanding of the Establishment Clause, and *Flast's* enforcement of that understanding, the Court vents that hostility under the guise of standing, 'to slam the courthouse door against plaintiffs who [as the Framers intended] are entitled to full consideration of their [Establishment Clause] claims on the merits.' Barlow v. Collins, 397 U.S. 159, 178 (1970) (Brennan, J., concurring in the result and dissenting)."

Justice Stevens also dissented, agreeing for the most part with Justice Brennan but writing separately and concluding that "[f]or the Court to hold that plaintiffs' standing depends on whether the Government's transfer was an exercise of its power to spend money, on the one hand, or its power to dispose of tangible property, on the other, is to trivialize the standing doctrine." After discussing *Flast* he continued:

"Today the Court holds, in effect, that the Judiciary has no greater role in enforcing the Establishment Clause than in enforcing other 'norm[s] of conduct which the federal government is bound to honor,' ... such as the Accounts Clause, United States v. Richardson, 418 U.S. 166, and the Incompatibility Clause, Schlesinger v. Reservists Committee to Stop the War, 418 U.S. 208. Ironically, however, its decision rests on the premise that the difference between a disposition of funds pursuant to the Spending Clause and a disposition of realty pursuant to the Property Clause is of fundamental jurisprudential significance. With all due respect, I am persuaded that the essential holding of Flast v. Cohen attaches special importance to the Establishment Clause and does not permit the drawing of a tenuous distinction between the Spending Clause and the Property Clause."

Does this 5-to-4 decision effectively limit federal taxpayer standing under *Flast* to the precise facts of that case — a spending power exercise challenged on establishment clause grounds by individuals?

Page 55. At the end of Note 5 add:

In Watt v. Energy Action Educational Foundation, — U.S. — , 102 S. Ct. 205, — L. Ed. 2d — (1981), the State of California brought suit to challenge the Secretary of the Interior's alleged failure to comply with a statutory outer continental shelf bidding procedure, as established in the O.C.S. Lands Act Amendments of 1978. Among the issues raised in the suit was the government's contention that California did not have standing to challenge the bidding procedure. Justice O'Connor, writing for a unanimous Court, addressed the standing issue:

"The 1978 Amendments require the federal government to turn over a fair share of the revenues of an OCS lease to the neighboring coastal State whenever the Federal Government and the State own adjoining portions of an OCS oil and gas pool.... California thus has a direct financial stake in federal OCS leasing off the California coast. In alleging that the bidding systems currently used by the Secretary of the Interior are incapable of producing a fair market return, California clearly asserts the kind of 'distinct and palpable injury' ... that is required for standing.... To demonstrate that it has standing, however, California must also show that there is a 'fairly traceable' causal connection between the injury it claims and the conduct it challenges, ... so that if the relief sought is granted, the injury will be redressed.... The essence of California's complaint ... is that the Secretary of the Interior, by failing to test non-cash-bonus [compensation] systems, has breached a statutory obligation to determine through experiment which bidding system works best. According to California, only by testing non-cash-bonus systems can the Secretary of the Interior carry out his duty to use the best bidding systems and thereby assure California a fair return for its resources.... For [these] reason[s], we agree with California that it has standing to challenge the Secretary['s] ... refusal to experiment with non-cash-bonus bidding systems."

Page 62. At the end of Note 4 add:

Note, The Precedential Value of Supreme Court Plurality Decisions, 80 Colum. L. Rev. 756 (1980).

Page 79. At the end of the second paragraph of Note 1 add:

In Santosky v. Kramer, — U.S. — , 102 S. Ct. 1388, — L. Ed. 2d — (1982), the Court held that New York's adoption of a "fair preponderance of the evidence standard" in a state-initiated parental rights termination hearing violated the due process clause of the Fourteenth Amendment. The Court further held that the state must prove its case by "clear and convincing evidence" before it may sever the rights of parents in their natural child. This resulted, the Court determined, from application of the three-factor analysis of Matthews v. Eldridge, as applied to the question of the proper standard of review in such a proceeding. *Lassiter* was distinguished, while *Stanley* and *Addington* were cited and relied upon. Justice Rehnquist, joined by Chief Justice Burger and Justices White and O'Connor, dissented.

Page 84. At the end of Note 1 add:

Zaccharias, Standing of Public Interest Litigating Groups to Sue on Behalf of Their Members, 39 U. Pitt. L. Rev. 453 (1978).

Page 84. At the end of Note 2 add:

Again relying on *Linda R.S.*, the Court disposed of Leeke v. Timmerman, — U.S. — , 102 S. Ct. 69, — L. Ed. 2d — (1981). In *Leeke* certain inmates of a South Carolina prison alleged that during the prison uprising they were unnecessarily beaten by prison guards. In support of those allegations respondent Timmerman presented sufficient evidence to a state court contending that petitioners conspired in bad faith to block issuance of the arrest warrants. The district court found for the respondents; the court of appeals affirmed, finding that the language of *Linda R.S.* did not foreclose the respondents' right to seek an arrest warrant. The Supreme Court reversed, holding that *Linda R.S.* controls. "As in *Linda R.S.*, there is a questionable nexus between [the] respondents' injury — the alleged beatings — and the action of the state officials in which they gave [ex parte] information to the magistrate prior to issuance of the arrest warrant.... It is ... clear that issuance of the arrest warrant in this case would *not* necessarily lead to a subsequent prosecution.... A private citizen therefore has no judicially cognizable right to prevent state officials from presenting information ... that will assist the magistrate in determining whether to issue the arrest warrant."

Justice Brennan, joined by Justice Marshall and Justice Blackmun, dissented, stating that *Linda R.S.* was "wholly inapposite," as the respondents had alleged that "conspiratorial acts have deprived them of their right to seek an arrest warrant, and thus denied them their constitutional rights of access to the courts." Thus, the dissenters found the Court's reliance on standing principles enunciated in *Linda R.S.* as misplaced.

Page 86. At the end of the carryover paragraph add:

Relying on *Gladstone*, the Court in Havens Realty Corp. v. Coleman, — U.S. — , 102 S. Ct. 1114, — L. Ed. 2d — (1982), held that the sole requirement for standing under §804 of the Fair Housing Act of 1968 is the Article III minimum of an injury in fact which is both distinct and palpable. In *Coleman* suit was brought by three individuals, as well as an orgaization named HOME (Housing Opportunities Made Equal), whose activities include counseling and referral services as well as investigating and processing complaints of housing discrimination. It was alleged that the defendant had committed illegally discriminatory steering practices. Each individual in the suit claimed an injury in fact based on either a direct denial of the opportunity to rent or the deprivation of the benefits of living in an integrated community. HOME also alleged injury, claiming that its members had been denied the benefits of interracial association. The Court began its inquiry by describing the statutory system designed by Congress in the Fair Housing Act of 1968, which includes §804(d) and which permits any person to test compliance with the provisions of the Act. The Court concluded that so-called "testers," without any intention of buying or renting a home, may nevertheless allege an injury in fact based on dissemination of false housing information. Justice Brennan, writing for the Court, found the allegations of injury in fact based upon the deprivation of an interracial environment to be sufficient to survive a motion to dismiss. Turning next to the issue of HOME's standing, Brennan stated that acceptance of HOME's allegation dictates the finding that the defendant's steering practices have perceptibly impaired HOME's ability to provide counseling and referral services for prospective purchasers of low- and moderate-income homes. Thus a sufficient injury in fact existed, and the case was then remanded to the district court for a trial on the merits.

Page 86. At the end of Note 4 add:

Cf. NAACP v. Alabama, Casebook p.1411, allowing third-party standing to an organization where essential for the effective assertion of the rights of individual members.

Page 87. At the end of Note 4 add:

Comment, The Burger Court's Approach to Jus Tertii Standing, 13 Gonzaga L. Rev. 961 (1977).

Page 90:

In line 2 of the second paragraph in the footnote, add "69" prior to "S. Ct."

Page 101. At the end of Note 6 add:

Comment, Political Questions and Sensible Answers, 57 Texas L. Rev. 1259 (1979).

Page 102:

In line 2 of the second paragraph of Note 1, delete "(1)," add a comma after "states," delete lines 3 and 4 entirely, and, in lines 5 and 6, delete the phrase "brought by" and insert the words "to which."

Page 102. At the end of Note 5 add:

Cf. Goldwater v. Carter, 444 U.S. 996, 100 S. Ct. 533, 63 L. Ed. 2d 479 (1979), where the Court granted certiorari and remanded the case to the district court with directions to dismiss the complaint. Senator Goldwater and other members of Congress had challenged President Carter's action in terminating treaties with Taiwan through executive action, asserting that this deprived them of their proper constitutional role with respect to foreign affairs and in particular with regard to treaty obligations. Justice Rehnquist, speaking also for Chief Justice Burger and Justices Stewart and Stevens, concluded that the matter involved a nonjusticiable political question because it related directly to the President's authority regarding foreign relations. Justice Powell concurred in the judgment on the ground that the issue was not yet ripe for judicial review. Justice Marshall concurred in the result. Justices White and Blackmun disagreed with the Court's disposition, stating that it should give plenary consideration to the issue of the President's power to terminate a treaty unilaterally and suggesting that it should not pass on the justiciability, standing, and ripeness questions at the threshold stage of the proceedings. Justice Brennan dissented, urging that the Court should affirm the judgment of the court of appeals "insofar as it rests upon the President's well-established authority to recognize, and withdraw recognition from, foreign governments." He also stated that the plurality "profoundly misapprehends the political question principle as it applies to matters of foreign relations." In Brennan's view "the doctrine does not pertain when a court is faced with the *antecedent* question whether a particular branch has been constitutionally designated as the repository of political decisionmaking," citing Powell v. McCormack.

Page 103. At the end of the carryover paragraph add:

For a discussion of the Supreme Court's original jurisdiction, see Maryland v. Louisiana, 451 U.S. 725, 101 S. Ct. 2114, 68 L. Ed. 2d 576 (1981), where several states, the United States government, and a number of pipeline companies challenged the constitutionality of a "first use tax," which Louisiana imposed upon natural gas brought into the state from the outer continental shelf. They brought the challenge pursuant to both the supremacy clause and the commerce clause. The Supreme Court held that the states, as major purchasers of natural gas, whose costs have increased as a result of Louisiana's "first use tax," are affected in a "substantial and real" way so as to justify the exercise of the Court's original jurisdiction. The Court also held that the states' attempt to raise the claim under the Supreme Court's original jurisdiction is further supported by the states' interest as *parens patriae.*

Justice Rehnquist dissented from the Court's invocation of its original jurisdiction. He stated that "[original jurisdiction] is obligatory only in appropriate cases," and that "because of the nature of the interests which the plaintiff states seek to vindicate in this original action, and because of the existence of alternate forums in which these interests can be vindicated, this [was not] an 'appropriate case' for the exercise of original jurisdiction." Rehnquist asserted that, "as a general rule, when a State's claim is indistinguishable from the claim of any private consumer it is insufficient to invoke [the Court's] original jurisdiction." Here the states had failed to show "some tangible relation to [their] sovereign interests." Nor was exercise of original jurisdiction on a *parens patriae* basis appropriate, he stated, for the states were "not suing to advance a sovereign or quasi-sovereign interest." Here, "the plaintiff states have not . . . established the 'strictest necessity' required for invoking this Court's original jurisdiction . . . and there-fore . . . Louisiana's motion to dismiss the complaint" should be granted. See infra in this Supplement, addition to Casebook p.410, for a complete discussion of the merits of this case.

Page 103. At the end of Note 1 add:

Simpson, Turning over the Reins: The Abolition of Mandatory Appellate Jurisdiction of the Supreme Court, 6 Hastings Const. L.Q. 297 (1979).

Page 105. At the end of the second full paragraph add:

Cf. San Diego Gas and Electric Co. v. City of San Diego, 450 U.S. 621, 101 S. Ct. 1287, 67 L. Ed. 2d 551 (1981), where the Court dismissed an appeal under 28 U.S.C. 1257 on the basis of the absence of a final judgment.

Justice Brennan, joined by Justices Stewart, Marshall, and Powell, dissented, finding the state appellate court's decision as constituting a final judgment, and thus reaching the constitutional issues in the case. Is such a decision consistent with the "rule of four"? See also Note, The Finality Rule for Supreme Court Review of State Court Orders, 91 Harv. L. Rev. 1004 (1978).

Page 108. At the end of the carryover paragraph add:

Incident to the 1980 revisions to the Supreme Court Rules, Rule 19 was renumbered so that it is now Rule 17 and was revised, so that it provides in pertinent part as follows:

"A review on writ of certiorari is not a matter of right, but of judicial discretion, and will be granted only when there are special and important reasons therefor. The following, while neither controlling nor fully measuring the Court's discretion, indicate the character of reasons that will be considered.

"(a) When a federal court of appeals has rendered a decision in conflict with the decision of another federal court of appeals on the same matter; or has decided a federal question in a way in conflict with a state court of last resort; or has so far departed from the accepted and usual course of judicial proceedings, or so far sanctioned such a departure by a lower court, as to call for an exercise of this Court's power of supervision.

"(b) When a state court of last resort has decided a federal question in a way in conflict with the decision of another state court of last resort or of a federal court of appeals.

"(c) When a state court or a federal court of appeals has decided an important question of federal law which has not been, but should be settled by this Court, or has decided a federal question in a way in conflict with applicable decisions of this Court."

While the Court has never attempted to spell out by rule the considerations that relate to giving plenary review to appeals, as distinguished from certiorari cases, it has as a practical matter utilized the same criteria specified in the rule relating to that category of cases, as now detailed in new Rule 17. In addition, new Rule 15, dealing expressly with appeals, provides that the jurisdictional statement in appeal cases coming from either state or federal courts should contain a "statement of the reasons why the questions presented are so substantial as to require plenary consideration, with briefs on the merits and oral argument, for their resolution." New Rule 16 suggests various reasons why the Court might determine to dispose of an appeal case summarily, pursuant to a motion to dismiss or affirm filed by the appellee, if "the appeal is not within this Court's jurisdiction, or ... not taken in conformity with statute or with these Rules," or if an appeal from a state court "does not present a substantial federal question," or "the federal question sought to be reviewed was not timely or properly raised and was not expressly passed on," or where "the judgment rests on an adequate non-federal basis"; with respect to cases coming from federal courts if "it is manifest that the questions on which the decision of the cause depends are so unsubstantial as not to need further argument"; and, finally, "on any other ground the appellee wishes to present as a reason why the Court should not set the case for argument." Both Rule 16.7 (dealing with appeals) and Rule 23.1 (relating to certiorari cases) state that the Court's order "may be a summary disposition on the merits."

Page 110. At the end of Note 6 add:

See Doe v. Delaware, 450 U.S. 382, 101 S. Ct. 1495, 67 L. Ed. 2d 312 (1981), where Justice Brennan, joined by Justice White, dissented from the Court's dismissal of an appeal based on the lack of a properly presented federal question. Brennan noted: "The practice in this Court has been to dismiss an appeal taken under 28 U.S.C. §1257(2) for want of a properly presented federal question only when the federal question was not raised at the proper juncture in the state court proceedings or in accordance with reasonable state rules. . . . If the record shows that a federal constitutional challenge to a state statute was brought to the attention of the state court 'with fair precision and in due time,' then 'the claim is ... regarded as having been adequately presented.' "

Justice Stevens, dissenting separately, displayed a willingness to decide the question presented on the merits, reserving the prerogative of remanding the case for consideration of the state law issues.

Comment, The Precedential Weight of Summary Disposition of Appeals, 29 Maine L. Rev. 325 (1978); Linzer, The Meaning of Certiorari Denials, 79 Colum. L. Rev. 1227 (1979).

Page 117. At the end of Note 7 add:

See United States v. Will, 449 U.S. 200, 101 S. Ct. 471, 66 L. Ed. 2d 392 (1980), where the Court was confronted with the question of when, if ever, the compensation clause of Article III prohibits Congress from repealing salary increases for federal judges which were to take effect automatically pursuant to a previously adopted formula. The Court stated that "[t]he Compensation Clause has its roots in the longstanding Anglo-American tradition of an independent judiciary ..., [and that] [our] Constitution promotes that independence specifically" through that provision. Interpreting the compensation clause, the Court held that the timing of the repealing legislation is determinative. Repealing legislation signed into law before the automatic increase becomes part of the judges' compensation in no manner diminishes their salaries, and thus such legislation is valid. However, an attempt to enact legislation which has the effect of repealing a salary increase already in force is a diminishment of judges' salaries and is therefore constitutionally infirm.

Page 124. At the end of the last paragraph add:

Note, Plurality Decisions and Judicial Decision-Making, 94 Harv. L. Rev. 1127 (1981); Hardisty, Reflections on Stare Decisis, 55 Ind. L.J. 41 (1979).

Page 126. At the end of the carryover paragraph add:

In its original form, the "federal question" jurisdictional statute, 28 U.S.C. 1331, contained a provision requiring that the amount in controversy exceed $10,000, exclusive of interest and costs (except where otherwise provided by statute). However, Congress recently changed §1331 by enacting the Federal Question Jurisdictional Amendments Act of 1980 (P.L. 96-486), which deleted the $10,000 amount in controversy requirement. As amended, §1331 reads as follows: "The district courts shall have original jurisdiction of all civil actions arising under the Constitution, Laws or Treaties of the United States." This amendment does not affect the $10,000 amount in controversy requirement for federal diversity jurisdiction under 28 U.S.C. 1332.

Page 127. At the end of the last full paragraph in Note 2 add:

Cf. United States v. Raddatz, 447 U.S. 667, 100 S. Ct. 2406, 65 L. Ed. 2d 424 (1980), holding that the procedural scheme of the Federal Magistrates Act, which gives district judges discretion to hear live testimony but the duty to make ultimate factual determinations on a *de novo* basis when a pretrial matter is heard and first resolved by a magistrate, violates neither Article III nor the Fifth Amendment's due process clause.

Page 128. At the end of the last full paragraph add:

Thornton, The Eleventh Amendment: An Endangered Species, 55 Ind. L.J. 293 (1980).

Page 129. At the end of the carryover paragraph add:

See also Florida Dept. of Health and Home Rehabilitative Services v. Florida Nursing Home Assn., 450 U.S. 47, 101 S. Ct. 1032, 67 L. Ed. 2d 132 (1981). The Court cited Edelman v. Jordan for the proposition that the Court "will find waiver [of state immunity] only where stated 'by the most express language or by such overwhelming implications from the text as [will] leave no room for any other reasonable construction.' " The Court further stated that the "mere fact that a State participates in a program through which the Federal Government provides assistance for the operation by the State of a system of public aid is not sufficient to establish consent on the part of the State to be sued in the federal courts."

Page 131. Add to the footnoted material:

In City of Milwaukee v. Illinois and Michigan, 451 U.S. 304, 101 S. Ct. 1784, 68 L. Ed. 2d 114 (1981), the Court held that federal common law, in an area of national concern, should be resorted to only in the absence of an applicable congressional act, and only then because the Court is compelled to consider federal questions which cannot be answered by federal statute alone.

See also Texas Industries, Inc. v. Radcliff Materials, Inc., — U.S. —, 101 S. Ct. 2061, 68 L. Ed. 2d 500 (1981), for another discussion of the application and scope of federal common law. Among the various issues presented, the Court was asked to determine whether the federal courts can and should afford the defendants in a successful antitrust suit a right to contribution based on federal common law. Writing for a unanimous Court, Chief Justice Burger stated: "The vesting of jurisdiction in the federal courts does not in and of itself give rise to authority to formulate federal common law; nor does the existence of congressional authority under Article I mean that federal courts are free to develop a common law to govern those areas until Congress acts. Rather, absent some congressional authority to formulate substantive rules of decision, federal common law exists only in such narrow areas as those concerned with the rights and obligations of the United States, interstate and international disputes implicating the conflicting rights of States or our relations with foreign nations, and admiralty cases. In these instances, our federal system does not permit the controversy to be resolved under state law, either because the authority and duties of the United States as sovereign are intimately involved or because the interstate or international nature of the controversy makes it inappropriate for state law to control." But, since "contribution among antitrust wrongdoers does not involve the duties of the Federal Government, the distribution of powers in our federal system, or matters necessarily subject to federal control even in the absence of statutory authority," it "does not implicate 'uniquely federal interests' of the kind that oblige the courts to formulate federal common law."

Page 133. Add to the footnoted material:

McMillan, Abstention — The Judiciary's Self-Inflicted Wound, 56 N. Carolina L. Rev. 527 (1978).

Page 134. At the end of the fourth paragraph add:

See Key v. Wise, — U.S. — , 102 S. Ct. 681, — L. Ed. 2d — (1981), where Justice Brennan, joined by Justices Marshall and Blackmun, entered a strong dissent to the Court's denial of certiorari. Key brought a quiet-title action against both Wise and the United States pursuant to the Federal Quiet Title Act, which vests exclusive jurisdiction of such suits in the federal district courts. The district court, *sua sponte*, entered an order of abstention requiring the parties to resolve the suit in state court. After a series of motions to reconsider and interlocutory appeals, petitioner filed an action in state court, raising the preemption objection in the Mississippi Supreme Court. The Mississippi Supreme Court rejected the objection raised to the state court's assertion of jurisdiction. In accordance with the federal district court's initial order, the parties returned to federal court following the final state court judgment. Upon return to federal court the respondents moved to dismiss the petitioner's suit on *res judicata* grounds. The district court granted the motion, and a divided Fifth Circuit panel affirmed. Justice Brennan, obviously disturbed by the resolution of the jurisdictional issue involved, characterized the district court's dismissal and the court of appeals' affirmation as "inexplicable," writing: "[T]his case is a most obvious candidate for summary reversal, or at the very least for the grant of plenary argument and decision. . . . What renders the Court's denial of the petition particularly inexplicable, indeed incredible, is that the Court of Appeals held that the order of abstention was clearly improper because it patently flouted the mandate of the Quiet Title Act and the District Court's original and exclusive jurisdiction of the case. . . ." Justice Brennan also addressed the *res judicata* effects of the Mississippi Supreme Court's rejection of the petitioner's preemption argument, finding it clear that "neither the District Court nor the Court of Appeals was bound by the state court's interpretation of the Quiet Title Act nor was either barred from reconsidering that Court's decision on the federal question."

Page 136. At the end of the last paragraph add:

Calhoun, Exhaustion Requirements in *Younger*-type Actions: More Mud in Already Clouded Waters, 13 Ind. L. Rev. 521 (1980).

Page 137. At the end of Note 7 add:

Cf. Allen v. McCurry, 449 U.S. 90, 101 S. Ct. 411, 66 L. Ed. 2d 308 (1980), where the Court reversed a court of appeals decision which held that since Stone v. Powell barred the respondent from maintaining a federal habeas corpus action in the district court, his only remaining route to a federal forum for his constitutional claims was provided by a §1983 suit. The lower court had held that the respondent's §1983 action would be proper, despite the apparent inconsistency with the doctrine of collateral estoppel. The Court stated that "[t]here is, in short, no reason to believe that Congress intended to provide a person claiming a federal right an unrestricted opportunity to relitigate an issue already decided in state court simply because the issue arose in a state proceeding in which he would rather not have been engaged at all."

Justice Blackmun, joined by Justices Brennan and Marshall, dissented, asserting that the Court was ignoring "the clear import of the legislative history of [§1983] and disregard[ing] the important federal policies that underlie its enforcement.... The legislative intent ... was to re-structure relations between the state and federal courts. Congress deliberately opened the federal courts to individual citizens in response to the States' failure to provide justice in their own courts. ..."

Along the same line as Stone v. Powell the Court in Sumner v. Mata, 449 U.S. 539, 101 S. Ct. 764, 66 L. Ed. 2d 722 (1981), held that §2254(d) applies to factual determinations made by state courts — trial or appellate. Section 2254 requires that "[i]n any proceeding instituted in a federal court by an application for a writ of habeas corpus by a person in custody pursuant to the judgment of a state court determination after a *hearing* on the merits of a *factual* issue ... evidenced by a written finding ... shall be presumed to be correct ..." (emphasis added). The respondent argued that §2254(d) requires a hearing to be conducted at the trial level. However, the Court declared that "[s]ection 2254(d) applies to cases in which a state court ... has made 'a determination after a hearing on the merits of a factual issue.' It makes no distinction between the factual determinations of a state trial court and those of a state appellate court. Nor does it specify any procedural requirements that must be satisfied for there to be a 'hearing on the merits of a factual issue,' other than [that] the habeas applicant and the state or its agent be parties to the state proceeding and that the state court determination be evidenced by a written finding.... Section 2254(d) by its terms thus applies to factual determinations made by state courts, whether the court be a trial court or appellate court.... This interest in federalism recognized by Congress in enacting §2254(d) requires deference by federal courts to factual determinations of all state courts."

A dissent authored by Justice Brennan, joined by Justices Marshall and Stevens, questioned the Court's determination that the issue presented to the court of appeals was purely a question of fact. In a terse reminder to the Court's majority, Justice Brennan warned that "[a] federal court need not — indeed, must not — defer to the state court's interpretation of federal law."

See Comment, Habeas Corpus After Stone v. Powell: The Opportunity for Full and Fair Litigation Standard, 13 Harv. Civ. Rights-Civ. Lib. L. Rev. 521 (1978).

Page 137. Add as a new Note 8, and change present Note 8 to 9:

8. In State of Minnesota v. Clover Leaf Creamery Co., 449 U.S. 539, 101 S. Ct. 715, 66 L. Ed. 2d 659 (1981), the Court upheld a Minnesota statute which prohibited the sale of retail milk in plastic non-returnable containers, but permitted such sale in other non-returnable containers such as paperboard cartons. The Minnesota Supreme Court had earlier found the statute to be constitutionally defective in light of equal protection and commerce clause principles. Justice Stevens, in dissent, questioned the majority's basis for upsetting the self-imposed rule that "a federal court is bound to respect the interpretation of state law announced by the highest judicial tribunal in a State." Justice Stevens pointed to "the factual conclusions drawn by the Minnesota courts," which are entitled to "as much deference as if drafted" by the legislature itself "and incorporated in a preamble to the state statute....There is no precedent in this Court's decisions for such federal oversight. [W]hen a state court has conducted the review [of the legislative record], it is not our business to disagree with the state tribunal's evaluation of the state's own lawmaking process. Even if the state court should tell us that a state statute has a meaning that we believe the State Legislature plainly did not intend, we are not free to take our own view of the matter."

Justice Stevens' dissent exemplifies another area of the inherent tension between state and federal courts. His opinion charged the majority with exceeding their authority to review state court judgments, which he stated is limited to determining if the state tribunal has applied the correct federal constitutional standards. In his words, the reversing of the Minnesota Supreme Court's decision based on a disagreement with that court's perception of its role in the state lawmaking process is "beyond [the U.S. Supreme] Court's authority."

Chapter Two

The Powers of Congress

Page 160. At the end of Note 1 add:

For a case holding that conversion of private property into navigable waters of the United States provides a basis for a valid claim for compensation under the Fifth Amendment's taking clause, despite the commerce clause aspects of the situation, see Kaiser Aetna v. United States, 444 U.S. 164, 100 S. Ct. 383, 62 L. Ed. 2d 332 (1979). Cf. Vaughn v. Vermilion Corp., 444 U.S. 206, 100 S. Ct. 399, 62 L. Ed. 2d 365 (1979), infra in this Supplement, addition to Casebook p.847.

Page 168. At the end of Note 2 add:

For a case holding that local real estate brokerage activities have a sufficiently appreciable effect on interstate commerce to provide a basis for a price-fixing claim under the Sherman Act, see McLain v. Real Estate Board of New Orleans, Inc., 444 U.S. 232, 100 S. Ct. 502, 62 L. Ed. 2d 441 (1980).

Page 175. At the end of Note 6 add:

See also the Privacy Protection Act of 1980 (P.L. 96-440), where Congress used the commerce clause as authority for enacting a statute restricting searches directed at the news media.

Page 203. At the end of Note 2 add:

Cf. Hodel v. Virginia Mining & Reclamation Assn., 452 U.S. 264, 101 S. Ct. 2352, 68 L. Ed. 2d 1 (1981), where the 1977 Surface Mining Control and Reclamation Act was subjected to a barrage of constitutional challenges involving the commerce clause, the Tenth Amendment, the just compensation clause, and due process and equal protection. Addressing the commerce clause challenge, the Court canvassed a number of commerce clause cases, including *Heart of Atlanta Motel, McClung, Jones & Laughlin Steel Corp.,* and Wickard v. Filburn, concluding that when an activity affects interstate commerce, the courts need only determine whether Congress could have had a rational basis for enacting the statute challenged. The Court then cited parts of the legislative history to support the district court's holding that Congress did in fact have such a basis for this statute. Although the act regulated land use, traditionally a local concern, the commerce power has consistently been held to extend to intrastate activities which affect interstate commerce. The Court concluded that the regulation of surface coal mining could be deemed necessary to protect interstate commerce from adverse effects that may result from that activity. This was sufficient to insulate the act from the appellee's commerce clause challenge.

Page 206:

In lines 1 and 2 of the second paragraph of Note 1, delete the comma after "810" and "45 U.S.L.W. 4895," and in line 10 change "Godfarb" to "Goldfarb."

Page 208:

In line 1 of Note 7 change "recent" to "various."

Page 226. At the end of Note 2 add:

Compare Hodel v. Virginia Mining & Reclamation Assn., 452 U.S. 264, 101 S. Ct. 2352, 68 L. Ed. 2d 1 (1981), infra in this Supplement, addition to Casebook p.529, discussing and limiting the holding in *National League of Cities*.

See also United Transportation Union v. Long Island R. Co., — U.S. —, 102 S. Ct. 1349, — L. Ed. 2d — (1982), where the Court again addressed a Tenth Amendment challenge to a congressional act. In this case the State of New York attempted to eliminate application of the Railway Labor Act to the Long Island Railroad by converting the private stock corporation to a public benefit corporation. The state's objective in so converting the railroad was to head off an impending strike, which was to take place at the expiration of the 60-day cooling-off period as provided for under the Railway Labor Act. If the state's actions were successful, New York's state statute (the "Taylor law") which prohibits strikes by public employees, would be applied. Suit was brought in district court, seeking a declaratory judgment. The district court held that the railroad was covered by the Railway Labor Act and not the Taylor law. The court of appeals reversed, holding that the rail operation became an integral state governmental function and that the Railway Labor Act operated to displace "essential governmental decisions" involving that operation. Chief Justice Burger delivered the opinion of a unanimous Court, stating:

"The key prong of the *National League of Cities* test applicable to this case is the third one, which examines whether 'the State's compliance with Federal law would directly impair their ability to structure integral operations in areas of traditional functions.' ... The determination of whether a Federal law impairs a State's authority with respect to 'areas of traditional [state] functions' may at times be a difficult one. In this case, however, we do not write upon a clean slate. As the District Court noted, in *National League of Cities* we explicitly reaffirmed our holding in United States v. California, 297 U.S. 175 (1936), and two other cases involving Federal regulation of railroads. ... It is thus clear that operation of a railroad engaged in interstate commerce is not an integral part of traditional state activities generally immune from Federal regulation under *National League of Cities*. ... The Long Island is concededly a railroad engaged in interstate commerce. ... [Therefore,] Federal regulation of state-owned railroads simply does not impair a State's ability to function as a State."

Chief Justice Burger went on to elucidate upon the meaning of *National League of Cities*, stating: "In essence, *National League of Cities* held that under most circumstances Federal power to regulate commerce could not be exercised in such a manner as to undermine the role of the States in our Federal system. This Court's emphasis on traditional governmental functions and traditional aspects of state sovereignty was not meant to impose a static historical view of state functions generally immune from Federal regulation. Rather it was meant to require an inquiry into whether the Federal regulation affects basic state prerogatives in such a way as would be likely to hamper the state government's ability to fulfill its role in the Union and endanger its 'separate and independent existence.' ... [However,] [j]ust as the Federal Government cannot usurp traditional state functions, there is no justification for a rule which would allow States, by acquiring functions previously performed by the private sector, to erode Federal authority in areas traditionally subject to Federal statutory regulation." The Chief Justice concluded: "To allow individual States, by acquiring railroads, to circumvent the Federal system of railway bargaining, or any of the other elements of Federal regulation of railroads, would destroy the uniformity thought essential by Congress and would endanger the efficient operation of the interstate rail system."

Page 250. At the end of Note 1 add:

For federal spending legislation designed to create new programs to care for and treat the developmentally disabled, see the Developmentally Disabled Assistance and Bill of Rights Act of 1975, 42 U.S.C. 6000 et seq. See Pennhurst State School and Hospital v. Halderman, 451 U.S. 1, 101 S. Ct. 1531, 67 L. Ed. 2d 694 (1981), for a case interpreting the act.

Page 253. At the end of Note 1 add:

For a discussion of congressional use of the spending power in the civil rights context, see Fullilove v. Klutznick, 448 U.S. 448, 100 S. Ct. 2758, 65 L. Ed. 2d 902 (1980), infra in this Supplement, addition to Casebook p.981.

Page 260. At the end of the carryover paragraph add:

Cf. Railway Labor Executives' Assn. v. Gibbons, — U.S. — , 102 S. Ct. 1169, — L. Ed. 2d — (1982), holding that a congressional act requiring a railroad's bankruptcy trustee to provide economic benefits to previous employees not hired by other carriers violated the constitutional requirement for "uniform" bankruptcy laws. While Congress may under the bankruptcy clause distinguish among classes of debtors or treat railroad bankruptcies as a distinctive problem, where only one railroad is singled out for special, beneficial treatment Congress exceeds its legislative authority under Art. I, Sec. 8, Cl. 4 of the Constitution.

Page 269. At the end of Note 6 add:

Cf. United States v. Nixon, Casebook p.329.

Page 274. At the end of the next to the last paragraph of Note 2 add:

In United States v. Gillock, 445 U.S. 360, 100 S. Ct. 1185, 63 L. Ed. 2d 454 (1980), the Court held the speech or debate clause inapplicable in a federal criminal prosecution brought against a state legislator. Such a privilege cannot be predicated on the separation of powers doctrine, which provides the conceptual underpinning for the immunity of members of Congress, or on notions of comity between the federal government and the states. Recognition of an evidentiary privilege for state legislators for their official acts would impair the legitimate governmental interest in enforcing federal criminal laws while providing only speculative benefits to the state legislative process. Tenney v. Brandhove, Casebook p.1446, was distinguished, as were *Helstoski, Brewster,* and like cases involving federal legislators. Instead, reliance was placed on Scheuer v. Rhodes, Casebook p.534, as well as O'Shea v. Littleton, 414 U.S. 488, 94 S. Ct. 669, 38 L. Ed. 2d 674 (1974), and Imbler v. Pachtman, 424 U.S. 409, 96 S. Ct. 984, 47 L. Ed. 2d 128 (1976).

Chapter Three

The Powers of the President

Page 297. At the end of Note 2 add:

See Goldwater v. Carter, supra in this Supplement, addition to Casebook p.102, where a majority of the Court concluded that a challenge to the President's authority to terminate a defense treaty through recognition of another government by executive agreement was a nonjusticiable political question; Justice Brennan dissented, relying on the President's power to recognize and withdraw recognition from foreign governments which, in his view, did not infringe upon the congressional role in the treatymaking process.

Page 297. At the end of the second paragraph of Note 3 add:

In Weinberger v. Rossi, – U.S. – , 102 S. Ct. 1510, – L. Ed. 2d – (1982), the Court interpreted the word "treaty," as contained in a United States statute prohibiting employment discrimination against United States citizens on military bases unless permitted by "treaty," to include executive agreements, stating: "Congress has not been consistent in distinguishing between Article II treaties and other forms of international agreements. . . . Thus it is not dispositive that Congress . . . used the term 'treaty' without specifically including international agreements that are not Article II treaties. . . . We think that some affirmative expression of congressional intent to abrogate the United States' international obligations is required in order to construe the word 'treaty' in [the statute in question] as meaning only Article II treaties." After reviewing the pertinent legislative history, the Court concluded that although the question is not free from doubt, the §106 "treaty" exception does extend to executive agreements.

Page 298. Add as new Note 4 after the carryover paragraph:

4. In Dames & Moore v. Regan, 453 U.S. 654, 101 S. Ct. 2972, 69 L. Ed. 2d 918 (1981), the Court sustained the President's agreeing to the termina-

tion of legal proceedings in American courts relating to Iranian assets that had effectively been "frozen," in exchange for the release by the Iranian government of Americans who had been held hostage there for over a year. Relying on the authorization provided to the Chief Executive by various Congressional enactments, in particular the International Emergency Economic Powers Act (50 U.S.C. 1701-1706), the Court, speaking through Justice Rehnquist, concluded:

"Because the President's action in nullifying the attachments and ordering the transfer of the assets was taken pursuant to specific congressional authorization, it is 'supported by the strongest of presumptions and the widest latitude of judicial interpretation, and the burden of persuasion would rest heavily upon any who might attack it.' *Youngstown,* 343 U.S., at 637 (Jackson, J., concurring). Under the circumstances of this case, we cannot say that petitioner has sustained that heavy burden. A contrary ruling would mean that the Federal Government as a whole lacked the power exercised by the President, see id., at 636-637, and that we are not prepared to say. . . .

Turning to the question of the President's power to suspend claims pending in American courts, the Court stated: "Although we have declined to conclude that the IEEPA or the Hostage Act directly authorizes the President's suspension of claims for the reasons noted, we cannot ignore the general tenor of Congress' legislation in this area in trying to determine whether the President is acting alone or at least with the acceptance of Congress. As we have noted, Congress cannot anticipate and legislate with regard to every possible action the President may find it necessary to take or every possible situation in which he might act. Such failure of Congress specifically to delegate authority does not, 'especially . . . in the areas of foreign policy and national security,' imply 'congressional disapproval' of action taken by the Executive, [quoting from Haig v. Agee, infra in this Supplement, addition to Casebook p.1597]. On the contrary, the enactment of legislation closely related to the question of the President's authority in a particular case which evinces legislative intent to accord the President broad discretion may be considered to 'invite' 'measures on independent presidential responsibility.' *Youngstown,* 343 U.S., at 637 (Jackson, J., concurring). At least this is so where there is no contrary indication of legislative intent and when, as here, there is a history of congressional acquiescence in conduct of the sort engaged in by the President. It is to that history which we now turn.

"Not infrequently in affairs between nations, outstanding claims by nationals of one country against the government of another country are 'sources of friction' between the two sovereigns. United States v. Pink, 315 U.S. 203, 225 (1942). To resolve these difficulties, nations have often entered into agreements settling the claims of their respective nationals. As one treatise writer puts it, international agreements settling claims by nationals of one state against the government of another 'are established international practice reflecting traditional international theory.' L. Henkin, Foreign Affairs and the Constitution 262 (1972). Consistent with that principle, the United States has repeatedly exercised its sovereign authority to settle the claims of its nationals against foreign countries. Though those settlements have sometimes been made by treaty, there has also been a longstanding practice of settling such claims by executive agreement without the advice and consent of the Senate. Under such agreements, the President has agreed to renounce or extinguish claims of United States nationals against foreign governments in return for lump sum payments or the establishment of arbitration procedures.... It is clear that the practice of settling claims continues today. Since 1952, the President has entered into at least 10 binding settlements with foreign nations, including an $80 million settlement with the People's Republic of China."

After discussing the International Claims Settlement Act (22 U.S.C. 1621 et seq.) in some detail, the Court further stated:

"In addition to congressional acquiescence in the President's power to settle claims, prior cases of this Court have also recognized that the President does have some measure of power to enter into executive agreements without obtaining the advice and consent of the Senate. In United States v. Pink, 315 U.S. 203 (1942), for example, the Court upheld the validity of the Litvinov Assignment, which was part of an Executive Agreement whereby the Soviet Union assigned to the United States amounts owed to it by American nationals so that outstanding claims of other American nationals could be paid. The Court explained that the resolution of such claims was integrally connected with normalizing United States' relations with a foreign state."

Rejecting several arguments "in opposition to" the proposition that Congress has acquiesced in this longstanding practice of claims settlement by executive agreement, Rehnquist asserted:

"In the first place, we do not believe that the President has attempted to divest the federal courts of jurisdiction. Executive Order No. 12294 purports only to 'suspend' the claims, not divest the federal courts of 'jurisdiction.' As we read the Executive Order, those claims not within the jurisdiction of the Claims Tribunal [contemplated by the agreement] will 'revive' and become judicially enforceable in United States courts. This case, in short, illustrates the difference between modifying federal court jurisdiction and directing the courts to apply a different rule of law.... The President has exercised the power, acquiesced in by Congress, to settle claims and, as such, has simply effected a change in the substantive law governing the lawsuit. Indeed, the very example of sovereign immunity belies petitioner's argument. No one would suggest that a determination of sovereign immunity divests the federal courts of 'jurisdiction.' Yet, petitioner's argument, if accepted, would have required courts prior to the enactment of the [Foreign Sovereign Immunities Act (28 U.S.C. 1330, 1602 et seq.)] to reject as an encroachment on their jurisdiction the President's determination of a foreign state's sovereign immunity."

In concluding, the Court stated: "In light of all of the foregoing – the inferences to be drawn from the character of the legislation Congress has enacted in the area, such as the IEEPA and the Hostage Act, and from the history of acquiescence in executive claims settlement — we conclude that the President was authorized to suspend pending claims pursuant to Executive Order No. 12294. As Justice Frankfurter pointed out in *Youngstown,* 343 U.S. at 610-611, 'a systematic, unbroken executive practice, long pursued to the knowledge of Congress and never before questioned . . . may be treated as a gloss on "Executive Power" vested in the President by §1 of Art. II.' . . . Such practice is present here and such a presumption is also appropriate. In light of the fact that Congress may be considered to have consented to the President's action in suspending claims, we cannot say that action exceeded the President's powers.

"Our conclusion is buttressed by the fact that the means chosen by the President to settle the claims of American nationals provided an alternate forum, the Claims Tribunal, which is capable of providing meaningful relief. [Perhaps] the provision of the Claims Tribunal will actually *enhance* the opportunity for claimants to recover their claims, in that the Agreement removes a number of jurisdictional and procedural impediments faced by claimants in United States courts. . . . Although being overly sanguine about the chances of United States claimants before the Claims Tribunal would require a degree of naivete which should not be demanded even of judges, the. . .point cannot be discounted. Moreover, it is important to remember that we have already held that the President has the *statutory* authority to nullify attachments and to transfer the assets out of the country. The Presidents's power to do so does not depend on his provision of a forum whereby claimants can recover on those claims. The fact that the President has provided such a forum here means that the claimants are receiving something in return for the suspension of their claims, namely, access to an international tribunal before which they may well recover something on their claims. Because there does appear to be a real 'settlement' here, this case is more easily analogized to the more traditional claim settlement cases of the past.

"Just as importantly, Congress has not disapproved of the action taken here. Though Congress has held hearings on the Iranian Agreement itself, Congress has not enacted legislation, or even passed a resolution, indicating its displeasure with the Agreement. Quite the contrary, the relevant Senate Committee has stated that the establishment of the Tribunal is 'of vital importance to the United States.' S. Rep. No. 97-71, 97th Cong., 1st Sess., 5 (1981). We are thus clearly not confronted with a situation in which Congress has in some way resisted the exercise of presidential authority.

"Finally, we re-emphasize the narrowness of our decision. We do not decide that the President possesses plenary power to settle claims, even as against foreign governmental entities. . . . But where, as here, the settlement of claims has been determined to be a necessary incident to the resolution of a major foreign policy dispute between our country and another, and where, as here, we can conclude that Congress acquiesced in the President's action, we are not prepared to say that the President lacks the power to settle such claims."

Justice Rehnquist concluded by asserting that it would be inappropriate "at the present time to address petitioner's contention that the suspension of claims, if authorized, would constitute a taking of property in violation of the Fifth Amendment... in the absence of just compensation," as the litigants themselves conceded that such a question "is not ripe for review." But, Rehnquist noted, "to the extent petitioner believes it has suffered an unconstitutional taking by the suspension of the claims, we see no jurisdictional obstacle to an appropriate action in the United States Court of Claims under the Tucker Act [28 U.S.C. 1491]."

Justice Powell concurred in part and dissented in part, agreeing with the "Court's opinion except its decision that the nullification of the attachments did not effect a taking of property interests giving rise to claims for just compensation."

Page 311. At the end of Note 3 add:

With respect to the authority of the executive branch to revoke an American citizen's passport on the ground that the individual's activities in foreign countries "are causing or are likely to cause serious damage to the national security or foreign policy of the United States," see Haig v. Agee, 453 U.S. 280, 101 S. Ct. 2766, 69 L. Ed. 2d 640 (1981), infra in this Supplement, addition to Casebook p.1597.

Page 320:

In line 25 of the carryover paragraph change "recessions" to "rescissions."

Page 324:

In line 2 of the first full paragraph insert "the" after "revoking."

Page 325. At the end of Note 10 add:

In Ferri v. Ackerman, 444 U.S. 193, 100 S. Ct. 402, 62 L. Ed. 2d 355 (1979), the Court held that appointed counsel representing indigent defendants in federal criminal trials are not entitled to absolute immunity in a malpractice action brought against them in a state court. The primary rationale for granting such immunity to judges, prosecutors, grand jurors, and other federal officers — freedom from intimidation — is absent with respect to appointed counsel, whose responsibilities are more analogous to those of privately retained counsel. Thus, "the federal officer immunity doctrine explicated in cases like Howard v. Lyons ... and Butz v. Economou ... is simply inapplicable...."

Page 326. At the end of Note 11 add:

Cf. Kissinger v. Reporters Committee for Freedom of the Press, 445 U.S. 136, 100 S. Ct. 960, 63 L. Ed. 2d 267 (1980), and Forsham v. Harris, 445 U.S. 169, 100 S. Ct. 978, 63 L. Ed. 2d 293 (1980), both dealing, *inter alia*, with the meaning of the phrase "agency records" as contained in the FOIA.

Page 340:

In line 2 of the last paragraph of Note 2 change "indicted" to "unindicted."

Page 342. At the end of Note 3 add:

See also the Classified Information Procedures Act (P.L. 96-456), which provides explicit procedures for requesting and obtaining "classified information" for use in criminal cases.

Chapter Four

Powers of the States in Areas of Federal Authority

Page 368. At the end of the first full paragraph add:

See also Kassel v. Consolidated Freightways Corp., 450 U.S. 662, 101 S. Ct. 1309, 67 L. Ed. 2d 580 (1981), where the Court invalidated an Iowa statute which restricted the maximum length of vehicles that may use its highways. Justice Powell announced the judgment of the Court, stating: "It is unnecessary to review in detail the evolution of the principles of Commerce Clause adjudication. The clause is both a 'prolific source of national power and an equally prolific source of conflict with legislation of the States[s]. . . .' The Clause permits Congress to legislate when it perceives that the national welfare is not furthered by the independent actions of the States. It is now well established, also, that the Clause itself is a 'limitation upon state power even without congressional implementation.' Hunt v. Washington State Apple Advertising Commn., 432 U.S. 333 (1977). The Clause requires that some aspects of trade generally must remain free from interference by the States. When a State ventures excessively into regulation of those aspects of commerce, it 'trespasses upon national interests' . . . and the courts will hold the State regulation invalid under the Clause alone."

Continuing, he stated: "The Commerce Clause does not, of course, invalidate all state restrictions on commerce. It has long been recognized that, 'in the absence of conflicting legislation by Congress, there is a residuum of power in the State to make laws governing matters of local concern which nevertheless in some measure affect interstate commerce or even, to some extent, regulate it.' Southern Pacific Co. v. Arizona, 325 U.S. 761, 767 (1945). The extent of the permissible state regulation is not always easy to measure. It may be said with confidence, however, that a state's power to regulate commerce is never greater than in matters traditionally of local concern. . . . But the incantation of a purpose to promote the public health and safety does not insulate a state law from Commerce Clause attack. Regulations designed for that salutary purpose nevertheless may further the purpose so marginally, and interfere with commerce so substantially, as to be invalid under the Commerce Clause."

After examining the Iowa statute to determine its legislative purpose and its regulatory effects, the Court concluded that the statute unconstitutionally burdened interstate commerce, without the promotion of any significant countervailing safety interest.

Justice Brennan, joined by Justice Marshall, concurred in the judgment, but on other grounds, finding that the Iowa law sought to discourage interstate truck traffic on its highways. The result of this characterization was to label the Iowa statute as a protectionist measure and therefore impermissible under the commerce clause.

Page 385. At the end of Note 3 add:

In State of Minnesota v. Clover Leaf Creamery Co., 449 U.S. 456, 101 S. Ct. 715, 66 L. Ed. 2d 659 (1981), the Court upheld a Minnesota statute which banned the sale of milk in plastic non-returnable containers, but permitted such sale in other non-returnable containers such as paperboard cartons. The purported purpose of the statute was to promote resource conservation, ease solid waste problems, and conserve energy.

The Court initiated its examination of the Minnesota statute by citing Hunt v. Washington State Apple Advertising Commn. for the proposition that when a state exercises its legislative duty "in areas of legitimate concern, such as environmental protection and resource conservation, [it is] nonetheless limited by the Commerce Clause." The Court continued, stating that it has applied a "[virtual] *per se* rule of invalidity" to laws purporting to promote environmental purposes, when they are in reality a disguised form of "economic protectionism." It then declared, however, that Minnesota's statute does not effect "simple protectionism," but regulates evenhandedly "by prohibiting all milk retailers from selling their products in plastic non-returnable milk containers, without regard to whether the milk, the containers, or the sellers are from outside the State. This statute is therefore unlike statutes discriminating against interstate commerce. . . ."

Since the Court found that the statute did not discriminate against interstate commerce, it framed the controlling question as "whether the incidental burden imposed on interstate commerce by the Minnesota act is 'clearly excessive in relation to the putative local benefits.' " It then concluded that "[t]he burden imposed on interstate commerce by the statute is relatively minor. Milk products may continue to move freely across the Minnesota border, and since most dairies package their products in more than one type of container, the inconvenience of having to conform to different packaging requirements in Minnesota and surrounding states should be slight." The Court also found it inconsequential that "pulpwood producers are the only Minnesota industry likely to benefit significantly from the Act at the expense of out-of-state firms." The Court's majority thus sustained the statute based on its finding of a legitimate state purpose, and the lack of a significant burden on interstate commerce.

For a discussion of Justice Stevens' dissent, see supra in this Supplement, addition to Casebook p.137.

Page 387. At the end of Note 1 add:

See also Lewis v. BT Investment Managers, Inc., 447 U.S. 27, 100 S. Ct. 2009, 64 L. Ed. 2d 702 (1980), distinguishing *Exxon Corp.* in holding that a Florida statute prohibiting out-of-state bank holding companies from owning or controlling businesses within the state that sell investment advisory services impermissibly discriminated against interstate commerce. While banking and related financial activities are of "profound local concern," they also have interstate attributes which provide a basis for congressional regulation and likewise support constitutional limitations on the powers of the states. The statutory scheme in question was found to be too "parochial," for it overtly prevented foreign financial institutions from competing in local markets. The Court found that the discrimination under the statute was not evenhanded because only banks, bank holding companies, and trust companies with principal operations outside Florida were prohibited from operating investment subsidiaries or giving investment advice within the state. Thus, the law discriminated among business entities according to the extent of their contacts with the local economy. Nor can the disparate treatment of out-of-state bank holding companies be justified as an incidental burden necessitated by legitimate local concerns.

Page 388. At the end of carryover paragraph add:

See also New England Power Co. v. New Hampshire, — U.S. —, 102 S. Ct. 1096, — L. Ed. 2d — (1982), where the Court was presented with the question whether a state can constitutionally prohibit the exportation of hydroelectric energy produced within its borders by a federally licensed facility. The Court held that the commerce clause precludes a state from giving its residents preferential rights of access to natural resources located within its borders, absent authorizing federal legislation. The Court went on to hold that Section 201(b) of the Federal Power Act, which provides in pertinent part that the Act "shall not ... deprive a State or State commission of its lawful authority now experienced over the exportation of hydroelectric energy ...," does not grant the states the affirmative power to burden interstate commerce in an impermissible manner. Speaking for a unanimous Court, Chief Justice Burger wrote: "Our cases have consequently held that the Commerce Clause ... precludes a State from mandating that its residents be given a preferred right of access, over out-of-state consumers, to natural resources located within its borders as to the products derived therefrom," citing, e.g., Philadelphia v. New Jersey. "[This] is precisely the sort of protectionist regulation that the Commerce Clause declares off-limits to the States. [Here the approach] is designed to gain an economic advantage for New Hampshire citizens at the expense of New England Power's customers in neighboring states." With respect to whether Congress had authorized the New Hampshire restriction, the Court stated that Section 201(b) of the Federal Power Act "is in no sense an affirmative grant of power to the States to widen interstate commerce [impermissibly]," but rather "did no more than leave standing whatever valid state laws then existed relating to the exportation of hydroelectric energy," thus "sav[ing] from [federal] pre-emption such state authority as was otherwise 'lawful.'" Concluding, Burger wrote: "[W]hen Congress has not 'expressly stated its intent and policy' to sustain state legislation from attack under the Commerce Clause, ... we have no authority to rewrite its legislation, based on what Congress 'probably had in mind.'" Section 201(b) was thus no more that it purported to be — "a standard 'non-preemption' clause."

Page 389. At the end of Note 3 add:

Cf. Reeves, Inc. v. Stake, 447 U.S. 429, 100 S. Ct. 2271, 65 L. Ed. 2d 244 (1980), holding that South Dakota's policy of preferring residents over out-of-state buyers with respect to sales of cement produced in a state-operated cement plant did not violate the commerce clause. Relying on Hughes v. Alexandria Scrap Corp., the Court stated that the commerce clause does not "limit the ability of the States themselves to operate freely in the free market." Since "state proprietary activities may be, and often are, burdened with the same restrictions imposed on private market participants,... [e]venhandedness suggests that, when acting as proprietors, States should similarly share existing freedoms from federal constraints, including the in-herent limits of the Commerce Clause." After rejecting the contention that the measure was "protectionist" in character, the Court distinguished situa-tions where natural resources "like coal, timber, wild game, or minerals" are involved. Justices Powell, Brennan, White, and Stevens dissented, stating that South Dakota's policy "represents precisely the kind of economic pro-tectionism that the Commerce Clause was intended to prevent" and express-ing concern that the majority's rationale might apply as well to state limitations on the access by nonresidents to scarce and important natural resources, despite the disclaimers in this regard.

Page 406:

In line 9 of the first full paragraph in the transitional note delete "Chief."

Page 410. At the end of Note 2 add:

Cf. Maryland v. Louisiana, 451 U.S. 725, 101 S. Ct. 2114, 68 L. Ed. 2d 576 (1981), where several states, together with the United States government and a number of pipeline companies, challenged Louisiana's imposition of a "first use tax" on natural gas brought into the state from the outer continental shelf. After discussing the exercise of the Court's original jurisdiction (supra in this Supplement, addition to Casebook p.103), the Court addressed the merits of the case.

Justice White delivered the opinion of the Court, stating:

"[The] plaintiffs argue that the First-Use Tax violates the Supremacy Clause because it interferes with federal regulation of the transportation and sale of natural gas in interstate commerce [and in particular] that §1303C of the First-Use Tax violates the Natural Gas Act, 15 U.S.C. §§717a-717w (Gas Act), as amended by the Gas Policy Act of 1978. In 1938, Congress enacted the Gas Act to assure that consumers of natural gas receive a fair price and also to protect against the economic power of the interstate pipeline. . . . The Gas Act was intended to provide the FPC, now the FERC, with authority to regulate the wholesale pricing of natural gas in the flow of interstate commerce from wellhead to delivery to consumers. Phillips Petroleum Co. v. Wisconsin, 347 U.S. 672, 682 (1954).

"Under the present law, natural gas owners are entitled to recover from their customers all legitimate costs associated with the production, processing, and transportation of natural gas. . . . As part of the First-Use Tax, Louisiana has directed that the amount of the Tax should be 'deemed a cost associated with uses made by the owner in preparation of marketing of the natural gas.' 47 La. Rev. Stat. §1303C. The Act further provides that an owner shall not have an enforceable right to seek reimbursement for payment of the Tax from any third party other than a purchaser of the gas, even though the third party may be the owner of marketable hydrocarbons that are extracted from the gas in the course of processing.

"The effect of §1303C is to interfere with the FERC's authority to regulate the determination of the proper allocation of costs associated with the sale of natural gas to consumers. The unprocessed gas obtained at the wellhead contains extractable hydrocarbons which are most often owned and sold separately from the 'dried' gas. The FERC normally allocates part of the processing costs between these related products, and insists that the owners of the liquefiable hydrocarbons bear a fair share of the expense associated with processing. . . . By specifying that the First-Use Tax is a processing cost to be either borne by the pipeline or other owner without compensation, an unlikely event in light of the large sums involved, or passed on to purchasers, Louisiana has attempted a substantial usurpation of the authority of the FERC by dictating to the pipelines the allocation of processing costs for the interstate shipment of natural gas. Owners of natural gas are foreclosed by the operation of §1303C from entering into valid contracts requiring the owners of the extracted hydrocarbons to reimburse the pipelines for costs associated with transporting and processing these products. The effect of §1303C is to shift the incidence of certain expenses, which the FERC insists are incurred substantially for the benefit of the owners of extractable hydrocarbons, to the ultimate consumer of the processed gas without the prior approval of the FERC....

"[Contrary to the Special Master, it] is our view... that the issue is ripe for decision without further evidentiary hearings. Under the Gas Act, determining pipeline and producer costs is the task of the FERC in the first instance, subject to judicial review. Hence, the further hearings contemplated by the Special Master to determine whether and how processing costs are to be allocated are as inappropriate as Louisiana's effort to pre-empt those decisions by a statute directing that processing costs be passed on to the consumer. Even if the FERC ultimately determined that such expenses should be passed on *in toto*, this kind of decisionmaking is within the jurisdiction of the FERC; and the Louisiana statute, like the state commission's order in [an earlier case], is inconsistent with the federal scheme and must give way.... The FERC need not adjust its rulings to accommodate the Louisiana statute. To the contrary, the State may not trespass on the authority of the federal agency. As we see it, plaintiffs are entitled to judgment on the pleadings that §1303C is invalid under the Supremacy Clause. To that extent, therefore, we sustain plaintiffs' exceptions to the Special Master's second report.

"Plaintiffs also argue that the First-Use Tax violates the Commerce Clause.... Initially, it is clear to us that the flow of gas from the OCS wells, through processing plants in Louisiana, and through interstate pipelines to the ultimate consumers in over 30 States constitutes interstate commerce. Louisiana argues that the taxable 'uses' within the State break the flow of commerce and are wholly local events. But although the Louisiana 'uses' may possess a sufficient local nexus to support otherwise valid taxation, we do not agree that the flow of gas from the wellhead to the consumer, even though 'interrupted' by certain events, is anything but a continual flow of gas in interstate commerce. Gas crossing a state line at any stage of its movement to the ultimate consumer is in interstate commerce during the entire journey....

"A state tax must be assessed in light of its actual effect considered in conjunction with other provisions of a State's tax scheme. 'In each case it is our duty to determine whether the statute under attack, whatever its name may be, will in its practical operation work discrimination against interstate commerce,' [citing cases]. In this case, the Louisiana First-Use Tax unquestionably discriminates against interstate commerce in favor of local interests as the necessary result of various tax credits and exclusions. No further hearings are necessary to sustain this conclusion. Under the specific provisions of the First-Use Tax, OCS gas used for certain purposes within Louisiana is exempted from the Tax. OCS gas consumed in Louisiana for (1) producing oil, natural gas, or sulphur; (2) processing natural gas for the extraction of liquefiable hydrocarbons; or (3) manufacturing fertilizer and anhydrous ammonia, is exempt from the First-Use Tax.... Competitive users in other States are burdened with the Tax. Other Louisiana statutes, enacted as part of the First-Use Tax package, provide important tax credits favoring local interests. Under the Severance Tax Credit, an owner paying the First-Use Tax on OCS gas receives an equivalent tax credit on any state severance tax owed in connection with production in Louisiana.... On its face, this credit favors those who both own OCS gas and engage in Louisiana production. The obvious economic effect of this Severance Tax Credit is to encourage natural gas owners involved in the production of OCS gas to invest in mineral exploration and development within Louisiana rather than to invest in further OCS development or in production in other States. Finally, under the Louisiana statutes, any utility producing electricity with OCS gas, any natural gas distributor dealing in OCS gas or any direct purchaser of OCS gas for consumption by the purchaser in Louisiana may recoup any increase in the cost of gas attributable to the First-Use Tax through credits against various taxes or a combination of taxes otherwise owed to the State of Louisiana.... Louisiana consumers of OCS gas are thus substantially protected against the impact of the First-Use Tax and have the benefit of untaxed OCS gas which because it is not subject to either a severance tax or the First-Use Tax may be cheaper than locally produced gas. OCS gas moving out of the State, however, is burdened with the First-Use Tax. ...

"In our view, the First-Use Tax cannot be justified as a compensatory tax. The concept of a compensatory tax first requires identification of the burden for which the State is attempting to compensate. Here, Louisiana claims that the First-Use Tax compensates for the effect of the State's severance tax on local production of natural gas. To be sure, Louisiana has an interest in protecting its natural resources and, like most States, has chosen to impose a severance tax on the privilege of severing resources from its soil.... But the First-Use Tax is not designed to meet these same ends since Louisiana has no sovereign interest in being compensated for the severance of resources from the federally-owned OCS land. The two events are not comparable in the same fashion as a use tax complements a sales tax. In that case, a State is attempting to impose a tax on a substantially equivalent event to assure uniform treatment of goods and materials to be consumed in the State. No such equality exists in this instance.

"The common thread running through the cases upholding compensatory taxes is the equality of treatment between local and interstate commerce.... As already demonstrated, however, the pattern of credits and exemptions allowed under the Louisiana statute undeniably violates this principle of equality. As we have said, OCS gas may generally be consumed in Louisiana without the burden of the First-Use Tax. Its principal application is to gas moving out of the State. Of course, it does equalize the tax burdens on OCS gas leaving the State and Louisiana gas going into the interstate market. But this sort of equalization is not the kind of 'compensating' effect that our cases have recognized.

"It may be true that further hearings would be required to provide a precise determination of the extent of the discrimination in this case, but this is an insufficient reason for not now declaring the Tax unconstitutional and eliminating the discrimination. We need not know how unequal the Tax is before concluding that it unconstitutionally discriminates. Accordingly, we grant plaintiffs' exception that the First-Use Tax is unconstitutional under the Commerce Clause because it unfairly discriminates against purchasers of gas moving through Louisiana in interstate commerce.

"In conclusion, we hold that §1303C violates the Supremacy Clause and that the First-Use Tax is unconstitutional under the Commerce Clause. Judgment to that effect and enjoining further collection of the Tax shall be entered. Jurisdiction over the case is retained in the event that further proceedings are required to implement the judgment."

Justice Powell took no part in the consideration or decision of this case, and Chief Justice Burger concurred separately. Justice Rehnquist, dissenting alone, questioned whether this was an "appropriate case" for the Court's exercising its original jurisdiction, stating:

"There is no question that this controversy falls within the literal terms of the constitutional and statutory grant of original jurisdiction to this Court. U.S. Const., Art. III, §2, cl. 2; 28 U.S.C. §1251(a) (Supp. III 1979). As the Court stated in Illinois v. Milwaukee, 406 U.S. 91, 93 (1972), however, '[w]e construe 28 U.S.C. §1251(a)(1), as we do Art. III, §2, cl. 2, to honor our original jurisdiction but to make it obligatory only in appropriate cases.' Because of the nature of the interests which the plaintiff States seek to vindicate in this original action, and because of the existence of alternate forums in which these interests can be vindicated, I do not consider this an 'appropriate case' for the exercise of original jurisdiction. The plaintiff States have not, in my view, established the 'strictest necessity' required for invoking this Court's original jurisdiction, Ohio v. Wyandotte Chemicals Corp., 401 U.S. 493, 505 (1971), and therefore I would grant defendant Louisiana's motion to dismiss the complaint."

Page 412. At the end of Note 3 add:

See also Commonwealth Edison Co. v. Montana, 453 U.S. 609, 101 S. Ct. 2946, 69 L. Ed. 2d 884 (1981), applying the modern test enunciated in *Complete Auto Transit* in upholding a much-disputed severance tax imposed by Montana on coal mined in the state, including coal mined on federal land. The tax is levied at varying rates depending on the value, energy content, and method of extraction of the coal, and may equal, at a maximum, 30 percent of the "contract sales price" of the mineral. Coal producers challenged the tax on commerce and supremacy clause grounds, alleging that it impermissibly burdened interstate commerce as well as frustrating the purposes of the Mineral Lands Leasing Act of 1920. After first rejecting a "mechanical" approach as to whether the incidence of the tax was on essentially "local" or interstate activity, the Court, speaking through Justice Marshall, assessed the severance tax "under *Complete Auto Transit's* four-part test." A nexus clearly existed, and there was not even the potential for multiple taxation, Marshall stated. Nor did the tax discriminate against interstate commerce, for it "is computed at the same rate regardless of the final destination of the coal, and there [was] no suggestion... that the tax is administered in a manner that departs from this even-handed formula." A state tax is not "considered discriminatory for purposes of the Commerce Clause [simply because] the tax burden is borne primarily by out-of-state consumers," he continued. And the Court similarly rejected an argument that "residents of one State [have] a right of access at 'reasonable' prices to resources located in another State that is richly endowed with resources, without regard to whether and on what terms residents of that resource-rich State have access to the resources. We are not convinced that the Commerce Clause, of its own force, gives residents of one State the right to control in this fashion the terms of resource development and depletion in a sister State." Marshall then turned to "the fourth prong of the *Complete Auto Transit* test: that the tax be 'fairly related to the services provided by the State,' 430 U.S., at 279." He stated:

"Appellants argue that they are entitled to an opportunity to prove that the amount collected under the Montana tax is not fairly related to the additional costs the State incurs because of coal mining. Thus, appellants' objection is to the *rate* of the Montana tax, and even then, their only complaint is that the *amount* the State receives in taxes far exceeds the *value* of the services provided to the coal mining industry. In objecting to the tax on this ground, appellants may be assuming that the Montana tax is, in fact, intended to reimburse the State for the cost of specific services furnished to the coal mining industry. Alternatively, appellants could be arguing that a State's power to tax an activity connected to interstate commerce cannot exceed the value of the services specifically provided to the activity. Either way, the premise of appellants' argument is invalid. Furthermore, appellants have completely misunderstood the nature of the inquiry under the fourth prong of the *Complete Auto Transit* test.... To accept appellants' apparent suggestion that the Commerce Clause prohibits the States from requiring an activity connected to interstate commerce to contribute to the general cost of providing governmental services, as distinct from those costs attributable to the taxed activity, would place such commerce in a privileged position. But as we recently reiterated, ' "[i]t was not the purpose of the commerce clause to relieve those engaged in interstate commerce from their just share of state tax burden even though it increases the cost of doing business." ' Colonial Pipeline Co. v. Traigle, 421 U.S. 100, 108 (1975), quoting Western Live Stock v. Bureau of Revenue, 303 U.S., at 254. The 'just share of state tax burden' includes sharing in the cost of providing 'police and fire protection, the benefit of a trained work force, and "the advantages of a civilized society." ' Exxon Corp. v. Wisconsin Dept. of Revenue, 447 U.S., at 228, quoting Japan Line, Ltd. v. County of Los Angeles, 441 U.S., at 445. See Washington Revenue Dept. v. Association of Wash. Stevedoring Cos., 435 U.S., at 750-751; id., at 764 (Powell, J., concurring); General Motors Corp. v. Washington, 377 U.S. 436, 440-441 (1964).

"Furthermore, there can be no question that Montana may constitutionally raise general revenue by imposing a severance tax on coal mined in the State. The entire value of the coal, before transportation, originates in the State, and mining of the coal depletes the resource base and wealth of the State, thereby diminishing a future source of taxes and economic activity.... In many respects, a severance tax is like a real property tax, which has never been doubted as a legitimate means of raising revenue by the situs State (quite apart from the right of that or any other State to tax income derived from use of the property).... When, as here, a general revenue tax does not discriminate against interstate commerce and is apportioned to activities occurring within the State, the State 'is free to pursue its own fiscal policies, unembarrassed by the Constitution, if by the practical operation of a tax the state has exerted its power in relation to opportunities which it has given, to protection which it has afforded, to benefits which it has conferred by the fact of being an orderly, civilized society.' Wisconsin v. J.C. Penney Co., 311 U.S. 435, 444 (1940).

"The relevant inquiry under the fourth prong of the *Complete Auto Transit* test 'is not, as appellants suggest, the *amount* of the tax or the *value* of the benefits allegedly bestowed as measured by the costs the State incurs on account of the taxpayer's activities.' Rather, the test is closely connected to the first prong of the *Complete Auto Transit* test. Under this threshold test, the interstate business must have a substantial nexus with the State before *any* tax may be levied on it. See National Bellas Hess, Inc. v. Illinois Revenue Dept., 386 U.S. 753 (1967). Beyond that threshold requirement, the fourth prong of the *Complete Auto Transit* test imposes the additional limitation that the *measure* of the tax must be reasonably related to the extent of the contact, since it is the activities or presence of the taxpayer in the State that may properly be made to bear a 'just share of state tax burden.' Western Live Stock v. Bureau of Revenue, 303 U.S., at 254. See National Geographic Society v. California Board of Equalization, 430 U.S. 551 (1977); Standard Pressed Steel Co. v. Washington Revenue Dept., 419 U.S. 360 (1975)....

"Against this background, we have little difficulty concluding that the Montana tax satisfies the fourth prong of the *Complete Auto Transit* test. The 'operating incidence' of the tax is on the mining of coal within Montana. Because it is measured as a percentage of the value of the coal taken, the Montana tax is in 'proper proportion' to appellants' activities within the State and, therefore, to their 'consequent enjoyment of the opportunities and protections which the State has afforded' in connection to those activities. Compare Nippert v. City of Richmond, 327 U.S., at 427. When a tax is assessed in proportion to a taxpayer's activities or presence in a State, the taxpayer is shouldering its fair share of supporting the State's provision of [public services].

"Appellants argue, however, that the fourth prong of the *Complete Auto Transit* test must be construed as requiring a factual inquiry into the relationship between the revenues generated by a tax and costs incurred on account of the taxed activity, in order to provide a mechanism for judicial disapproval under the Commerce Clause of state taxes that are excessive. This assertion reveals that appellants labor under a misconception about a court's role in cases such as this. The simple fact is that the appropriate level or rate of taxation is essentially a matter for legislative, and not judicial, resolution. . . . In essence, appellants ask this Court to prescribe a test for the validity of state taxes that would require state and federal courts, as a matter of federal constitutional law, to calculate acceptable rates or levels of taxation of activities that are conceded to be legitimate subjects of taxation. This we decline to do.

"In the first place, it is doubtful whether any legal test could adequately reflect the numerous and competing economic, geographic, demographic, social, and political considerations that must inform a decision about an acceptable rate or level of state taxation, and yet be reasonably capable of application in a wide variety of individual cases. But even apart from the difficulty of the judicial undertaking, the nature of the factfinding and judgment that would be required of the courts merely reinforces the conclusion that questions about the appropriate level of state taxes must be resolved through the political process. Under our federal system, the determination is to be made by state legislatures in the first instance and, if necessary, by Congress, when particular state taxes are thought to be contrary to federal interests. Cf. Mobil Oil Corp. v. Commissioner of Taxes, 445 U.S., at 448-449; Moorman Manufacturing Co. v. Bair, 437 U.S., at 280. . . . We are satisfied that the Montana tax, assessed under a formula that relates the tax liability to the value of appellant coal producers' activities within the State, comports with the requirements of the *Complete Auto Transit* test."

The Court's consideration of the supremacy clause issue is discussed infra in this Supplement, addition to Casebook p.469.

Justice Blackmun, joined by Justices Powell and Stevens, dissented, maintaining that, under *Complete Auto Transit,* a tax allegedly "tailored to single out interstate commerce" and assertedly bearing no relationship to the services provided by the taxing state should be given "careful scrutiny." At the least, the dissenters suggested, "appellants [should be] entitled to a *trial* on this claim." After noting that "the imposition of this severence tax has generated enormous revenues for" Montana, which "has approximately 25% of all known United States coal reserves," Blackmun wrote:

"We have not interpreted this requirement of 'fair relation' in a narrow sense; interstate commerce may be required to share equally with intrastate commerce the cost of providing [public services]. Moreover, interstate commerce can be required to 'pay its own way' in a narrower sense as well: the

State may tax interstate commerce for the purpose of recovering those costs attributable to the activity itself. . . . [But the] Court has never suggested, however, that interstate commerce may be required to pay *more* than its own way. The Court today fails to recognize that the Commerce Clause does impose limits upon the State's power to impose even facially neutral and properly apportioned taxes. . . . Accordingly, while the Commerce Clause does not require that interstate commerce be placed in a privileged position it does require that it not be unduly burdened. . . .

"[A] mineral-rich State [may] require that those who consume its resources pay a fair share of the general costs of government, as well as the specific costs attributable to the commerce itself. Thus, the mere fact that the burden of a severance tax is largely shifted forward to out-of-state consumers does not, standing alone, make out a Commerce Clause violation. . . . But the Clause *is* violated when, as appellants allege is the case here, the State effectively selects a 'class of out-of-state taxpayers to shoulder a tax burden grossly in excess of any costs imposed directly or indirectly by such taxpayers on the State.' "

In concluding, Justice Blackmun acknowledged that the task of the judiciary in applying the "fairly related" facet of *Complete Auto Transit's* test would be "a formidable one" in a complex situation such as the one presented by the Montana tax. But, since the case "poses grave issues that threaten both to 'polarize the Nation'. . . and to reawaken 'the tendencies toward economic Balkanization' that the Commerce Clause was designed to remedy," the courts "should not lightly abandon [their proper] role."

Justice White concurred separately, resolving his doubts about the case by relying on the potential exercise of congressional authority "to protect interstate commerce from intolerable or even undesirable burdens," together with the executive branch's counsel "not to overturn the Montana tax as inconsistent with either the Commerce Clause or federal statutory policy in the field of energy or otherwise. The constitutional authority and the machinery to thwart efforts such as those of Montana, if thought unacceptable, are available to Congress, and surely Montana and other similarly situated States do not have the political power to impose their will on the rest of the country."

Page 455. At the end of the carryover paragraph add:

For a recent case decided along the same lines as *LaRue,* see New York State Liquor Authority v. Bellanca, 452 U.S. 714, 101 S. Ct. 2599, 69 L. Ed. 2d 357 (1981), where the Court, in a per curiam decision, held that a New York statute which prohibited nude dancing in establishments licensed by the state to sell liquor for on-premises consumption is not unconstitutional. The Court explained its holding by citing and quoting from both California v. LaRue and Doran v. Salem Inn, Inc., 422 U.S. 922 (1974), for the proposition that a state may, pursuant to its power to regulate the sale of liquor within its boundaries, ban topless dancing in establishments granted a license to serve liquor.

Page 456. At the end of Note 3 add:

In Mobil Oil Corp. v. Commissioner of Taxes of Vermont, 445 U.S. 425, 100 S. Ct. 1223, 63 L. Ed. 2d 510 (1980), the Court held that Vermont's imposition of an income tax, on income received by a New York corporation in the form of "foreign source" dividends ... from its subsidiaries and affiliates doing business abroad, violated neither the due process nor commerce clauses nor imposed an undue burden on foreign commerce. There was a sufficient nexus so as to satisfy the due process clause, the Court concluded, for Mobil was a single unitary business with substantial contacts with Vermont, and there was a rational relationship between the income attributed to the state and the intrastate activities of the corporation. Mobil had failed to establish that dividends from foreign subsidiaries and affiliates were so unrelated to its sale of petroleum products in Vermont so as to require exemption of such foreign source income from fairly apportioned income taxation by Vermont.

Nor did the income taxation in question impose an impermissible burden on interstate or foreign commerce. Although New York was the corporation's "commercial domicile," there was no reason why, as a result, it should have the exclusive authority to tax Mobil's dividend income. That income is part of the income of a functionally integrated entity and thus is reasonably related to the benefits and privileges conferred on the corporation by several states, in addition to New York. Thus, although the Court declined to decide what the "constituent elements" of a fair apportionment formula might be, it found that Vermont's three-factor formula, based on sales, payroll, and property, resulted in no multiple taxation within the meaning of the Court's applicable precedents, as applied to Mobil's dividend income. Moreover, there was no burden on foreign commerce, for the focus of concern was on domestic rather than foreign taxation of commerce. Japan Line, Ltd. v. County of Los Angeles, Casebook p.400, was inapposite, for there the Court had "focused on problems of duplicative taxation at the international level," instead of "the wholly different sphere of multiple taxation among our States" as presented here.

Finally, the Court rejected Mobil's arguments based on "federal tax policy," for the "federal statutes and treaties [cited] concern problems of multiple taxation at the international level and simply are not germane to the issue of multiple state taxation [the corporation] has framed. Concurrent federal and state taxation of income, of course, is a well-established norm. Absent some explicit directive from Congress, we cannot infer that treatment of foreign income at the federal level mandates identical treatment by the States. The absence of any explicit directive to that effect is attested by the fact that Congress has long debated, but has not enacted, legislation designed to regulate state taxation of income." *Northwestern States Portland Cement* was discussed at length, and the Court also referred to "several recent cases" where it had "attempted to clarify apparently conflicting precedents" regarding the impact of the commerce clause on state taxation, citing *Moorman Manufacturing Co., Association of Washington Stevedoring Cos.,* and *Complete Auto Transit.*

Justice Stevens was the sole dissenter from Justice Blackmun's majority opinion, although Justices Stewart and Marshall did not participate.

How significant a case is *Mobil Oil*? Does it add anything of doctrinal consequence to the previously established framework? If so, what? Assuming it is reflective of the Court's increasingly permissive attitude toward state taxation, does it extend that approach several steps beyond its previous reach?

Applying the recently decided *Mobil Oil Corp.* case, the Court in Exxon Corp. v. Wisconsin Department of Revenue, 447 U.S. 207, 100 S. Ct. 2109, 65 L. Ed. 2d 66 (1980), held that Wisconsin could, consistent with the due process and commerce clauses, impose a net income tax on the statutorily apportioned total income of a vertically integrated petroleum company doing business in several states. Although Exxon had no exploration, production, or refining operations in Wisconsin, the Court determined that its marketing activities within the state were an integral part of one unitary business so that the necessary "minimal connection" or "nexus" existed between the taxing state and the interstate aspects of the company's business. Moreover, since the company did not show actual multiple taxation, the Wisconsin statute did not violate the commerce clause. Wisconsin's three-pronged apportionment sought to ensure that the amount of income taxed was fairly related to services provided by that state to a company having a substantial nexus with the taxing jurisdiction, citing *Moorman Manufacturing Co.* along with *Mobil Oil.* Quoting from the latter case the Court stated that "[t]he 'linchpin of apportionability' for state income taxation of an interstate enterprise is the 'unitary business principle.'" Interestingly, there were no dissents.

Page 465. At the end of Note 4 add:

But cf. Justice White's dissent from the Court's denial of certiorari in United Air Lines, Inc. v. Division of Industrial Safety of the State of California, — U.S. — , 102 S. Ct. 485, — L. Ed. 2d — (1981), where the petitioner, United Air Lines, challenged California's OSHA system as it is applied to aircraft operation and maintenance facilities in California. United argued that the operation of the federal scheme of FAA supervision preempts enforcement of the state scheme. The district court granted United's motion for injunctive relief, which prohibited further enforcement by Cal./OSHA. The Court of Appeals for the Ninth Circuit reversed, holding that the complaint should be dismissed for lack of subject matter jurisdiction.

Justice White stated: "Petitioner [here] alleged that the state action interfered with and disrupted the federal statutory scheme. This can only be read as a claim of federal pre-emption. The Court of Appeals responded erroneously, in my view, to this issue of pre-emption by characterizing it as defensive [in posture] and an inadequate basis for federal court jurisdiction." Continuing, Justice White stated: "The suggestion that a defendant in a pending or threatened state action based on state law is foreclosed on jurisdictional grounds from seeking a federal declaratory judgment or an injunction based on the claim that the state action is barred by a federal statute or the Federal Constitution makes little sense in light of the [prior] holdings of the Court. . . . [If] there is never jurisdiction when a state defendant has a defense grounded in federal law, the Anti-Injunction Act [see Casebook p.136] would be surplusage. Under this theory, all litigants would be required to pursue their federal claims in state court. Perhaps they should, but that is not what the present jurisdictional statutes and our cases construing them require."

Page 466. At the end of Note 7 add:

Cf. New England Power Co. v. New Hampshire, supra in this Supplement, addition to Casebook p. 388.

Page 468. At the end of Note 12 add:

In Maryland v. Louisiana, 451 U.S. 725, 101 S. Ct. 2114, 68 L. Ed. 2d 576 (1981), the Supreme Court held Louisiana's "first use tax" on natural gas brought into the state from the outer continental shelf invalid under the supremacy clause. The Court found that the Natural Gas Act, 15 U.S.C. 717a-717w, was amended by the Gas Policy Act of 1978, gave the Federal Power Commission "paramount and exclusive authority" to regulate the "intricate relationship between the purchaser's cost structures and eventual costs to wholesale customers who sell to consumers in other states." Thus, the "first use tax" was inconsistent with the federal scheme, and, as such, the federal act preempted the Louisiana statute. For a more complete discussion of the merits, see supra in this Supplement, addition to Casebook p.410.

Page 469. At the end of Note 13 add:

Cf. Commonwealth Edison Co. v. Montana, 453 U.S. 609, 101 S. Ct. 2946, 69 L. Ed. 2d 884 (1981), rejecting a contention that a Montana severance tax, as applied to the mining of federally owned coal, violated the supremacy clause because it conflicted with the purposes of the Mineral Lands Leasing Act of 1920 (30 U.S.C. 181 et seq.).

"Congress expressly authorized the States to impose severance taxes on federal lessees without imposing any limits on the amount of such taxes," the Court pointed out. Neither the language nor the legislative history of the federal statute indicates that the Montana tax, by effectively appropriating directly to Montana a major portion of the "economic rents" from the lands, conflicts with the purpose of the congressional act. Nor, the Court determined, was the Montana tax unconstitutional because it allegedly "substantially frustrates national energy policies, [as] reflected in several federal statutes." The Court found no congressional interest "to pre-empt all state legislation that may leave an adverse impact on the use of coal."

For discussion of the commerce clause aspects of the case, see supra in this Supplement, addition to Casebook p.412.

Page 470. At the end of Note 2 add:

Cf. McCarty v. McCarty, 453 U.S. 210, 101 S. Ct. 2728, 69 L. Ed. 2d 589 (1981), where the Court was faced with a challenge to a federal military retirement statute in the context of a divorce proceeding in California, a community-property state. After examining and explaining the policy that the field of domestic relations is one which belongs primarily to the individual states, the Court further stated that a "[state's] family and family-property law must do 'major damage' to 'clear and substantial federal interests before the Supremacy Clause will demand that state law be overridden. . . .' " The Court went on to characterize California's community property statute as one which impairs the federal interest in providing military retirement pay to such a degree as to require application of supremacy clause principles, holding:

"We conclude, therefore, that there is a conflict between the terms of the federal retirement statute and the community property right asserted by the appellee here. . . . [T]he question remains whether the 'consequences of that [community property right] sufficiently injure the objective of the federal program to require nonrecognition.' . . . This inquiry, however, need be only a brief one, for it is manifest that the application of community property principles to military retired pay threatens grave harm to 'clear and substantial' federal interests. . . . Under the Constitution, Congress has the power '[t]o raise and support armies,' '[t]o provide and maintain a navy,' and '[t]o make rules for the Government and Regulation of the land and Naval Forces.' U.S. Const., Art. I, §8, cls. 12, 13, and 14. . . . Pursuant to this grant of authority, Congress has enacted a military retirement system designed to accomplish two major goals: to provide for the retired service member, and to meet the personal management needs of the active military forces. The community property division of retired pay has the potential to frustrate each of these objectives."

Justice Rehnquist dissented, joined by Justice Brennan and Justice Stewart, essentially stating his belief that unless the federal statutory scheme authorizing the military retirement system explicitly states that state laws are to be pre-empted, the Court should not read this language into the legislation.

See also Ridgway v. Ridgway — U.S. — , 102 S. Ct. 49, — L. Ed. 2d — (1981), where the Court held that pursuant to provisions of the Servicemen's Group Life Insurance Act of 1965, the designated beneficiary of the insurance proceeds prevails over an inconsistent state court divorce judgment imposing a constructive trust upon the insurance proceeds in favor of the decedent's children. The Court grounded its decision on both the legislative history of the act and the supremacy clause.

Page 479. At the end of Note 2 add:

Allgeyer. Justice Black dissented.

Page 480. At the end of the first full paragraph in Note 3 add:

Compare California Retail Liquor Dealers Association v. Midcal Aluminum, Inc., 445 U.S. 97, 100 S. Ct. 937, 63 L. Ed. 2d 233 (1980), holding that the Twenty-first Amendment did not bar application of the Sherman Act to California's wine resale price maintenance system, as the asserted state interests were less substantial than the national policy favoring competition.

Chapter Five

Intergovernmental Relations

Page 504. Add to the first paragraph of the footnoted material:

Comment, Federal Immunity from State Taxation: A Reassessment, 45 U. Chi. L. Rev. 695 (1978).

Page 510. At the end of Note 5 add:

Wells & Hellerstein, The Governmental-Proprietary Distinction in Constitutional Law, 66 Virginia L. Rev. 1073 (1980).

See also United States v. New Mexico, — U.S. — , 102 S. Ct. 1373, — L. Ed. 2d — (1982), where Justice Blackmun delivered a unanimous opinion dealing with the constitutional question of the extent to which a state may impose taxes on contractors that conduct business with the federal government. After characterizing the Court's earlier attempts to resolve this question as "confusing," Blackmun urged a return to underlying constitutional principles to guide the application of federal tax immunity, writing: "The one constant here, of course, is simple enough to express: A state may not, consistent with the Supremacy Clause, ... lay a tax 'directly upon the United States,' Mayo v. United States, 319 U.S. 441, 447 (1943). While '[o]ne could, and perhaps should, read *McCulloch* ... simply for the principle that the Constitution prohibits a state from taxing discriminatorily a federally established instrumentality,' First Agricultural Bank v. State Tax Commn., 392 U.S. 339, 350 (1968) (dissenting opinion), the Court has never questioned the propriety of absolute Federal immunity from state taxation.... But limits on the immunity doctrine are, for present purposes, as significant as the rule itself. This immunity may not be conferred simply because the tax has an effect on the United States, or even because the Federal Government shoulders the entire economic burden of the levy.... Similarly, immunity cannot be conferred simply because the state tax falls on the earnings of contractors providing services to the Government. James v. Dravo Contracting Co.... And where a use tax is involved, immunity cannot be conferred simply because the state is levying the tax on the use of

Federal property in private hands, United States v. City of Detroit, ... even if the private entity is using the Government property to provide the United States with goods, United States v. Township of Muskegon.... In such a situation the contractor's use of property 'in connection with commercial activities carried on for profit is a separate and distinct taxable activity.' ... Indeed immunity cannot be conferred simply because the tax is paid with Government funds."

Continuing, Justice Blackmun added: "What the Court's cases leave room for, then, is the conclusion that tax immunity is appropriate in only one circumstance: when the levy falls on the United States itself, or on an agency or instrumentality so closely connected to the Government that the two cannot realistically be viewed as separate entities, at least insofar as the activity being taxed is concerned.... Thus, a finding of constitutional tax immunity requires something more than the invocation of traditional agency notions: to resist the State's taxing power, a private taxpayer must actually 'stand in the Government's shoes.' "

Applying this analysis, the Court went on to hold that the doctrine of federal immunity does not shield funds advanced by the federal government to federal contractors from imposition of New Mexico's gross receipts and compensating use taxes.

Page 513. At the end of the next to the last paragraph of Note 8 add:

See also White Mountain Apache Tribe v. Bracker, 448 U.S. 136, 100 S. Ct. 2518, 65 L. Ed. 2d 665 (1980), and Central Machinery Co. v. Arizona State Tax Commn., 448 U.S. 160, 100 S. Ct. 2592, 65 L. Ed. 2d 684 (1980), holding that comprehensive federal regulation of Indian affairs precludes application of state excise and sales taxes to on-reservation business activities, even those not immediately involving Indians. Cf. Washington v. Confederated Tribes of Colville Indian Reservation, 447 U.S. 134, 100 S. Ct. 2069, 65 L. Ed. 2d 10 (1980), regarding the permissible scope of state and tribal taxation of purchases from tribal smokeshops.

Page 520:

In line 6 of Note 1 change "approval" to "approach."

Page 526. At the end of the carryover paragraph add:

In Merrion v. Jicarilla Apache Tribe, — U.S. —, 102 S. Ct. 894, — L. Ed. 2d — (1982), the respondent Indian Tribe imposed a severance tax on oil and gas production on tribal lands, although oil and gas extracted and consumed by the tribe are exempted from the tax. Petitioner, a lessee under a long-term lease with the tribe to extract oil and gas, brought an action to enjoin enforcement of the tax. The district court entered a permanent injunction holding that the tax violated the commerce clause. Justice Marshall delivered the opinion of the Court, quoting Worcester v. Georgia, 6 Pet. 515 (1832), where Chief Justice Marshall observed that Indian tribes had "always been considered as distinct, independent political communities retaining their original natural rights." Justice Marshall here concluded: "Although the tribes are subject to the authority of the Federal Government, the 'weaker power does not surrender its independence — its right to self-government, by associating with a stronger and taxing its protection.' Adhering to this understanding we conclude that the Tribe did not surrender its authority to tax the mining activities of petitioners, whether this authority is deemed to arise from the Tribe's inherent power of self-government or from its inherent power to exclude nonmembers. Therefore, the Tribe may enforce its severance tax unless and until Congress divests this power, an action that Congress has not taken to date. Finally, the severance tax imposed by the Tribe cannot be invalidated on the ground that it violates the 'negative implications' of the Commerce Clause."

Page 529:

In the last line of the first paragraph of Note 2, change "cl. 2" to "cl. 3."

Page 529. At the end of Note 2 add:

See Hodel v. Virginia Mining & Reclamation Assn., 452 U.S. 264, 101 S. Ct. 2352, 69 L. Ed. 2d 1 (1981), where the Court was called upon to determine whether the 1977 Surface Mining Control and Reclamation Act violated the Tenth Amendment by displacing the states' interests in regulating land use. The act requires coal operators to return the site of excavation to its "approximate original contour." The Court began its discussion of the Tenth Amendment challenge by clarifying the implications of National League of Cities v. Usery, Casebook p.218, stating: "It should be apparent from this discussion that in order to succeed [on a Tenth Amendment challenge] a claim that congressional commerce power legislation is invalid under the reasoning of National League of Cities must satisfy each of three requirements. First, there must be a showing that the challenged statute regulates 'States as States.' ... Second, the federal regulation must address matters that are indisputably 'attributes of state sovereignty.' ... And third, it must be apparent that the States' compliance with the federal law would directly impair their ability 'to structure integral operations in areas of traditional functions.' ... When the Surface Mining Act is examined in light of these principles, it is clear that appellee's Tenth Amendment challenge must fail because the first of the three requirements is not satisfied. ... There [has been] no suggestion that the Act commandeers the legislative processes of the States by directly compelling them to enact and enforce a federal regulatory program.... The most that can be said is that the Surface Mining Act establishes a program of cooperative federalism that allows the States, within limits established by federal minimum standards, to enact and administer their own regulatory programs, structured to meet their own particular needs.... In this respect, the Act resembles a number of other federal statutes that have survived Tenth Amendment challenges in the lower federal courts.... Although [some] congressional enactments obviously curtail or prohibit the States' prerogatives to make legislative choices respecting subjects the States may consider important, the Supremacy Clause permits... [such determinations].... As the Court long ago stated: '[I]t is elementary and well settled that there can be no divided authority over interstate commerce, and that the acts of Congress on [a federal] subject are supreme and exclusive.' ... Thus, [conceivably,] Congress could constitutionally have enacted a statute prohibiting any state regulation of surface coal mining.... [This] Court long ago rejected the suggestion that Congress invades areas reserved to the States by the Tenth Amendment simply because it exercises its authority under the Commerce Clause in a manner that displaces the States' exercise of their police powers.... It would therefore be a radical departure from long-established precedent for this Court to hold that the Tenth Amendment prohibits Congress from displacing state police power laws regulating private activity. Nothing in *National League of Cities* compels or even hints at such a departure."

Page 534. At the end of the third paragraph of Note 3 add:

Cf. Gomez v. Toledo, 446 U.S. 635, 100 S. Ct. 1920, 64 L. Ed. 2d 572 (1980), infra in this Supplement, addition to Casebook p.654. See also Supreme Court of Virginia v. Consumers Union of the United States, 446 U.S. 719, 100 S. Ct. 1967, 64 L. Ed. 2d 641 (1980), where the Court decided that the Virginia Supreme Court and its members were immune from suit under 42 U.S.C. 1983 when acting in a legislative capacity in promulgating the Virginia Code of Professional Responsibility. However, the Virginia court and its chief justice were properly held amenable to a suit for declaratory and injunctive relief when acting in their enforcement capacity in regulating and disciplining attorneys, even though they could not be subjected to liability for damages for such activities.

Page 534. At the end of Note 4 add:

See also United States v. Gillock, supra in this Supplement, addition to Casebook p.274, holding that state legislators have no privilege which bars the introduction of evidence of their official legislative acts in the course of a federal criminal prosecution.

Page 534. At the end of Note 5 add:

Cf. Maher v. Gagne, 448 U.S. 122, 100 S. Ct. 2570, 65 L. Ed. 2d 653 (1980) (Eleventh Amendment does not bar awarding attorney's fees of a prevailing party against a state).

Page 536. At the end of the fifth paragraph add:

Cf. Allstate Insurance Co. v. Hague, 449 U.S. 302, 101 S. Ct. 633, 66 L. Ed. 2d 521 (1981), in which the Court stated that "[i]n deciding constitutional choice-of-law questions, whether under the Due Process Clause or the Full Faith and Credit Clause, this Court has traditionally examined the contacts of the State, whose law was applied, with the parties and with the occurrence or transaction giving rise to the litigation. In order to ensure that the choice of law is neither arbitrary nor fundamentally unfair, ... the Court has invalidated the choice of law of a State which has had no significant contact or significant aggregation of contacts, creating state interests, with the parties and the occurrence or transaction." Applying this principle the Court found that the aggregation of Minnesota contacts with the parties and the occurrence (decedent had lived in Wisconsin, but was employed in Minnesota, petitioner Allstate was and is continuing to do business in Minnesota, and respondent became a Minnesota resident prior to the institution of this suit) created a sufficient state interest as to justify imposition of Minnesota law.

Page 536. At the end of the last paragraph add:

Cf. Thomas v. Washington Gas Light Co., 448 U.S. 261, 100 S. Ct. 2647, 65 L. Ed. 2d 757 (1980), reversing a Fourth Circuit holding that the full faith and credit clause bars a supplemental award under the District of Columbia's worker's compensation act to an injured employee who had previously received an award under the Virginia statute. Justice Stevens' plurality opinion contains an extensive discussion of pertinent full faith and credit clause cases. Justice White, joined by Chief Justice Burger and Justice Powell, concurred separately; Justices Rehnquist and Marshall dissented.

Page 537. At the end of the second full paragraph add:

In Underwriters National Ins. Co. v. North Carolina Life and Accident and Health Ins. Guaranty Assn., — U.S. —, 102 S. Ct. 1357, — L. Ed. 2d — (1982), the Court required full faith and credit to be given to an Indiana court decision relating to a financially troubled Indiana insurance company's deposit that was held in trust by North Carolina for the benefit of North Carolina policyholders, where the North Carolina company actively participated in the Indiana "rehabilitation" proceedings. The court held, relying on Durfee v. Duke, that even the jurisdictional questions were *res judicata* since all issues nad been fully and fairly litigated in the Indiana court

Page 539. At the end of the second paragraph in Section B, add:

To the same effect as *Sweeney*, see Pacielo v. Walker, 449 U.S. 86, 101 S. Ct. 308, 66 L. Ed. 2d 304 (1980), where the Court also cited and quoted from Michigan v. Doran, 439 U.S. 282, 99 S. Ct. 530, 58 L. Ed. 2d 521 (1978), concluding that "interstate extradition was intended to be a summary and mandatory executive proceeding derived from the language of Article IV, §2, cl. 2 of the Constitution." Thus, a habeas corpus action in the courts of the "asylum" state was improper despite the petitioner's Eighth Amendment claim.

Chapter Six

The Bill of Rights, the Fourteenth Amendment, and the Concept of "State Action"

Page 550. Add to the footnoted material:

Oaks, The Proper Role of the Federal Courts in Enforcing the Bill of Rights, 54 N.Y.U.L. Rev. 911 (1979).

Page 553. At the end of Note 3 add:

Cf. City of Memphis v. Greene, 451 U.S. 100, 101 S. Ct. 1584, 67 L. Ed. 2d 769 (1981), where the Court upheld the legitimacy of the city's decision to close a street at a point which separated an all-white community from a predominantly black one, despite challenges based on both 42 U.S.C. 1982 and the Thirteenth Amendment. The majority concluded that "[t]he interests motivating the city's actions are ... sufficient to justify an adverse impact on motorists who are somewhat inconvenienced by the street closing. [This] inconvenience cannot [however] be equated to an actual restraint on the liberty of black citizens that is in any sense comparable to the odious practice[s] the Thirteenth Amendment was designed to eradicate."

Justice Marshall, writing in dissent, addressed the Thirteenth Amendment challenge, stating: "Assuming with the majority that the amendment would, even without implementing legislation, ban more than the mere practice of slavery, I would conclude that official action causing harm of the magnitude suffered here plainly qualifies as a 'badge or incident' of slavery.... I do not mean to imply that all municipal decisions that affect Negroes adversely and benefit whites are prohibited by the Thirteenth Amendment. I would, however, insist that the government carry a heavy burden of justification before I would sustain against Thirteenth Amendment challenge conduct as egregious as erection of a barrier to prevent predominantly-Negro traffic from entering a historically all-white neighborhood."

Justice Marshall also concluded that a §1982 violation is, *a fortiori*, a violation of the Thirteenth Amendment as well.

Page 600. At the end of Note 2 add:

Cf. Brown v. Louisiana, 447 U.S. 323, 100 S. Ct. 2214, 65 L. Ed. 2d 159 (1980), holding that the rule announced in *Burch* applies retroactively in cases still pending on direct review; Justice Brennan wrote the plurality opinion, but Justice Powell's concurring opinion, joined by Justice Stevens, was determinative with respect to the extent of retroactivity.

Page 618. At the end of Note 3 add:

See also Fedorenko v. United States, 449 U.S. 490, 101 S. Ct. 737, 66 L. Ed. 2d 686 (1981), where the government sought revocation of the petitioner's United States citizenship, based upon §1451(a) of the Immigration and Nationality Act of 1952. The district court accepted Fedorenko's argument that through the use of its equity power, the court could exercise its discretion not to revoke Fedorenko's citizenship. The court of appeals rejected this argument and the Supreme Court affirmed, holding that "district courts lack equitable discretion to refrain from entering a judgment of denaturalization against a naturalized citizen whose citizenship was procured illegally or by willful misrepresentation of material facts." Agreeing with the court of appeals, the Court stated that "[o]nce it has been determined that a person does not qualify for citizenship, . . . the district court has no discretion to ignore the defect and grant citizenship."

Page 618. At the end of Note 4 add:

In Vance v. Terrazas, 444 U.S. 248, 100 S. Ct. 540, 62 L. Ed. 2d 461 (1980), the Court held that, consistent with the *Afroyim* decision and with the citizenship clause generally, Congress could prescribe the evidentiary standards to be used in expatriation proceedings. Thus, §349(c) of the Immigration and Nationality Act, which provides that the government must prove by a preponderance of the evidence that the individual specifically intended to renounce his citizenship, in addition to committing the expatriating act, and that the voluntariness of the expatriating act is rebuttably presumed to exist and is not constitutionally infirm under either the citizenship clause of the Fourteenth Amendment or the due process clause of the Fifth Amendment. Justices Brennan, Stewart, Marshall, and Stevens dissented, maintaining that under *Afroyim* citizenship could be lost only by formal renunciation and that 8 U.S.C. 1481(a)(6) contained the congressionally prescribed procedure for such a voluntary renunciation, which had concededly not been followed here.

Page 621. At the end of Note 2 add:

Cf. Haig v. Agee, 453 U.S. 280, 101 S. Ct. 2766, 69 L. Ed. 2d 640 (1981), infra in this Supplement, addition to Casebook p.1597, upholding State Department revocation of a citizen's passport on national security grounds.

Page 639. Add to the footnoted material:

Schwartz, A New Fourteenth Amendment: The Decline of State Action, Fundamental Rights and Suspect Classifications Under the Burger Court, 56 Chi.-Kent L. Rev. 865 (1980).

Page 650:

In line 6 of Note 1, delete "he took" and insert "dissenters'" before "approach."

Page 654. At the end of the first full paragraph of Note 1 add:

The rationale of *Monnell* was explicated and applied in Owen v. City of Independence, 445 U.S. 622, 100 S. Ct. 1398, 63 L. Ed. 2d 673 (1980), where the Court held that a muncipality, sued for damages for its constitutional violations under §1983, has no immunity from liability and may not assert the good faith of its officials as a defense to such liability.

Cf. Board of Regents v. Tomanio, 446 U.S. 478, 100 S. Ct. 1790, 64 L. Ed. 2d 440 (1980), holding that 42 U.S.C. 1988, which refers federal courts to state statutes when federal law provides no rule of decision for §1983 actions, unless state law is "inconsistent" with federal law, required a federal court to apply a state tolling rule. This resulted in the §1983 suit being barred by the state statute of limitations, since time for filing suit was not suspended while related but independent remedies were pursued.

See also City of Newport v. Fact Concerts, Inc., 450 U.S. 1028, 101 S. Ct. 2478, 69 L. Ed. 2d 616 (1981), where the Court held that municipalities are immune from punitive damages in §1983 actions. The Court reasoned that neither the legislative history of §1983 nor public policy supported exposure of municipal governments to such damage awards.

Page 654. At the end of the last paragraph of Note 1 add:

Cf. Gomez v. Toledo, 446 U.S. 635, 100 S. Ct. 1920, 64 L. Ed. 2d 572 (1980), holding that in a §1983 action against a public official the plaintiff need not allege that the defendant acted in bad faith; such officials, who might be entitled to claim qualified immunity, must plead good faith as an affirmative defense.

See also Maine v. Thiboutot, 448 U.S 1, 100 S. Ct. 2502, 65 L. Ed. 2d 555 (1980), and Maher v. Gagne, 448 U.S. 122, 100 S. Ct. 2570, 65 L. Ed. 2d 653 (1980), holding that 42 U.S.C. 1983 provides a basis for suits relating not only to alleged constitutional violations but also to violations of federal statutes that protect civil rights, and also that the Civil Rights Attorney's Fees Awards Act of 1976 (42 U.S.C. 1988) authorizes awards in §1983 actions based on federal statutory rights. Justice Powell, joined by Chief Justice Burger and Justice Rehnquist, dissented.

See also Dennis v. Sparks, 449 U.S. 24, 101 S. Ct. 183, 66 L. Ed. 2d 185 (1980), holding that private persons jointly participating with a state trial judge to commit an act in violation of §1983 are not entitled to the benefit of that judge's absolute immunity from liability. Further, despite the dismissal of the §1983 action against the judge based on this immunity, the Court concluded that the private litigants acted under color of law and are therefore potentially liable for damages.

Page 655. At the end of Note 3 add:

Where a parolee committed a murder five months after his release from incarceration by state officials, he was not an "agent" of the releasing jurisdiction for "state action" purposes, with respect to a suit brought under 42 U.S.C. 1983 by the victim's survivors. Moreover, a state statute that grants parole officers absolute immunity from state tort claims is rationally related to the legitimate state interest in promoting the rehabilitation of prisoners, and thus is not violative of the Fourteenth Amendment's due process clause. Martinez v. California, 444 U.S. 277, 100 S. Ct. 553, 62 L. Ed. 2d 481 (1980).

Page 670. At the end of Note 2 add:

Cf. PruneYard Shopping Center v. Robins, 447 U.S. 74, 100 S. Ct. 2035, 64 L. Ed. 2d 741 (1980), infra in this Supplement, addition to Casebook p.1235, where the Court distinguished *Lloyd* and found it inapplicable where the state courts had held that expressional activity in a privately owned shopping center was protected by *state* constitutional provisions. So long as restrictions on property rights do not violate the federal Constitution, a state under its police power may protect the exercise of free speech and petition rights, regardless of whether state action in the federal constitutional sense is involved so as to trigger application of the First Amendment. Thus, a state may not only adopt a more expansive view of individual liberties than that under the federal Constitution, but in effect a broader concept of "state action" than if the federal Constitution alone were relied upon.

Page 677:

In line 9 of the second full paragraph change "not" to "now."

Page 686. At the end of Note 3 add:

Cf. City of Memphis v. Greene, infra in this Supplement, addition to Casebook p.986, in which the Court sustained the city's decision to close a street at a point which divided an all-white community from a predominantly black one, for the purpose of reducing the flow of traffic through the white neighborhood. The Court characterized the injury to the affected black citizens as a "slight inconvenience," while finding the city's interest in promoting health and safety of the members of the white community both legitimate and non-discriminatory.

Justice Marshall, joined by Justice Brennan and Justice Blackmun, entered a strong dissent, describing the impact of the city's actions as "carv[ing] out racial enclaves." After examining the record, Justice Marshall's conclusions regarding the city's action differed significantly from those of the majority. Marshall first cited the trial court's finding that the adverse impact of closing the street on blacks was greater than on whites. Turning next to the possible psychological effects of closing the street, Marshall cited the trial court testimony of a professor of psychology from the University of Tennessee, who predicted that the street closing "would reinforce feelings about the city's 'favoritism' towards whites and also serve as a 'monument to racial hostility.'" Finally, Marshall examined the city's motives for closing the street, by applying the tests enunciated in Arlington Heights v. Metropolitan Housing Development Corp., 429 U.S. 252 (1972). Concluding that the respondent black citizens had provided ample evidence of discriminatory intent, Marshall stated: "[I]n this picture a group of white citizens has decided to act to keep Negro citizens from traveling through their urban 'utopia' and the city has placed its seal of approval on the scheme. It is this action that I believe is forbidden, and it is for that reason that I dissent."

Page 692. At the end of Note 1 add:

Cf. Norwood v. Harrison, Casebook p.948.

Chapter Seven

Due Process — Substantive and Procedural — and the Protection of Liberty, Property, and Economic Interests

Page 710. Add to the first paragraph of the footnoted material:

Preston & Mehlman, The Due Process as a Limitation on the Reach of State Legislation: A Historical and Analytical Examination of Substantive Due Process, 8 U. Balt. L. Rev. 1 (1978).

Page 723. At the end of Note 1 add:

See also Little v. Streater, 452 U.S. 1, 101 S. Ct. 2202, 68 L. Ed. 2d 627 (1981), infra in this Supplement, addition to Casebook p.785.

Page 735:

In line 10 of the first full paragraph in Ferguson v. Skrupa, change "stated" to "disclaimed."

Page 740. Add as a new Note following O'Connor v. Donaldson:

Cf. Pennhurst State School and Hospital v. Halderman, 451 U.S. 1, 101 S. Ct. 1531, 67 L. Ed. 2d 694 (1981), where the Court rejected the argument that §6010 of the Developmentally Disabled Assistance and Bill of Rights Act creates substantive rights in favor of the mentally retarded. In *Pennhurst,* the court of appeals had held that §6010 of the act, the "bill of rights" provision, granted mentally retarded persons a right to "appropriate treatment, services, and habilitation" in "the setting that is least restrictive of . . . personal liberty." After examining the structure of the act, the Supreme Court concluded that "like other federal-state cooperative programs, the act is voluntary and the states are given the choice of complying with the

conditions set forth in the act, or foregoing the benefit of Federal funding."
Although the act lists a variety of conditions for receipt of federal funds,
Justice Rehnquist, writing for the majority, noted an absence of any language suggesting that §6010 should be viewed as a "condition" for the
receipt of federal funding under the act. Therefore, the issue before the
Supreme Court was one of statutory construction: did Congress intend
§6010 to create enforceable individual rights and governmental obligations?
Addressing this issue, the Court cited two longstanding principles of statutory construction: (1) "[t]he case for inferring intent is at its weakest where, as
here, the rights asserted impose *affirmative* obligations on the States to fund
certain services," and (2) "legislation enacted pursuant to the Spending
Power is much in the nature of a contract: in return for federal funds, the
States agree to comply with federally imposed conditions. The legitimacy of
Congress's power to legislate under the Spending Power thus rests on
whether the State voluntarily and knowingly accepts the terms of the contract. . . . There can, of course, be no knowing acceptance if a state is unaware of the conditions or is unable to ascertain what is expected of it.
Accordingly, if Congress intends to impose a condition of the grant of federal moneys, it must do so unambiguously."

Justice White, joined by Justices Brennan and Marshall, dissented in
part from the Court's holding, stating: "The language and scheme of the
Act make it plain enough to me that Congress intended §6010, although
couched in terms of right, to serve as requirements that the participating
states must observe in receiving under the provisions of the Act. . . . As
clearly as words can, §6010. . . declares that the developmentally disabled
have the right to appropriate treatment, services and habilitation. . . .
[Section 6010] cannot be treated as only wishful thinking on the part of
Congress or as playing some fanciful role in the implementation of the
Act."

Page 740. Add to the second paragraph of the footnoted material:

Schoenfeld, Civil Rights for the Handicapped Under the Constitution and
Section 504 of the Rehabilitation Act, 49 U. Cin. L. Rev. 580 (1980).

Page 751. At the end of Note 1 add:

Cf. Vitek v. Jones, infra in this Supplement, addition to Casebook p.792,
holding that the involuntary transfer of a convicted felon from a state prison
to a mental hospital without procedural safeguards violated due process.

Page 751. At the end of Note 2 add:

Comment, The Constitution and the Family, 93 Harv. L. Rev. 1157 (1980);
Tribe, The Puzzling Persistence of Process-Based Constitutional Theories, 89
Yale L.J. 1063 (1980).

Cf. Little v. Streater, 452 U.S. 1, 101 S. Ct. 2202, 68 L. Ed. 2d 627 (1981), infra in this Supplement, addition to Casebook p.785, where the Court again found itself confronted with questions involving familial relationships and the rights of indigents.

Page 753. At the end of Note 1 add:

But compare Texaco, Inc. v. Short, — U.S. — , 102 S. Ct. 781, — L. Ed. 2d — (1982), where the Court upheld the Indiana Mineral Lapse Act, which provides for the automatic reversion, without notice, of a severed mineral interest to the surface owner after 20 years of non-use. The Court intimated that property owners are charged with knowledge of relevant statutory provisions affecting their interest in property, and thus have no constitutional right to be advised that the 20-year period of non-use is about to expire.

Page 757. At the end of the second paragraph of Note 1 add:

Cf. Allstate Insurance Co. v. Hague, 449 U.S. 302, 101 S. Ct. 633, 66 L. Ed. 2d 521 (1981), where the Court reviewed the contacts the forum state had with the parties and occurrence to determine if the state had sufficient "state interests" to apply its law. The Court determined that because the decedent was employed in Minnesota for a period of 15 years, and that Allstate did and is continuing to do business there, together with the fact that the respondent moved to Minnesota prior to the initiation of this suit, Minnesota did in fact have a sufficient state interest in applying its own laws.

Justice Stevens, in a separate concurrence, took occasion to address specifically the question of whether the full faith and credit clause "require[s] the forum State to apply foreign law whenever another State has a valid interest in the litigation." He suggested that it does not and intimated that "the Clause should not invalidate a state court's choice of forum law unless that choice threatens the federal interest in national unity by unjustifiably infringing upon the legitimate interests of another State." After examining the facts he concluded that the Minnesota court did not unjustifiably infringe upon the legitimate interests of the state of Wisconsin.

Page 758. At the end of Note 3 add:

In another case applying the minimum contacts requirements of *International Shoe*, the Court concluded that the mere fortuitous circumstance that a single automobile sold in New York to New York residents happened to suffer an accident while passing through Oklahoma did not empower Oklahoma courts to exercise jurisdiction under that state's long-arm statute, consistent with due process. Foreseeability alone was not a sufficient predicate for the attempted exercise of *in personam* jurisdiction, the Court stated, since there was a total absence of those affiliating circumstances that are necessary to satisfy the *International Shoe* test. Justices Marshall and Blackmun dissented, stating that the majority took an unnecessarily narrow view of the requirements of a sufficient relationship between the "defendant, the forum, and the litigation," quoting from Shaffer v. Heitner. An automobile importer and distributor could reasonably anticipate being sued in a foreign state with which it had only a limited relationship, the dissent concluded. World-Wide Volkswagen Corp. v. Woodson, 444 U.S. 286, 100 S. Ct. 559, 62 L. Ed. 2d 490 (1980). Similarly, in Rush v. Savchuk, 444 U.S. 320, 100 S. Ct. 571, 62 L. Ed. 2d 516 (1980), again relying on *International Shoe* and *Shaffer,* the Court held that a state may not exercise *quasi in rem* jurisdiction over a defendant who has no forum contacts by attaching the contractual obligation of an insurer licensed to do business in the state to defend and indemnify him in connection with the suit. The fictional presence in the jurisdiction of the insurance policy obligation did not provide the state with a basis for determining the nonresident defendant's liability for an out-of-state accident, the Court determined, as there were no "significant contacts between the litigation and the forum." Moreover, the Court stated, the "requirements of *International Shoe* ... must be met as to each defendant over whom a state court exercises jurisdiction." Justice Stevens dissented in *Rush,* while Justice Brennan wrote an extensive dissent in both cases, essentially maintaining that the majority was reading "*International Shoe* and its progeny too narrowly" and suggesting that the "standards enunciated by those cases may already be obsolete as constitutional boundaries."

Page 761. At the end of the first paragraph add:

See also Logan v. Zimmerman Brush Co., — U.S. —, 102 S. Ct. 1148, — L. Ed. 2d — (1982), where the Court was presented with the question whether a state may terminate a complainant's cause of action because a state official failed to process his complaint in a timely fashion as required by state. The Illinois Supreme Court held that the statutory provision in question is mandatory, and accordingly held that failure to comply stripped the Illinois Fair Employment Practices Commission of jurisdiction to consider the petitioner's charge. Logan had argued that his due process rights would be violated if the Commission's error were allowed to extinguish his cause of action. The Court began its inquiry by first characterizing the complainant's discrimination claim as a constitutionally protected one in the form of a property interest. Justice Blackmun, writing the Court's opinion, stated: "The hallmark of property ... is an individual entitlement grounded in state law, which cannot be removed except 'for cause.' ... Because the state scheme has deprived Logan of a property right, then, we turn to the determination of what process was due him." Justice Blackmun continued: "As our decisions have emphasized time and again, the Due Process Clause grants the aggrieved party the opportunity to present his case and have its merits fairly judged. Thus it has become a truism that 'some form of hearing' is required before the owner is finally deprived of a protected property interest. . . . To put it plainly as possible, the State may not finally destroy a property interest without giving the putative owner an opportunity to present his claim of entitlement. . . . [This] Court has acknowledged that the timing and nature of the required hearing 'will depend on appropriate accommodation of the competing interests involved.' . . . Obviously, nothing we have said entitles every civil litigant to a hearing on the merits of every case. The State may erect reasonable procedural requirements for triggering the right of adjudication, be they statutes of limitation . . . or, in appropriate cases, filing fees. . . . And the State certainly accords *due* process when it terminates a claim for failure to comply with a reasonable procedural or evidentiary rule. . . . What the Fourteenth Amendment does require, however, 'is an *opportunity* . . . granted at a meaningful time and in a meaningful manner . . . for [a] hearing appropriate to the nature of the case. . . .' It is such an opportunity that Logan was denied."

Page 764:

In line 2 of the second paragraph of Note 6, change "namely" to "originally."

Page 773. At the end of Note 2 add:

Compare Haig v. Agee, 452 U.S. 280, 101 S. Ct. 2766, 69 L. Ed. 2d 640 (1981), infra in this Supplement, addition to Casebook p.1597, concluding that procedural due process was satisfied, in the context of revocation of a passport for national security reasons, by the government's providing the respondent with a statement of reasons and an opportunity for a prompt post-revocation hearing. A pre-revocation hearing was not required because of the substantial likelihood of "serious damage" to national security or American foreign policy from the respondent's activities.

Page 779:

In line 11 of the second paragraph of Note 3 change "changes" to "charges."

Page 780. At the end of Note 3 add:

Cf. Delaware State College v. Ricks, 449 U.S. 250, 101 S. Ct. 498, 66 L. Ed. 2d 431 (1980).

Page 780. At the end of the carryover paragraph add:

Cf. Gomez v. Toledo, supra in this Supplement, addition to Casebook p.654.

Page 785. At the end of Note 1 add:

LASSITER v. DEPARTMENT OF SOCIAL SERVICES OF DURHAM COUNTY, 452 U.S. 18, 101 S. Ct. 2153, 68 L. Ed. 2d 640 (1981). A North Carolina court transferred the petitioner's child from her care to the Durham County Department of Social Services, finding that the child had been neglected by the mother. Following this action the petitioner was convicted of second-degree murder, and a long prison sentence was imposed. The department petitioned the lower court to terminate Ms. Lassiter's parental rights. The petitioner, in prison, did not aver that she was indigent, and the court did not appoint counsel for her. At the termination hearing the petitioner cross-examined the social worker involved and testified on her own behalf. The court soon after terminated the petitioner's parental rights, and the court of appeals rejected the petitioner's argument that, because she was in fact indigent, the due process clause of the Fourteenth Amendment required the state to provide counsel for her. The North Carolina Supreme Court denied review. Justice Stewart delivered the opinion of the Court upholding this determination, stating:

"The pre-eminent generalization that emerges from this Court's precedents on an indigent's right to appointed counsel is that such a right has been recognized to exist only where the litigant may lose his physical liberty if he loses the litigation. Thus, when the Court overruled the principle of Betts v. Brady, 316 U.S. 455, that counsel in criminal trials need be appointed only where the circumstances in a given case demand it, the Court did so in the case of a man sentenced to prison for five years. Gideon v. Wainwright, 372 U.S. 335. And thus Argersinger v. Hamlin, 407 U.S. 25, established that counsel must be provided before any indigent may be sentenced to prison, even where the crime is petty and the prison term brief.

"That it is the defendant's interest in personal freedom, and not simply the special Sixth and Fourteenth Amendments' right to counsel in criminal cases, which triggers the right to appointed counsel is demonstrated by the Court's announcement in In re Gault, 387 U.S. 1, that 'the Due Process Clause of the Fourteenth Amendment requires that in respect of proceedings to determine delinquency *which may result in commitment to an institution in which the juvenile's freedom is curtailed,*' the juvenile has a right to appointed counsel even though those proceedings may be styled 'civil' and not 'criminal.'...

"Significantly, as a litigant's interest in personal liberty diminishes, so does his right to appointed counsel. In Gagnon v. Scarpelli, 411 U.S. 778, the Court gauged the due process rights of a previously sentenced probationer at a probation-revocation hearing. In Morrissey v. Brewer, 408 U.S. 471, 480, which involved an analogous hearing to revoke parole, the Court had said: 'Revocation deprives an individual, not of the absolute liberty to which every citizen is entitled, but only of the conditional liberty properly dependent on observance of special parole restrictions.' Relying on that discussion, the Court in *Scarpelli* declined to hold that indigent probationers have, *per se*, a right to counsel at revocation hearings, and instead left the decision whether counsel should be appointed to be made on a case-by-case basis.

"Finally, the Court has refused to extend the right to appointed counsel to include prosecutions which, though criminal, do not result in the defendant's loss of personal liberty. The Court in Scott v. Illinois, 440 U.S. 367, for instance, interpreted the 'central premise of *Argersinger*' to be 'that actual imprisonment is a penalty different in kind from fines or the mere threat of imprisonment,' and the Court endorsed that premise as 'eminently sound and warrant[ing] adoption of actual imprisonment as the line defining the constitutional right to appointment of counsel.' Id., at 373. The Court thus held 'that the Sixth and Fourteenth Amendments to the United States Constitution require only that no indigent criminal defendant be sentenced to a term of imprisonment unless the State has afforded him the right to assistance of appointed counsel in his defense.' Ibid.

"In sum, the Court's precedents speak with one voice about what 'fundamental fairness' has meant when the Court has considered the right to appointed counsel, and we thus draw from them the presumption that an indigent litigant has a right to appointed counsel only when, if he loses, he may be deprived of his physical liberty. It is against this presumption that all the other elements in the due process decision must be measured.

"The case of Mathews v. Eldridge, 424 U.S. 319, 335, propounds three elements to be evaluated in deciding what due process requires, viz., the private interests at stake, the government's interest, and the risk that the procedures used will lead to erroneous decisions. We must balance these elements against each other, and then set their net weight in the scales against the presumption that there is a right to appointed counsel only where the indigent, if he is unsuccessful, may lose his personal freedom.

"This Court's decisions have by now made plain beyond the need for multiple citation that a parent's desire for and right to 'the companionship, care, custody, and management of his or her children' is an important interest that 'undeniably warrants deference and, absent a powerful countervailing interest, protection.' Stanley v. Illinois, 405 U.S. 645, 651. Here the State has sought not simply to infringe upon that interest, but to end it. If the State prevails, it will have worked a unique kind of deprivation.... A parent's interest in the accuracy and justice of the decision to terminate his or her parental status is, therefore, a commanding one.

"Since the State has an urgent interest in the welfare of the child, it shares the parent's interest in an accurate and just decision. For this reason, the State may share the indigent parent's interest in the availability of appointed counsel. If, as our adversary system presupposes, accurate and just results are most likely to be obtained through the equal contest of opposed interests, the State's interest in the child's welfare may perhaps best be served by a hearing in which both the parent and the State acting for the child are represented by counsel, without whom the contest of interests may become unwholesomely unequal. North Carolina itself acknowledges as much by providing that where a parent files a written answer to a termination petition, the State must supply a lawyer to represent the child. . . .

"The State's interests, however, clearly diverge from the parent's insofar as the State wishes the termination decision to be made as economically as possible and thus wants to avoid both the expense of appointed counsel and the cost of the lengthened proceedings his presence may cause. But though the State's pecuniary interest is legitimate, it is hardly significant enough to overcome private interests as important as those here, particularly in light of the concession in the respondent's brief that the 'potential costs of appointed counsel in termination proceedings. . . are admittedly *de minimis* compared to the costs in all criminal actions.'

"Finally, consideration must be given to the risk that a parent will be erroneously deprived of his or her child because the parent is not represented by counsel. North Carolina law now seeks to assure accurate decisions by establishing [extensive and detailed] procedures. . . .

"The dispositive question, which must now be addressed, is whether the three *Eldridge* factors, when weighed against the presumption that there is no right to appointed counsel in the absence of at least a potential deprivation of physical liberty, suffice to rebut that presumption and thus to lead to the conclusion that the Due Process Clause requires the appointment of counsel when a State seeks to terminate an indigent's parental status. To summarize the above discussion of the *Eldridge* factors: the parent's interest is an extremely important one (and may be supplemented by the dangers of criminal liability inherent in some termination proceedings); the State shares with the parent an interest in a correct decision, has a relatively weak pecuniary interest, and, in some but not all cases, has a possibly stronger interest in informal procedures; and the complexity of the proceeding and the incapacity of the uncounselled parent could be, but would not always be, great enough to make the risk of an erroneous deprivation of the parent's rights insupportably high.

"If, in a given case, the parent's interests were at their strongest, the State's interests were at their weakest, and the risks of error were at their peak, it could not be said that the *Eldridge* factors did not overcome the presumption against the right to appointed counsel, and that due process did not therefore require the appointment of counsel. But since the *Eldridge* factors will not always be so distributed, and since 'due process is not so rigid as to require that the significant interests in informality, flexibility and economy must always be sacrificed,' Gagnon v. Scarpelli, supra, 411 U.S., at 788, neither can we say that the Constitution requires the appointment of counsel in every parental termination proceeding. We therefore adopt the standard found appropriate in Gagnon v. Scarpelli, and leave the decision whether due process calls for the appointment of counsel for indigent parents in termination proceedings to be answered in the first instance by the trial court, subject, of course, to appellate review. . . ."

After enunciating that a case-by-case standard should be applied to the due process right to appointed counsel for indigent parents at a parental termination proceeding, the Court examined the facts of the instant case, finding that because no expert witnesses testified and because of the absence of specially troublesome points of law, the trial court did not err in failing to appoint counsel for Ms. Lassiter.

Justice Blackmun, joined by Justices Brennan and Marshall, dissented, stating:

"The Court today denies an indigent mother the representation of counsel in a judicial proceeding initiated by the State of North Carolina to terminate her parental rights with respect to her youngest child. The Court most appropriately recognizes that the mother's interest is a 'commanding one,' . . . and it finds no countervailing state interest of even remotely comparable significance. . . . Nonetheless, the Court avoids what seems to me the obvious conclusion that due process requires the presence of counsel for a parent threatened with judicial termination of parental rights, and, instead, revives an ad hoc approach thoroughly discredited nearly 20 years ago in Gideon v. Wainwright, 372 U.S. 335 (1963). Because I believe that the unique importance of a parent's interest in the care and custody of his or her child cannot constitutionally be extinguished through formal judicial proceedings without the benefit of counsel, I dissent.

"This Court is not unfamiliar with the problem of determining under what circumstances legal representation is mandated by the Constitution. In Betts v. Brady, 316 U.S. 455 (1942), it reviewed at length both the tradition behind the Sixth Amendment right to counsel in criminal trials and the historical practices of the States in that area. The decision in *Betts* — that the Sixth Amendment right to counsel did not apply to the States and that the due process guarantee of the Fourteenth Amendment permitted a flexible, case-by-case determination of the defendant's need for counsel in state criminal trials — was overruled in Gideon v. Wainwright, 372 U.S., at 345. The Court in *Gideon* rejected the *Betts* reasoning to the effect that counsel for indigent criminal defendants was ' "not a fundamental right, essential to a fair trial." ' Id., at 340 (quoting Betts v. Brady, 316 U.S. at 471). Finding the right well-founded in its precedents, the Court further concluded that 'reason and reflection require us to recognize that in our adversary system of criminal justice, any person haled into court, who is too poor to hire a lawyer, cannot be assured a fair trial unless counsel is provided him.' 372 U.S., at 344. Similarly, in Argersinger v. Hamlin, 407 U.S. 25 (1972), assistance of counsel was found to be a requisite under the Sixth Amendment, as incorporated into the Fourteenth, even for a misdemeanor offense punishable by imprisonment for less than 6 months.

"Outside the criminal context, however, the Court has relied on the flexible nature of the due process guarantee whenever it has decided that counsel is not constitutionally required. The special purposes of probation revocation determinations, and the informal nature of those administrative proceedings, including the absence of counsel for the State, led the Court to conclude that due process does not require counsel for probationers. Gagnon v. Scarpelli, 411 U.S. 778, 785-789 (1973). In the case of school disciplinary proceedings, which are brief, informal, and intended in part to be educative, the Court also found no requirement for legal counsel. Goss v. Lopez, 419 U.S. 565, 583 (1975). Most recently, the Court declined to intrude the presence of counsel for a minor facing voluntary civil commitment by his parent, because of the parent's substantial role in that decision and because of the decision's essentially medical and informal nature. Parham v. J.R., 442 U.S. 584, 604-609 (1979).

"In each of these instances, the Court has recognized that what process is due varies in relation to the interests at stake and the nature of the governmental proceedings. Where the individual's liberty interest is of diminished or less than fundamental stature, or where the prescribed procedure involves informal decisionmaking without the trappings of an adversarial trial-type proceeding, counsel has not been a requisite of due process. Implicit in this analysis is the fact that the contrary conclusion sometimes may be warranted. Where an individual's liberty interest assumes sufficiently weighty constitutional significance, and the State by a formal and adversarial proceeding seeks to curtail that interest, the right to counsel may be necessary to ensure fundamental fairness. See In re Gault, 387 U.S. 1 (1967). To say this is simply to acknowledge that due process allows for the adoption of different rules to address different situations or contexts.

"It is not disputed that state intervention to terminate the relationship between petitioner and her child must be accomplished by procedures meeting the requisites of the Due Process Clause. Nor is there any doubt here about the kind of procedure North Carolina has prescribed. North Carolina law requires notice and a trial-type hearing before the State on its own initiative may sever the bonds of parenthood. The decisionmaker is a judge, the rules of evidence are in force, and the State is represented by counsel. The question, then, is whether proceedings in this mold, that relate to a subject so vital, can comport with fundamental fairness when the defendant parent remains unrepresented by counsel. As the Court today properly acknowledges, our consideration of the process due in this context, as in others, must rely on a balancing of the competing private and public interests, an approach succinctly described in Mathews v. Eldridge, 424 U.S. 319, 335 (1976). . . . As does the majority, I evaluate the 'three distinct factors' specified in *Eldridge:* the private interest affected; the risk of error under the procedure employed by the State; and the countervailing governmental interest in support of the challenged procedure. . . .

"In this case, the State's aim is not simply to influence the parent-child relationship but to *extinguish* it. A termination of parental rights is both total and irrevocable. Unlike other custody proceedings, it leaves the parent with no right to visit or communicate with the child, to participate in, or even to know about, any important decision affecting the child's religious, educational, emotional, or physical development. It is hardly surprising that this forced dissolution of the parent-child relationship has been recognized as a punitive sanction by courts, Congress, and commentators. The Court candidly notes, as it must, . . . that termination of parental rights by the State is a 'unique kind of deprivation.'

"The magnitude of this deprivation is of critical significance in the due process calculus, for the process to which an individual is entitled is in part determined 'by the extent to which he may be "condemned to suffer grievous loss." ' Goldberg v. Kelly, 397 U.S., at 263, quoting Joint Anti-Fascist Refugee Committee v. McGrath, 341 U.S. 123, 168 (1951) (Frankfurter, J., concurring). . . . Surely there can be few losses more grievous than the abrogation of parental rights. Yet the Court today asserts that this deprivation somehow is less serious than threatened losses deemed to require appointed counsel, because in this instance the parent's own 'personal liberty' is not at stake. . . .

"Rather than opting for the insensitive presumption that incarceration is the only loss of liberty sufficiently onerous to justify a right to appointed counsel, I would abide by the Court's enduring commitment to examine the relationships among the interests on both sides, and the appropriateness of counsel in the specific type of proceeding. The fundamental significance of the liberty interests at stake in a parental termination proceeding is undeniable, and I would find this first portion of the due process balance weighing heavily in favor of refined procedural protections. The second *Eldridge* factor, namely, the risk of error in the procedure provided by the State, must then be reviewed with some care."

Justice Blackmun next examined North Carolina's parental termination proceedings, characterizing them as similar in many respects to a criminal prosecution. After noting various junctures where error could enter the termination proceeding, Justice Blackmun concluded that the second *Eldridge* factor had been satisfied. Continuing, Justice Blackmun wrote:

"The final factor to be considered, the interests claimed for the State, do not tip the scale against providing appointed counsel in this context. . . .

"The State may, and does, properly assert a legitimate interest in promoting the physical and emotional well-being of its minor children. But this interest is not served by terminating the rights of any concerned, responsible parent. Indeed, because North Carolina is committed to 'protect[ing] all children from the unnecessary severance of a relationship with biological or legal parents,' 'the State spites its own articulated goals when it needlessly separates' the parent from the child. Stanley v. Illinois, 405 U.S., at 653.

"The State also has an interest in avoiding the cost and administrative inconvenience that might accompany a right to appointed counsel. But, as the Court acknowledges, the State's fiscal interest 'is hardly significant enough to overcome private interests as important as those here.' . . . The

State's financial concern indeed is a limited one, for the right to appointed counsel may well be restricted to those termination proceedings that are instituted by the State. Moreover, no difficult line-drawing problem would arise with respect to other types of civil proceedings. The instant due process analysis takes full account of the fundamental nature of the parental interest, the permanency of the threatened deprivation, the gross imbalance between the resources employed by the prosecuting State and those available to the indigent parent, and the relatively insubstantial cost of furnishing counsel. An absence of any one of these factors might yield a different result. But where, as here, the threatened loss of liberty is severe and absolute, the State's role is so clearly adversarial and punitive, and the cost involved is relatively slight, there is no sound basis for refusing to recognize the right to counsel as a requisite of due process in a proceeding initiated by the State to terminate parental rights.

"The Court's analysis is markedly similar to mine; it, too, analyzes the three factors listed in Mathews v. Eldridge, and it, too, finds the private interest weighty, the procedure devised by the State fraught with risks of error, and the countervailing governmental interest insubstantial. Yet, rather than follow this balancing process to its logical conclusion, the Court abruptly pulls back and announces that a defendant parent must await a case-by-case determination of his or her need for counsel. ... This conclusion is not only illogical, but it also marks a sharp departure from the due process analysis consistently applied heretofore. The flexibility of due process, the Court has held, requires case-by-case consideration of different decisionmaking *contexts,* not of different *litigants* within a given context. In analyzing the nature of the private and governmental interests at stake, along with the risk of error, the Court in the past has not limited itself to the particular case at hand. Instead, after addressing the three factors as generic elements in the context raised by the particular case, the Court then has formulated a rule that has general application to similarly situated cases.

"The Court's own precedents make this clear. In Goldberg v. Kelly, the Court found that the desperate economic conditions experienced by welfare recipients *as a class* distinguished them from other recipients of governmental benefits, 397 U.S., at 264. In Mathews v. Eldridge, the Court concluded that the needs of Social Security disability recipients were *not* of comparable urgency, and, moreover, that existing pretermination procedures, based largely on written medical assessments, were likely to be more objective and evenhanded than typical welfare entitlement decisions. 424 U.S., at 339-345. These cases established rules translating due process in the welfare context as requiring a pretermination hearing but dispensing with that requirement in the disability benefit context. A showing that a particular welfare recipient had access to additional income, or that a disability recipient's eligibility turned on testimony rather than written medical reports, would not result in an exception from the required procedural norms. ...

"There are sound reasons for this. Procedural norms are devised to ensure that justice may be done in every case, and to protect litigants against unpredictable and unchecked adverse governmental action. Through experience with decisions in varied situations over time, lessons emerge that reflect a general understanding as to what is minimally necessary to assure fair play. Such lessons are best expressed to have general application which guarantees the predictability and uniformity that underlie our society's commitment to the rule of law. By endorsing, instead, a retrospective review of the trial record of each particular defendant parent, the Court today undermines the very rationale on which this concept of general fairness is based. . . .

"Assuming that this ad hoc review were adequate to ensure fairness, it is likely to be both cumbersome and costly. And because such review involves constitutional rights implicated by state adjudications, it necessarily will result in increased federal interference in state proceedings. The Court's implication to the contrary. . . is belied by the Court's experience in the aftermath of Betts v. Brady. The Court was confronted with innumerable post-verdict challenges to the fairness of particular trials, and expended much energy in effect evaluating the performance of state judges. This level of intervention in the criminal processes of the States prompted Justice Frankfurter, speaking for himself and two others, to complain that the Court was performing as a 'super-legal-aid bureau.' Uveges v. Pennsylvania, 335 U.S. 437, 450 (1948) (dissenting opinion). I fear that the decision today may transform the Court into a 'super-family-court.' "

Justice Stevens, dissenting separately, stated that application of the *Eldridge* factors required the trial court to appoint counsel in this type of case.

Compare Little v. Streater, 452 U.S. 1, 101 S. Ct. 2202, 68 L. Ed. 2d 627 (1981), decided the same day as *Lassiter*, where the Court was presented with the question "whether a Connecticut statute, which provides that in paternity actions the cost of blood grouping tests [as exculpatory evidence] is to be borne by the party requesting them, violates the Due Process Clause and Equal Protection Clause of the Fourteenth Amendment when applied to deny such tests to indigent defendants."

Because the appellee's child was a recipient of public assistance, Connecticut law compelled appellee under penalty of fine and imprisonment "to disclose the name of the putative father under oath and to institute an action to establish the paternity of said child." This, the appellant argued, unlike a common dispute between private parties, involves the state in the paternity proceeding in a substantial way, thus giving rise to a constitutional duty to provide for the cost of blood group tests for indigent putative fathers.

After examining the appellant's argument under an *Eldridge* analysis, the Court concluded that the "appellant did not receive the process he was constitutionally due. Without obtaining blood test evidence in a paternity case, an indigent defendant, who faces the State as an adversary when the child is a recipient of public assistance and who must overcome the evidentiary burden Connecticut imposes [adverse presumption against the defendant's testimony by elevating the weight to be accorded to a mother's imputation of him] lacks 'a meaningful opportunity to be heard.' ... Therefore 'the requirement of fundamental fairness' expressed by the Due Process Clause was not satisfied here." Boddie v. Connecticut, among other decisions, was cited and relied upon.

Page 786. At the end of Note 2 add:

Cf. Schweiker v. McClure, — U.S. — , 102 S. Ct. 1665, — L. Ed. 2d — (1982), where the Court held that the procedure for reviewing disputed Medicare claims, under which a claimant's nonappealable final review is before a hearing officer chosen by the private insurance carrier that originally made the claim determination under review, does not violate the claimant's due process rights. While due process "demands impartiality on the part of those who function in ... quasi-judicial capacities," the presumption that the hearing officers were "unbiased" had not been rebutted in the instant case. Moreover, there was no serious risk of erroneous decision, despite the role of carrier-appointed hearing officers.

Page 791. At the end of Note 2 add:

In Connecticut Board of Pardons v. Dumshat, 452 U.S. 458, 101 S. Ct. 2460, 69 L. Ed. 2d 158 (1981), the Court rejected a claim by prisoners serving life sentences in Connecticut state prisons that they have a constitutionally protected "entitlement" to a statement of reasons why commutation of their prison sentences had not been granted. The respondent prisoners had contended that the Board's consistent practice of granting commutations to most life inmates was sufficient to create a protectable liberty interest. Chief Justice Burger stated that because pardon and parole boards had "unfettered discretion" the prisoners possessed "simply a unilateral hope" of commutation or pardon.

See also Jago v. Van Curen, — U.S. — , 102 S. Ct. 31, — L. Ed. 2d — (1981), where the Court rejected a prisoner's argument that he gained a "protected liberty interest" in an early release from incarceration, after notification by the parole board but before the actual release. Characterizing the parole revocation decision as involving a "grievous loss," the Court quoted from Morrissey v. Brewer, stating: " '[T]he question is not merely the 'weight' of the individual's interest, but whether the nature of the interest is one within the contemplation of the liberty or property language of the Fourth Amendment.' "

Justice Stevens, joined by Justices Brennan and Marshall, dissented from the Court's holding, essentially criticizing what Justice Stevens termed as a "dubious distinction" being made between the decision to revoke parole and the decision to grant or deny parole.

Page 791. At the end of Note 3 add:

Cf. Marshall v. Jerrico, Inc., 446 U.S. 238, 100 S. Ct. 1610, 64 L. Ed. 2d 182 (1980), holding that the Fair Labor Standards Act's requirement that civil penalties assessed by the Labor Department for violations of the child labor laws be used to defray the cost of enforcing such legislation did not create a sufficient potential for bias on the part of administrative officials so as to violate the Fifth Amendment's due process clause. Distinguishing Tumey v. Ohio, 273 U.S. 510, 47 S. Ct. 437, 71 L. Ed. 2d 749 (1927), and Ward v. Village of Monroeville, 409 U.S. 57, 93 S. Ct. 80, 34 L. Ed. 2d 267 (1972), the Court concluded that strict due process requirements as to the neutrality of decisionmakers performing judicial or quasi-judicial functions are not applicable to determination of administrators whose functions resemble those of a prosecutor more closely than a judge.

Page 792. At the end of Note 5 add:

Compare Vitek v. Jones, 445 U.S. 480, 100 S. Ct. 1254, 63 L. Ed. 2d 552 (1980), invalidating a Nebraska statute authorizing the transfer of a convicted felon from a state prison to a mental hospital, upon the determination by a doctor that this was medically necessary, as violative of procedural due process. Such an involuntary transfer implicates a liberty interest protected by the Fourteenth Amendment's due process clause, and thus must be accompanied by adequate notice, an adversary hearing before an independent decisionmaker, a written statement by the factfinder of the evidence relied on and the reasons for the decision, and, finally, the availability of appointed counsel for indigent prisoners. Only a plurality of the justices agreed on the latter point, with Justice Powell, who otherwise joined Justice White's majority opinion, stating that appointed counsel was not required in such a situation in order to satisfy the requirements of due process. Meachum v. Fano, 427 U.S. 215, 96 S. Ct. 2532, 49 L. Ed. 2d 451 (1976) (holding that the transfer of a prisoner from one prison to another does not infringe a protected liberty interest), and *Greenholtz* were distinguished, and *Morrissey* and *Wolff* cited and relied upon by the Court. Chief Justice Burger and Justices Stewart, Blackmun, and Rehnquist dissented on the ground that the case was moot because of appellee's return to incarceration in a state prison. See also Santosky v. Kramer, supra this Supplement, addition to Casebook p.79.

Page 794. Add to the footnoted material:

Schwartz, Administrative Law and the Burger Court, 8 Hofstra L. Rev. 325 (1980).

Page 805:

In line 8 of the first paragraph change "mortgages" to "mortgagees."

Page 813:

In line 12 of the second full paragraph change "bearing" to "barring."

Page 822. At the end of the first full paragraph add:

See United States v. Darusmont, 449 U.S. 292, 101 S. Ct. 549, 66 L. Ed. 2d 513 (1981), where the Court, in a per curiam decision, reaffirmed *Hudson* and *Welch*, quoting Judge Learned Hand to the effect that "[n]obody has a vested right in the rate of taxation, which may be retroactively changed at the will of Congress at least for periods of less than twelve months; Congress has done so from the outset. . . ."

Page 822. As an addendum to the footnote add:

For a recent application of the ex post facto clause in the criminal area, see Weaver v. Graham, 450 U.S. 24, 101 S. Ct. 960, 67 L. Ed. 2d 17 (1981). Restating the principles of the *ex post facto* clause, Justice Marshall, writing for a unanimous Court, stated: "The *ex post facto* prohibition forbids the Congress and the States from enacting any law 'which imposes a punishment for an act which is not punishable at the time it was committed, or imposes additional punishment to that then prescribed.' ... Through this prohibition, the Framers sought to assure that legislative acts give fair warning of their effect and permit individuals to rely on their meaning until explicitly changed. ... The ban also restricts governmental power by restraining arbitrary and potentially vindictive legislation. ... In accord with those purposes, our decisions prescribe that two critical elements must be present for a criminal or penal law to be *ex post facto*: it must be retrospective, that is it must apply to events occurring before its enactment, and it must disadvantage the offender affected by it."

Page 827. At the end of Note 1 add:

See Hodel v. Virginia Mining & Reclaimation Assn., 452 U.S. 264, 101 S. Ct. 2352, 69 L. Ed. 2d 1 (1981), where the Court addressed a due process challenge to the 1977 Surface Mining Control and Reclamation Act, which gives the Secretary of the Interior the power to order the immediate cessation of surface mining when he determines that the operation is in violation of the act. Justice Marshall, writing for the Court, stated: "Our cases have indicated that due process ordinarily requires an opportunity for 'some kind of hearing' prior to the deprivation of a significant property interest. ... [However,] [t]he Court has often acknowledged. . . that summary administrative action[s] may be justified in emergency situations. . . .The question, then, is whether the issuance of immediate cessation orders under. . . [the act] falls under this emergency situation exception to the normal rule that due process requires a hearing prior to deprivation of a property right. We believe that it does. . . . The immediate cessation order provisions reflect Congress' concern about the devastating damage that may result from mining disasters. They represent an attempt to reach an accommodation between the legitimate desire of mining companies to be heard before submitting to administrative regulation and the governmental interest in protecting the public health and safety and the environment from imminent danger. Protection of the health and safety of the public," Marshall concluded, "is a paramount governmental interest which justifies summary administrative action." Justice Marshall also rejected a challenge to the act on the ground that it failed to establish objective criteria to govern the issuance of the cessation orders, finding that due process is satisfied when at some stage statutory procedures afford a property owner an opportunity for a hearing and a judicial determination.

Page 828. At the end of Note 3 add:

Cf. Texaco, Inc. v. Short, — U.S. —, 102 S. Ct. 781, — L. Ed. 2d — (1982), where the Court held, *inter alia*, that the Indiana Mineral Lapse Act, which provides that a severed mineral interest that is unused for a period of 20 years will automatically revert back to the surface owner unless the owner of the mineral rights files a statement of claim within that 20-year period, is not a taking without just compensation because the property is considered abandoned after 20 years, and thus the former owner retains no legal property interest.

Page 836. At end of Note 6 add:

Compare the approach of the Court in Andrus v. Allard, 444 U.S. 51, 100 S. Ct. 318, 62 L. Ed. 2d 210 (1979), where the Court upheld the constitutionality of the Eagle Protection Act and the Migratory Bird Treaty Act, described as "conservation statutes designed to prevent the destruction of certain species of birds," even though the pertinent regulations construed the statutes "to authorize the prohibition of commercial transactions in pre-existing avian artifacts." There was no violation of the taking clause, the Court concluded, even though the regulations "prevent the most profitable use of [the] property" and cause a reduction in its value. Citing and relying on a number of earlier taking clause cases, including the recent *Penn Central Transportation Co.* case (Casebook p.840), the Court noted that there was no compelled surrender of the artifacts and "no physical invasion or restraint upon them. Rather, a significant restriction has been imposed on one means of disposing of the artifacts. But the denial of one traditional property right does not always amount to a taking. At least where an owner possesses a full 'bundle' of property rights, the destruction of one 'strand' of the bundle is not a taking, because the aggregate must be viewed in its entirety. . . . [I]t is crucial that appellees retain the right to possess and transport their property, and to donate or devise the protected birds."

It is noteworthy that the Court, while rejecting the claim on the merits, assumed as obvious the application of the taking clause to personal as well as real property.

Page 840. At the end of Note 1 add:

Van Alstyne, The Recrudescence of Property Rights as the Foremost Principle of Civil Liberties: The First Decade of the Burger Court, 43 Law & Contemp. Prob. 66 (1980).

At issue in Agins v. City of Tiburon, 447 U.S. 255, 100 S. Ct. 2138, 65 L. Ed. 2d 106 (1980), was the constitutionality, under the taking clause, of a municipality's open-space land zoning ordinances, which restricted a previously purchased five-acre tract to single-family residences and open-space use. Concluding that the ordinances, which permitted construction of one to five residences on the zoned tracts of land, did not result in an impermissible taking without just compensation, the Court stressed that the legislation advanced the legitimate governmental goal of discouraging premature and disorderly development of open space, and neither prevented the best use of the land nor extinguished a fundamental attribute of ownership so as to burden the landowners' enjoyment of their property in such a way as to constitute a taking. The Court pointed out that the landowners will share in the benefits as well as the burdens of this zoning policy, and that such benefits must be considered along with the immediate loss in market value. Reliance was placed on the *Euclid* and *Belle Terre* cases, as well as the more recent decisions in *Penn Central* and *Kaiser Aetna.*

Page 840. At the end of Note 2 add:

See also City of Memphis v. Greene, infra in this Supplement, addition to Casebook p.986.

Page 847. At the end of Note 2 add:

Requiring the owners of a shipping center to permit members of the public to exercise state-protected rights of free assembly and expression on privately owned shopping-center property does not constitute a violation of the Fifth Amendment's taking clause, since the owners failed to demonstrate that the "right to exclude others" was essential to the use or economic value of the property. Time, place, and manner restrictions of orderly activity are sufficient to protect the property interests involved; *Kaiser Aetna* was distinguished. PruneYard Shopping Center v. Robins, 447 U.S. 74, 100 S. Ct. 2035, 64 L. Ed. 2d 741 (1980).

Page 847. At the end of Note 3 add:

Speaking for the Court's majority in Kaiser Aetna v. United States, 444 U.S. 164, 100 S. Ct. 383, 62 L. Ed. 2d 332 (1979), Justice Rehnquist concluded that the commerce clause does not create a blanket exemption to application of the taking clause of the Fifth Amendment. Thus, if the federal government determined to make a public park of a private pond and in doing so converted the property into "navigable waters" of the United

States, it must invoke the power of eminent domain and provide just compensation for the property interests taken. "Here," the Court concluded, "the Government's attempt to create a public right of access to the improved pond goes so far beyond ordinary regulation or improvement for navigation as to amount to a taking under the logic of Pennsylvania Coal Co. v. Mahon. . . ." Justices Blackmun, Brennan, and Marshall dissented, viewing a federal navigational servitude as precluding any cognizable taking clause claim.

In a related case the Court concluded that no general public right of use arises when canals built with private funds on private property join navigable waters. Vaughn v. Vermilion Corp., 444 U.S. 206, 100 S. Ct. 399, 62 L. Ed. 2d 365 (1979). However, the Court noted, if a preexisting waterway were diverted by such an action, a public right of way would be permitted.

Page 851. At the end of Note 2 add:

In Webb's Fabulous Pharmacies Inc. v. Beckwith, 449 U.S. 155, 101 S. Ct. 466, 66 L. Ed. 2d 358 (1980), the Court held that the county's withholding of interest earned on an interpleader fund was an unconstitutional "taking" in violation of the Fifth and Fourteenth Amendments, especially since a fee had already been assessed for the court clerk's services in administering the fund.

Page 859. At the end of Note 3 add:

See also Dames & Moore v. Regan, — U.S. — , 101 S. Ct. 2972, 69 L. Ed. 2d 918 (1981), supra in this Supplement, addition to Casebook p.298, concluding that the question whether presidential action incident to the agreement with Iran for release of American hostages constituted a compensable taking without just compensation for claims against Iranian assets located in this country, which were "unfrozen" under the agreement, was "not [yet] ripe for review." Compare Justice Powell's separate opinion, concluding that "[t]he extraordinary powers of the President and Congress upon which our decision rests cannot, in the circumstances of this case, displace the Just Compensation Clause of the Constitution."

Chapter Eight

Equal Protection and Privileges and Immunities

Page 861:

In line 4 of the introductory note change "1953" to "1954."

Page 865. At the end of Note 1 add:

Although the Fourteenth Amendment was not officially a part of the Constitution when *Crandall* was decided, and there is no express reference to the provision in the Court's opinion, it has historically been viewed as a privileges and immunities clause case.

Page 874:

In line 9 of the carryover paragraph in Note 3, change "simple" to "single."

Page 874. At the end of the first full paragraph of Note 3 add:

Cf. Reeves, Inc. v. Stake, 447 U.S. 429, 100 S. Ct. 2271, 65 L. Ed. 2d 244 (1980). In this regard, cf. Commonwealth Edison Co. v. Montana, supra in this Supplement, addition to Casebook p.410, regarding the impact on interstate commerce of a severance tax imposed in the mining of coal by a resource-rich state. Cf. New England Power Co. v. New Hampshire, – U.S. – ,102 S. Ct. 1096, – L. Ed. 2d – (1982), invalidating a state's prohibition of the transmission of electricity to out-of-state buyers, on commerce clause grounds, at least without congressional authorization.

Page 874. At the end of the second full paragraph add:

See also Weinberger v. Rossi, – U.S. – , 102 S. Ct. 1510, L. Ed. 2d – (1982), which upheld an executive agreement with the Philippine government providing for preferential employment opportunities for Filipino citizens on United States bases in the Philippines. The Court construed a

Congressional statute prohibiting employment discrimination against United States citizens on military bases overseas unless permitted by "treaty" to include a general exception for executive agreements to the same effect.

Page 875. Add to the footnoted material:

Weidner, The Equal Protection Clause: The Continuing Search for Judicial Standards, 57 U. Det. J. Urb. L. 867 (1980).

Page 885:

In line 2 of the third full paragraph change "faces" to "races."

Page 891. At the end of the carryover paragraph add:

Cf. City of Memphis v. Greene, infra in this Supplement, addition to Casebook p.986, where the Court upheld the city's closing of a street at a point which divided an all-white neighborhood from a predominantly black one. The court rejected the respondents' claim that the city's actions violated both 42 U.S.C. 1982 and the Thirteenth Amendment.

Page 893. At the end of the carryover paragraph add:

Cf. State of Minnesota v. Clover Leaf Creamery Co., 449 U.S. 456, 101 S. Ct. 715, 66 L. Ed. 2d 659 (1981), in which the Court sustained a state statute banning the retail sale of milk in plastic non-returnable containers, but permitted such sale in other non-returnable containers such as paperboard cartons. Cf. Texaco Inc. v. Short, — U.S. — , 102 S. Ct. 781, — L. Ed. 2d — (1982) (sustaining a statutory exception to the Indiana Mineral Lapse Act for owners of 10 or more mineral rights interests because such owners are more likely to be able to engage in actual production of mineral resou. .es).

Page 893. At the end of the second full paragraph add:

Bice, Rationality Analysis in Constitutional Law, 65 Minn. L. Rev. 1 (1980); Delgado, Active Rationality in Judicial Review, 64 Minn. L. Rev. 467 (1980).

Page 895. At the end of Note 2 add:

In Schweiker v. Wilson, 450 U.S. 221, 101 S. Ct. 1074, 67 L. Ed. 2d 186 (1981), the Court was presented with an equal protection challenge to a statutory classification created by the 1972 amendments to the Social Security Act. Among the various provisions of the act, Congress designed a Supplemental Security Income (SSI) program to provide a subsistence allowance to the country's needy aged, blind, and disabled. Despite the apparent reach of this program, it excluded from eligibility persons who are "inmate[s] of a public institution." However, Congress also created a specific exemption to this exclusion by providing that "otherwise eligible person[s] in a hospital, extended care facility, nursing home, or intermediate care facility receiving payments ... under a State plan approved under the [Medicaid program]," would receive a reduced allowance. As a result, Congress directly linked the eligibility to receive this reduced benefit to residents of institutions which receive Medicaid benefits for the care of its eligible individuals. Appellees attacked the constitutionality of this classification, arguing that the exclusion of their class of mentally ill (disabled) persons bears no rational relationship to any legitimate objective of the SSI program.

Justice Blackmun, writing for a five-member majority, stated: "The equal protection obligation imposed by the Due Process Clause of the Fifth Amendment is not an obligation to provide the best governance possible. This is a necessary result of different institutional competences, and its reasons are obvious. Unless a statute employs a classification that is inherently invidious or that impinges on fundamental rights, areas in which the judiciary then has a duty to intervene in the democratic process, the Court properly exercises only a limited review power over Congress, the appropriate representative body through which the public makes democratic choices among alternative solutions to social and economic programs.... Thus, the pertinent inquiry is whether the classification employed ... advances legitimate legislative goals in a rational fashion.... As long as the classificatory scheme chosen by Congress rationally advances a reasonable and identifiable governmental objective, we must disregard the existence of other methods of allocation that we, as individuals, perhaps would have preferred."

The Court then examined the legislative history of the SSI program and determined that Congress deliberately incorporated the Medicaid eligibility standards. Having found the adoption of the Medicaid standards intentional, the Court concluded that Congress could rationally decide, in view of budgetary constraints and other relevant considerations, that the Medicaid recipients in public institutions are most in need and deserving of the relatively small monthly income supplements.

Justice Powell, joined by Justices Brennan, Marshall, and Stevens, dissented from the Court's holding, finding that the legislative history of the SSI program neither identifies nor suggests any policy reasonably intended to be served by denying the appellees the SSI allowance. Powell stated: "In my view, the Court should receive with some skepticism *post hoc* hypotheses about legislative purpose, unsupported by the legislative history. When no indication of legislative purpose appears other than the current position of the Secretary, the Court should require that the classification bear a 'fair and substantial relation' to the asserted purpose.... This marginally more demanding scrutiny indirectly would test the plausibility of the tendered purpose, and preserve equal protection review as something more than 'a mere tautological recognition of the fact that Congress did what it intended to do.' "

See also United States Railroad Retirement Board v. Fritz, 449 U.S. 166, 101 S. Ct. 453, 66 L. Ed. 2d 368 (1980), where petitioners challenged, on equal protection grounds, a system of classifications designed by Congress to determine which persons who worked for both railroad and non-railroad employers would be eligible to collect both railroad retirement benefits and social security benefits. The legislative history of the Railroad Retirement Act of 1974 recognized that the payment of these so-called "windfall" benefits threatened the railroad retirement system with bankruptcy. As a result, Congress, determined to place the system on a "sound financial basis," eliminated the future accruals of the "windfall" benefits, but included a grandfather clause (45 U.S.C. 231b(h)) which expressly preserved these benefits to certain classes of employees.

Justice Rehnquist delivered the opinion of the Court, stating in an almost summary fashion that "the distinctions drawn in §231b(h) do not burden fundamental constitutional rights or create 'suspect' classifications, such as race or national origin, [so that] we may put cases involving judicial review of such claims to one side." Following a brief examination of the equal protection claims based on the legislative classifications, Rehnquist cited Dandridge v. Williams for the proposition that economic and social legislation must simply meet the rational basis test. He concluded further that when "there are plausible reasons for Congress' action, our inquiry is at an end. It is of course 'constitutionally irrelevant whether the reasoning in fact underlay the legislative decision' ... because this Court has never insisted that a legislative body articulate its reasons for enacting a statute. This is particularly true where the legislature must necessarily engage in a process of line drawing. The 'task of classifying persons for ... benefits ... inevitably requires that some persons who have an almost equally strong claim to favorite treatment be placed on different sides of the line' ... and the fact that the line may have been drawn differently at some points is a matter of legislative, rather than judicial, consideration."

Justice Stevens concurred separately in the judgment, stating essentially that to satisfy the rational basis test, a system of classifications must bear a close correlation to either the actual purpose of the statute or a legitimate purpose which could have conceivably motivated an impartial legislature. He continued: "If the adverse impact on the disfavored class is an apparent aim of the legislature, its impartiality would be suspect. If, however, the adverse impact may reasonably be viewed as an acceptable cost of achieving a larger goal, an impartial lawmaker could rationally decide that that cost should be incurred."

Justice Brennan, joined by Justice Marshall, wrote a dissenting opinion which accepted the majority's use of the rational basis test, but which chastised the Court for its failure to "scrutinize the challenged classification in the manner established by ... governing precedents." Brennan stated that "the rational basis standard 'is not a toothless one' and will not be satisfied by flimsy or implausible justifications for the legislative classification, professed after the fact by government attorneys.... When faced with a challenge to a legislative classification under the rational basis test, the Court should ask, first, what the purposes of the statute are, and second, whether the classification is rationally related to achievement of those purposes."

Page 896. At the end of the first full paragraph in Note 3 add:

In Searle & Co. v. Cohn, – U.S. – , 102 S. Ct. 1137, – L. Ed. 2d – (1982), the Court held that a New Jersey tolling provision, applied in an action against a foreign corporation that is not presently represented within the state, does not violate the equal protection clause because the increased difficulty of out-of-state service of process provides the necessary rational basis for this legislative choice. Justice Stevens dissented, finding the total deprivation of the benefit of the statute of limitations to unregistered foreign corporations as constitutionally impermissible, even under the rational basis test.

Page 896. At the end of the first paragraph of Note 4 add:

See also Western & Southern Life Insurance Co. v. State Board of Equalization of California, 451 U.S. 648, 101 S. Ct. 2070, 68 L. Ed. 2d 514 (1981), where the appellant insurance companies challenged California's practice of imposing a "retaliatory" tax on foreign insurers when the insurer's state of incorporation imposes higher taxes on California insurers doing business in that state than California would otherwise impose on that state's insurers doing business in California. The challenge was based on both the commerce clause and equal protection clause of the Fourteenth Amendment.

The Court dismissed the appellant's commerce clause challenge to the retaliatory tax, relying on the McCarran Act, which removes entirely any commerce clause restriction upon California's power to tax the insurance business.

Justice Brennan, writing for the Court, addressed the equal protection challenge raised by the appellants, stating: "The Fourteenth Amendment forbids the States to 'deny to any person within [their] jurisdiction the equal protection of the laws'... but does not prevent the States from making reasonable classifications among such persons. Thus, California's retaliatory insurance tax should be sustained if we find that its classification is rationally related to achievement of a legitimate state purpose.... But as [the] appellee points out, state tax provisions directed against out-of-state parties have not always been subject to such scrutiny.... Since California courts have defined the retaliatory tax as a 'privilege' tax... application of the reasoning of [earlier] cases would require us to sustain the tax without further inquiry into its rational basis. We must therefore decide first whether California's retaliatory tax is subject to such further inquiry.

"Some past decisions of this Court have held that a State may exclude a foreign corporation from doing business or acquiring a holding property within its borders. . . . From this principle . . . the theory that a State may attach such conditions as it chooses upon the grant of the privilege to do business within the state [has arisen]. . . . While this theory would suggest that a state may exact any condition, no matter how onerous or otherwise unconstitutional, on a foreign corporation desiring to do business within it, this Court has also held that a State may not impose *unconstitutional* conditions on the grant or the privilege. Sherbert v. Verner, 734 U.S. 398, 404 (1963). . . .

"These two principles are in obvious tension. If a *State* cannot impose unconstitutional conditions on a grant of a privilege, then its right to withhold the privilege is less than absolute. But if the State's right to withhold the privilege is absolute then no one has the right to challenge the terms under which the State chooses to exercise that right. In view of this tension, it is not surprising that the Court's attempt to accommodate both principles that produced results that seem inconsistent or illogical. . . ."

The Court then examined a series of cases involving both privilege taxes and retaliatory taxes, concluding: "It [is] now established that, whatever the extent of a State's authority to exclude foreign corporations from doing business within its boundaries, that authority does not justify imposition of more onerous taxes or other burdens on foreign corporations, unless the discrimination between foreign and domestic corporations bears a rational relation to a legitimate state purpose. . . . In determining whether a challenged classification is rationally related to achievement of a legitimate state purpose we must answer two questions: (1) Does the challenged legislation have a legitimate purpose?, and (2) Was it reasonable for the lawmakers to believe that use of the challenged classification would promote that purpose? . . .

"Many may doubt the wisdom of California's retaliatory tax; indeed, the retaliatory tax has often been criticized as a distortion of the tax system and an impediment to the raising of revenue from the taxation of insurance. . . . [However,] there can be no doubt that promotion of domestic industries by deterring barriers to interstate business is a legitimate state purpose. This Court has recognized the legitimacy of state efforts to maintain the profit level of a domestic industry, Parker v. Brown, 317 U.S. 341, 363-367 (1943), and of efforts to 'protect and enhance the reputation' of a domestic industry so that it might compete more effectively in the interstate market, Pike v. Bruce Church, Inc., 397 U.S. 137, 143 (1970). California's effort on behalf of its domestic insurance industry is no less legitimate. . . . The mere fact that California seeks to promote its insurance industry by influencing the policies of other States does not render the purpose illegitimate. United States Steel Corp. v. Multistate Tax Commn., 434 U.S. 452, 478 (1978). . . . Having established that the purpose of California's lawmakers in enacting the retaliatory tax was legitimate, we turn to the second element in our analysis: whether it was reasonable for California's lawmakers to believe that use of the challenged classification would promote that purpose.... [W]hether *in fact* the provision will accomplish *its* objective is not the question: the Equal Protection Clause is satisfied if we conclude that the California Legislature *rationally could have believed* that the retaliatory tax would promote its objective.... [W]e cannot say that the California Legislature's conclusions were irrational, or even unreasonable. Assuming that the lawmakers of each State are motivated in part by a desire to promote the interests of their domestic insurance industry, it is reasonable to suppose that California's retaliatory tax will induce them to lower the burdens on California insurers in order to spare their domestic insurers the cost of the retaliatory tax in California."

The Court therefore concluded that "the California retaliatory insurance tax withstands the strictures of the Fourteenth Amendment."

Justice Stevens, joined by Justice Blackmun, dissented.

Page 897. At the end of Note 6 add:

In Hodel v. Indiana, 452 U.S. 314, 101 S. Ct. 2376, 69 L. Ed. 2d 40 (1981), the Court rejected an equal protection challenge to the 1977 Surface Mining Control and Reclamation Act, which provides, *inter alia*, for variances from the act's requirements that an operator must return the land to its approximate original contour for steep-slope and mountaintop operations, but does not provide similar variances for operators in nonmountainous areas. Justice Marshall delivered the opinion of the Court, stating: "Social and economic legislation like the Surface Mining Act that does not employ suspect classifications or impinge on fundamental rights must be upheld against equal protection attack when the legislative means are rationally related to a legitimate governmental purpose.... As the Court explained in Vance v. Bradley, 440 U.S. 93, 97 (1979), social and economic legislation is valid unless 'the varying treatment of different groups or persons is so unrelated to the achievement of any combination of legitimate purposes that [a court] can only conclude that the legislature's actions were irrational.' This is a heavy burden, and [the] appellees have not carried it.... The characteristics of surface coal mining obviously will vary according to the different conditions present in the affected States. Congress has determined that the measures appropriate for steep-slope mines are not necessarily desirable in flatter terrain and prime farmland areas. In allowing variances from the approximate original contour requirement applicable to steep-slope mines, Congress may have been influenced by the relative shortage of level land in the steep-slope areas of the country which does not exist in the flatter terrain areas of the Midwest. Similarly, Congress presumably concluded that allowing variances from prime farmland provisions would undermine the effort to preserve the productivity of such lands. In our view, Congress acted rationally in drawing these distinctions, and the fact that a particular State has more of one kind of mining operation than another does not establish impermissible discrimination under the Fifth Amendment's Due Process Clause."

Page 906. At the end of Note 1 add:

Horowitz, The Jurisprudence of *Brown* and the Dilemmas of Liberalism, 14 Harv. Civ. Rights-Civ. Lib. L. Rev. 599 (1980).

Page 911. At the end of Note 5 add:

Cf. Prince Edward School Foundation v. United States, 450 U.S. 944, 101 S. Ct. 1408, 67 L. Ed. 2d 376 (1981) (infra in this Supplement, addition to Casebook p.948).

Page 948. At the end of Note 2 add:

Comment, The Constitutionality of Public School Financing Laws, 8 Fordham Urb. L.J. 673 (1980).

Page 948. At the end of Note 3 add:

Justice Rehnquist, joined by Justices Stewart and Powell, dissented from the Court's denial of certiorari in Prince Edward School Foundation v. United States, 450 U.S. 944, 101 S. Ct. 1408, 67 L. Ed. 2d 376 (1981). The case presented an appeal from the Internal Revenue Service action which removed the foundation's tax-exempt status. The IRS took the action pursuant to a position adopted in 1970 that it would no longer recognize the tax-exempt status of any private school that did not adopt and administer a non-discriminatory admissions policy. Affidavits had been entered into evidence asserting that the private school operated by petitioner did in fact have an open admissions policy. Among these affidavits were statistics which indicated that no black student had ever applied for admission to the school.

Justice Rehnquist's dissent expressed his concern over the district court's determination that the record supported the IRS action.

Cf. City of Memphis v. Greene, infra in this Supplement, addition to Casebook p.986, where the Court held that simply because one race may be "inconvenienced" to a greater degree than another, this cannot by itself be equated with an actual impairment of statutory or constitutionally protected rights.

Page 956. At the end of Note 5 add:

Justice Rehnquist, joined by Chief Justice Burger and Justice Powell, dissented from the denial of certiorari in Cleveland Board of Education v.

Reed, 445 U.S. 935, 100 S. Ct. 1329, 63 L. Ed. 2d 770 (1980). While he agreed that segregative intent on the part of the school board has been shown, he felt that the court of appeals had neglected to address the propriety of the consequences of the systemwide remedy that had been ordered. Stating that "the traditional rule [is] that the remedy imposed by a United States District Court exercising its equitable powers must restore, as nearly as possible, the situation which would have existed had the wrong not occurred," he would have granted review of this issue. Referring to Justice Powell's dissent (joined by Justices Stewart and himself) in Estes v. Metropolitan Branches of Dallas NAACP, 444 U.S. 437, 100 S. Ct. 716, 62 L. Ed. 2d 626 (1980), dismissing the case as having been improvidently taken for plenary consideration, Rehnquist said that the district court's discretion did not extend to restructuring the entire demography of a city such as Cleveland, as reflected in its school system, unless the school board itself was responsible for the racial composition of various parts of the city. Citing and quoting from *Swann* and *Bradley,* he concluded: "Even if the Constitution required it, and it were possible for federal courts to do it, no equitable decree can fashion an 'emerald city' where all races, ethnic groups, and persons of various income levels live side by side in a large metropolitan area." In the *Dallas* case Powell wrote that "this case presents a long-needed opportunity to re-examine the considerations relevant to framing a remedy in a desegregation suit," stating that "[i]t is increasingly evident that use of the busing remedy to achieve racial balance can conflict with the goals of equal educational opportunity and quality schools" and that "[i]n all too many cities, well-intentioned court decrees have had the primary effect of stimulating resegregation," as occurred in *Dallas.* He concluded: "The promise of Brown v. Board of Education ... cannot be fulfilled by continued imposition of self-defeating remedies." Finally, see also Delaware State Board of Education v. Evans, 446 U.S. 923, 100 S. Ct. 1862, 64 L. Ed. 2d 278 (1980), where Justice Rehnquist (joined by Justices Stewart and Powell) again dissented from the denial of certiorari in a school desegregation case, stating that the *Dayton* case and like precedents require district courts to impose changes in a school system only to the extent necessary to cure the violation. He felt that the court of appeals' departure from earlier decisions warranted review and that the need for specific findings was especially compelling when a district court imposes a remedy curtailing local control of public education, as in the Wilmington case before the Court.

Page 979. At the end of Note 2 add:

See also Edwards, Affirmative Action or Reverse Discrimination, 13 Creighton L. Rev. 713 (1980); Wright, Color-Blind Theories and Color-Conscious Remedies, 47 U. Chi. L. Rev. 213 (1980); A Symposium on Affirmative Action, 26 Wayne L. Rev. (1980); Abraham, Some Post-*Bakke-Weber* Reflections on "Reverse Discrimination," 13 U. Rich. L. Rev. 373 (1979).

Page 981. After United Steelworkers of America v. Weber add:

FULLILOVE v. KLUTZNICK
448 U.S. 448, 100 S. Ct. 2758, 65 L. Ed. 2d 902 (1980)

[Section 103(f)(2) of the Public Works Employment Act of 1977 (P.L. 95-28, 91 Stat. 116) provided that at least 10 percent of federal funds granted for local public works projects must be used by the state or local grantee to procure services or supplies from businesses owned principally by "minority group members," defined as American citizens who are "Negroes, Spanish-speaking, Orientals, Indians, Eskimos, and Aleuts." This "minority business enterprise" (MBE) set-aside provision was challenged by contractors who alleged that they had sustained economic injury as a result of its enforcement by the Secretary of Commerce and related federal agencies; they alleged that the MBE requirement on its face violated the Fourteenth Amendment's equal protection clause and the equal protection component of the Fifth Amendment's due process clause. The lower federal courts upheld the provision's constitutionality. Dividing 6-to-3 and with no majority opinion, the Supreme Court affirmed, concluding that the MBE set-aside provision was not in conflict with the equal protection concept.]

Mr. Chief Justice BURGER announced the judgment of the Court and delivered an opinion in which Mr. Justice WHITE and Mr. Justice POWELL joined. . . .

The clear objective of the MBE provision is disclosed by our necessarily extended review of its legislative and administrative background. The program was designed to ensure that, to the extent federal funds were granted under the Public Works Employment Act of 1977, grantees who elect to participate would not employ procurement practices that Congress had decided might result in perpetuation of the effects of prior discrimination which had impaired or foreclosed access by minority businesses to public contracting opportunities. The MBE program does not mandate the allocation of federal funds according to inflexible percentages solely based on race or ethnicity.

Our analysis proceeds in two steps. At the outset, we must inquire whether the *objectives* of this legislation are within the power of Congress. If so, we must go on to decide whether the limited use of racial and ethnic criteria, in the context presented, is a constitutionally permissible *means* for achieving the congressional objectives and does not violate the equal protection component of the Due Process Clause of the Fifth Amendment.

In enacting the MBE provision, it is clear that Congress employed an amalgam of its specifically delegated powers. The Public Works Employment Act of 1977, by its very nature, is primarily an exercise of the Spending Power. U.S. Const., Art. I, §8, cl. 1. This Court has recognized that the power to "provide for the . . . general Welfare" is an independent grant of legislative authority, distinct from other broad congressional powers. Buckley v. Valeo, 424 U.S. 1, 90-91 (1976); United States v. Butler, 297 U.S. 1, 65-66 (1936). Congress has frequently employed the Spending Power to further broad policy objectives by conditioning receipt of federal monies upon compliance by the recipient with federal statutory and administrative directives. This Court has repeatedly upheld against constitutional challenge the use of this technique to induce governments and private parties to cooperate voluntarily with federal policy. [Citations omitted.]

The MBE program is structured within this familiar legislative pattern. The program conditions receipt of public works grants upon agreement by the state or local governmental grantee that at least 10% of the federal funds will be devoted to contracts with minority businesses, to the extent this can be accomplished by overcoming barriers to access and by awarding contracts to bona fide MBE's. It is further conditioned to require that MBE bids on these contracts are competitively priced, or might have been competitively priced but for the present effects of prior discrimination. Admittedly, the problems of administering this program with respect to these conditions may be formidable. Although the primary responsibility for ensuring minority participation falls upon the grantee, when the procurement practices of the grantee involve the award of a prime contract to a general or prime contractor, the obligations to assure minority participation devolve upon the private contracting party; this is a contractual condition of eligibility for award of the prime contract.

Here we need not explore the outermost limitations on the objectives attainable through such an application of the Spending Power. The reach of the Spending Power, within its sphere, is at least as broad as the regulatory powers of Congress. If, pursuant to its regulatory powers, Congress could have achieved the objectives of the MBE program, then it may do so under the Spending Power. And we have no difficulty perceiving a basis for accomplishing the objectives of the MBE program through the Commerce Power insofar as the program objectives pertain to the action of private contracting parties, and through the power to enforce the equal protection guarantees of the Fourteenth Amendment insofar as the program objectives pertain to the action of state and local grantees.

We turn first to the Commerce Power. U.S. Const., Art. I, §8, cl. 3. Had Congress chosen to do so, it could have drawn on the Commerce Clause to regulate the practices of prime contractors on federally funded public works projects. Katzenbach v. McClung, 379 U.S. 294 (1964); Heart of Atlanta Motel, Inc. v. United States, 379 U.S. 241 (1964). The legislative history of the MBE provision shows that there was a rational basis for Congress to conclude that the subcontracting practices of prime contractors could perpetuate the prevailing impaired access by minority businesses to public contracting opportunities, and that this inequity has an effect on interstate commerce. Thus Congress could take necessary and proper action to remedy the situation. Ibid.

It is not necessary that these prime contractors be shown responsible for any violation of antidiscrimination laws. Our cases dealing with application of Title VII of the Civil Rights Act of 1964, 78 Stat. 253, as amended, express no doubt of the congressional authority to prohibit practices "challenged as perpetuating the effects of [not unlawful] discrimination occurring prior to the effective date of the Act." Franks v. Bowman Transportation Co., 424 U.S. 747, 761 (1976). Insofar as the MBE program pertains to the actions of private prime contractors, the Congress could have achieved its objectives under the Commerce Clause. We conclude that in this respect the objectives of the MBE provision are within the scope of the Spending Power.

[Chief Justice Burger's discussion of Katzenbach v. Morgan (Casebook p.1118), Oregon v. Mitchell (Casebook p.1125), and City of Rome v. United States (infra in this Supplement, addition to Casebook p.1113) is omitted. He concluded that "[o]ur cases reviewing the parallel power of Congress to enforce the provisions of the Fifteenth Amendment ... confirm that congressional authority [under the Fourteenth Amendment] extends beyond the prohibition of purposeful discrimination to encompass state action that has discriminatory impact perpetuating the effects of past discrimination," and thus Section 5 of the Fourteenth Amendment provides a separate basis "for the power to regulate the procurement practices of state and local grantees of federal funds." The Chief Justice continued:]

With respect to the MBE provision, Congress had abundant evidence from which it could conclude that minority businesses have been denied effective participation in public contracting opportunities by procurement practices that perpetuated the effects of prior discrimination. Congress, of course, may legislate without compiling the kind of "record" appropriate with respect to judicial or administrative proceedings. Congress had before it, among other data, evidence of a long history of marked disparity in the percentage of public contracts awarded to minority business enterprises. This disparity was considered to result not from any lack of capable and qualified minority businesses, but from the existence and maintenance of barriers to competitive access which had their roots in racial and ethnic discrimination, and which continue today, even absent any intentional discrimination or other unlawful conduct. Although much of this history related to the experience of minority businesses in the area of federal procurement, there was direct evidence before the Congress that this pattern of disadvantage and discrimination existed with respect to state and local construction contracting as well. In relation to the MBE provision, Congress acted within its competence to determine that the problem was national in scope.

Although the Act recites no preambulary "findings" on the subject, we are satisfied that Congress had abundant historical basis from which it could conclude that traditional procurement practices, when applied to minority businesses, could perpetuate the effects of prior discrimination. Accordingly, Congress reasonably determined that the prospective elimination of these barriers to minority firm access to public contracting opportunities generated by the 1977 Act was appropriate to ensure that those businesses were not denied equal opportunity to participate in federal grants to state and local governments, which is one aspect of the equal protection of the laws. Insofar as the MBE program pertains to the actions of state and local grantees, Congress could have achieved its objectives by use of its power under §5 of the Fourteenth Amendment. We conclude that in this respect the objectives of the MBE provision are within the scope of the Spending Power.

[Turning then "to the question whether, as a *means* to accomplish those plainly constitutional objectives, Congress may use racial and ethnic criteria, in this limited way, as a condition attached to a federal grant," and "stress[ing] the limited scope of our inquiry," Burger noted "the need for careful judicial evaluation to assure that any congressional program that employs racial or ethnic criteria to accomplish the objective of remedying the present effects of past discrimination is narrowly tailored to the achievement of that goal." He continued:]

Our review of the regulations and guidelines governing administration of the MBE provision reveals that Congress enacted the program as a strictly remedial measure; moreover, it is a remedy that functions prospectively, in the manner of an injunctive decree. Pursuant to the administrative program, grantees and their prime contractors are required to seek out all available, qualified, bona fide MBE's; they are required to provide technical assistance as needed, to lower or waive bonding requirements where feasible, to solicit the aid of the Office of Minority Business Enterprise, the Small Business Administration or other sources for assisting MBE's to obtain required working capital, and to give guidance through the intricacies of the bidding process. The program assumes that grantees who undertake these efforts in good faith will obtain at least 10% participation by minority business enterprises. It is recognized that, to achieve this target, contracts will be awarded to available, qualified, bona fide MBE's even though they are not the lowest competitive bidders, so long as their higher bids, when challenged, are found to reflect merely attempts to cover costs inflated by the present effects of prior disadvantage and discrimination. There is available to the grantee a provision authorized by Congress for administrative waiver on a case-by-case basis should there be a demonstration that, despite affirmative efforts, this level of participation cannot be achieved without departing from the objectives of the program. There is also an administrative mechanism, including a complaint procedure, to ensure that only bona fide MBE's are encompassed by the remedial program, and to prevent unjust participation in the program by those minority firms whose access to public contracting opportunities is not impaired by the effects of prior discrimination.

As a threshold matter, we reject the contention that in the remedial context the Congress must act in a wholly "color-blind" fashion, [citing and discussing *Swann* and similar school desegregation cases]. . . .

In these school desegregation cases we dealt with the authority of a federal court to formulate a remedy for unconstitutional racial discrimination. However, the authority of a court to incorporate racial criteria into a remedial decree also extends to statutory violations. Where federal anti-discrimination laws have been violated, an equitable remedy may in the appropriate case include a racial or ethnic factor, [citing Title VII cases]. In another setting, we have held that a state may employ racial criteria that are reasonably necessary to assure compliance with federal voting rights legislation, even though the state action does not entail the remedy of a constitutional violation, [citing *United Jewish Organizations,* Casebook p.979].

Here we deal, as we noted earlier, not with the limited remedial powers of a federal court, for example, but with the broad remedial powers of Congress. It is fundamental that in no organ of government, state or federal, does there repose a more comprehensive remedial power than in the Congress, expressly charged by the Constitution with competence and authority to enforce equal protection guarantees. Congress not only may induce voluntary action to assure compliance with existing federal statutory or constitutional antidiscrimination provisions, but also, where Congress has authority to declare certain conduct unlawful, it may, as here, authorize and induce state action to avoid such conduct.

A more specific challenge to the MBE program is the charge that it impermissibly deprives nonminority businesses of access to at least some portion of the government contracting opportunities generated by the Act. It must be conceded that by its objective of remedying the historical impairment of access, the MBE provision can have the effect of awarding some contracts to MBE's which otherwise might be awarded to other businesses, who may themselves be innocent of any prior discriminatory actions. Failure of nonminority firms to receive certain contracts is, of course, an incidental consequence of the program, not part of its objective; similarly, past impairment of minority-firm access to public contracting opportunities may have been an incidental consequence of "business-as-usual" by public contracting agencies and among prime contractors.

It is not a constitutional defect in this program that it may disappoint the expectations of nonminority firms. When effectuating a limited and properly tailored remedy to cure the effects of prior discrimination, such "a sharing of the burden" by innocent parties is not impermissible. The actual "burden" shouldered by nonminority firms is relatively light in this connection when we consider the scope of this public works program as compared with overall construction contracting opportunities. Moreover, although we may assume that the complaining parties are innocent of any discriminatory conduct, it was within congressional power to act on the assumption that in the past some nonminority businesses may have reaped competitive benefit over the years from the virtual exclusion of minority firms from these contracting opportunities. . . .

The Congress has not sought to give select minority groups a preferred standing in the construction industry, but has embarked on a remedial program to place them on a more equitable footing with respect to public contracting opportunities. There has been no showing in this case that Congress has inadvertently effected an invidious discrimination by excluding from coverage an identifiable minority group that has been the victim of a degree of disadvantage and discrimination equal to or greater than that suffered by the groups encompassed by the MBE program. It is not inconceivable that on very special facts a case might be made to challenge the congressional decision to limit MBE eligibility to the particular minority groups identified in the Act. But on this record we find no basis to hold that Congress is without authority to undertake the kind of limited remedial effort represented by the MBE program. Congress, not the courts, has the heavy burden of dealing with a host of intractable economic and social problems. . . .

[The Burger opinion's discussion rejecting contentions that the MBE program was underinclusive, on the one hand, and overinclusive, on the other, is omitted.]

[Noting that "[i]t is significant that the administrative scheme provides for waiver and exemption" and also "contains measures to effectuate the congressional objective of assuring legitimate participation by disadvantaged MBE's," Burger concluded:]

That the use of racial and ethnic criteria is premised on assumptions rebuttable in the administrative process gives reasonable assurance that application of the MBE program will be limited to accomplishing the remedial objectives contemplated by Congress and that misapplications of the racial and ethnic criteria can be remedied. In dealing with this facial challenge to the statute, doubts must be resolved in support of the congressional judgment that this limited program is a necessary step to effectuate the constitutional mandate for equality of economic opportunity. The MBE provision may be viewed as a pilot project, appropriately limited in extent and duration, and subject to reassessment and reevaluation by the Congress prior to any extension or reenactment. Miscarriages of administration could have only a transitory economic impact on businesses not encompassed by the program, and would not be irremediable.

Congress, after due consideration, perceived a pressing need to move forward with new approaches in the continuing effort to achieve the goal of equality of economic opportunity. In this effort, Congress has necessary latitude to try new techniques such as the limited use of racial and ethnic criteria to accomplish remedial objectives; this especially so in programs where voluntary cooperation with remedial measures is induced by placing conditions on federal expenditures. That the program may press the outer limits of congressional authority affords no basis for striking it down.

Petitioners have mounted a facial challenge to a program developed by the politically responsive branches of Government. For its part, the Congress must proceed only with programs narrowly tailored to achieve its objectives, subject to continuing evaluation and reassessment; administration of the programs must be vigilant and flexible; and, when such a program comes under judicial review, courts must be satisfied that the legislative objectives and projected administration give reasonable assurance that the program will function within constitutional limitations. But, [quoting from Justices Jackson and Brandeis, while considerations of judicial self-restraint and the desirability of encouraging legislative experimentation argued for upholding the MBE provision, still] . . . . [a]ny preference based on racial or ethnic criteria must necessarily receive a most searching examination to make sure that it does not conflict with constitutional guarantees. This case is one which requires, and which has received, that kind of examination. This opinion does not adopt, either expressly or implicitly, the formulas of analysis articulated in such cases as University of California Regents v. Bakke, 438 U.S. 265 (1978). However, our analysis demonstrates that the MBE provision would survive judicial review under either test articulated in the several *Bakke* opinions. The MBE provision of the Public Works Employment Act of 1977 does not violate the Constitution.

Affirmed.

Mr. Justice POWELL, concurring. . . .

[Justice Powell, while joining the Burger opinion, wrote a separate concurring opinion "to apply the analysis set forth by [his] opinion in . . . *Bakke*." While "Section 102(f)(2) employs a racial classification that is constitutionally prohibited unless it is a necessary means of advancing a compelling governmental interest," Powell concluded that "it is justified as a remedy that serves the compelling governmental interest in eradicating the continuing effects of past discrimination identified by Congress." He continued:]

Because the distinction between permissible remedial action and impermissible racial preference rests on the existence of a constitutional or statutory violation, the legitimate interest in creating a race-conscious remedy is not compelling unless an appropriate governmental authority has found that such a violation has occurred. In other words, two requirements must be met. First, the governmental body that attempts to impose a race-conscious remedy must have the authority to act in response to identified discrimination. Second, the governmental body must make findings that demonstrate the existence of illegal discrimination. In *Bakke,* the Regents failed both requirements. They were entrusted only with educational functions, and they made no findings of past discrimination. Thus, no compelling governmental interest was present to justify the use of a racial quota in medical school admissions. *Bakke,* 438 U.S., at 309-310.... [Moreover,] [o]ur past cases also establish that even if the government proffers a compelling interest to support reliance upon a suspect classification, the means selected must be narrowly drawn to fulfill the governmental purpose.... [Thus, in] reviewing the constitutionality of §103(f)(2), we must decide: (i) whether Congress is competent to make findings of unlawful discrimination; (ii) if so, whether sufficient findings have been made to establish that unlawful discrimination has affected adversely minority business enterprises; and (iii) whether the 10% set-aside is a permissible means for redressing identifiable past discrimination. None of these questions may be answered without explicit recognition that we are reviewing an Act of Congress.

[Justice Powell then engaged in a detailed analysis of these three questions, resolving each of them affirmatively after canvassing cases relating to the congressional power to enforce the Civil War amendments and the legislative history of the MBE provision, and then turning to the third issue and stating:]

Under this Court's established doctrine, a racial classification is suspect and subject to strict judicial scrutiny.... The conclusion that Congress found a compelling governmental interest in redressing identified discrimination against minority contractors therefore leads to the inquiry whether use of a 10% set-aside is a constitutionally appropriate means of serving that interest. In the past, this "means" test has been virtually impossible to satisfy. Only two of this Court's modern cases have held the use of racial classifications to be constitutional. See Korematsu v. United States, 323 U.S. 214 (1944); Hirabayshi v. United States, 320 U.S. 81 (1943). Indeed, the failure of legislative action to survive strict scrutiny has [led] some to wonder whether our review of racial classifications has been strict in theory, but fatal in fact....

Enactment of the set-aside is designed to serve the compelling governmental interest in redressing racial discrimination. As this Court has recognized, the implementation of any affirmative remedy for redress of racial discrimination is likely to affect persons differently depending upon their race. Although federal courts may not order or approve remedies that exceed the scope of a constitutional violation, this Court has not required remedial plans to be limited to the least restrictive means of implementation....

I believe that the enforcement clauses of the Thirteenth and Fourteenth Amendments give Congress a similar measure of discretion to choose a suitable remedy for the redress of racial discrimination. The legislative history of §5 of the Fourteenth Amendment is particularly instructive.... But that authority must be exercised in a manner that does not erode the guarantees of these Amendments. The Judicial Branch has the special responsibility to make a searching inquiry into the justification for employing a race-conscious remedy. Courts must be sensitive to the possibility that less intrusive means might serve the compelling state interest equally as well. I believe that Congress' choice of a remedy should be upheld, however, if the means selected are equitable and reasonably necessary to the redress of identified discrimination. Such a test allows the Congress to exercise necessary discretion but preserves the essential safeguard of judicial review of racial classifications.

[Finding this test to be satisfied here, Powell noted:] By the time Congress enacted §103(f)(2) in 1977, it knew that other remedies had failed to ameliorate the effects of racial discrimination in the construction industry. Although the problem had been addressed by antidiscrimination legislation, executive action to remedy employment discrimination in the construction industry, and federal aid to minority businesses, the fact remained that minority contractors were receiving less than 1% of federal contracts. . . .

[Moreover,] [t]he §103(f)(2) set-aside is not a permanent part of federal contracting requirements. As soon as the PWEA program concludes, this set-aside program ends. The temporary nature of this remedy ensures that a race-conscious program will not last longer than the discriminatory effects it is designed to eliminate. It will be necessary for Congress to re-examine the need for a race-conscious remedy before it extends or re-enacts §103(f)(2). . . .

The percentage chosen for the set-aside is within the scope of congressional discretion [citing court of appeals' cases, and noting that] [t]he choice of a 10% set-aside thus falls roughly halfway between the present percentage of minority contractors and the percentage of minority group members in the Nation.

[Finally, while a] race-conscious remedy should not be approved without consideration of an additional crucial factor — the effect of the set-aside upon innocent third parties, [here the] burden is [not] so great that the set-aside must be disapproved. . . .

In the history of this Court and this country, few questions have been more divisive than those arising from governmental action taken on the basis of race. Indeed, our own decisions played no small part in the tragic legacy of government-sanctioned discrimination. See Plessy v. Ferguson, 163 U.S. 537 (1896); Dred Scott v. Sanford, 19 How. (60 U.S.) 393 (1857). At least since the decision in Brown v. Board of Education, 347 U.S. 483 (1954), the Court has been resolute in its dedication to the principle that the Constitution envisions a Nation where race is irrelevant. The time cannot come too soon when no governmental decision will be based upon immutable characteristics of pigmentation or origin. But in our quest to achieve a society free from racial classification, we cannot ignore the claims of those who still suffer from the effects of identifiable discrimination.

Distinguishing the rights of all citizens to be free from racial classifications from the rights of some citizens to be made whole is a perplexing, but necessary, judicial task. When we first confronted such an issue in *Bakke*, I concluded that the Regents of the University of California were not competent to make, and had not made, findings sufficient to uphold the use of the race-conscious remedy they adopted. As my opinion made clear, I believe that the use of racial classifications, which are fundamentally at odds with the ideals of a democratic society implicit in the Due Process and Equal Protection Clauses, cannot be imposed simply to serve transient social or political goals, however worthy they may be. But the issue here turns on the scope of congressional power, and Congress has been given a unique constitutional role in the enforcement of the post-Civil War Amendments. In this case, where Congress determined that minority contractors were victims of purposeful discrimination and where Congress chose a reasonably necessary means to effectuate its purpose, I find no constitutional reason to invalidate §103(f)(2).[15]

Mr. Justice MARSHALL, with whom Mr. Justice BRENNAN and Mr. Justice BLACKMUN join, concurring in the judgment....

[Indicating that his "resolution of the constitutional issue in this case is governed by the separate opinion [he] coauthored in ... *Bakke*" and that "the 10% minority set-aside provision ... passes constitutional muster under the standard announced in that opinion," Justice Marshall further stated that "principles outlawing the irrelevant or promiscuous use of race [are] inappropriate to racial classifications that provide benefits to minorities for the purpose of remedying the present effects of past racial discrimination. Such classifications may disadvantage some whites, but whites as a class lack the 'traditional indicia of suspectness'" possessed by blacks and other racial minorities.] Because the consideration of race is relevant to remedying the continuing effects of past racial discrimination, and because governmental programs employing racial classifications for remedial purposes can be crafted to avoid stigmatization, we concluded [in *Bakke*] that such programs should not be subjected to conventional "strict scrutiny" — scrutiny that is strict in theory, but fatal in fact....

Nor did we determine that such programs should be analyzed under the minimally rigorous rational-basis standard of review. We recognized that race has often been used to stigmatize politically powerless segments of society, and that efforts to ameliorate the effects of past discrimination could be based on paternalistic stereotyping, not on a careful consideration of modern social conditions. In addition, we acknowledged that governmental classification on the immutable characteristic of race runs counter to the

15. Petitioners also contend that §103(f)(2) violates Title VI of the Civil Rights Act of 1964, 42 U.S.C. §2000d et seq. Because I believe that the set-aside is constitutional, I also conclude that the program does not violate Title VI. See *Bakke*, 438 U.S., at 287 (opinion of Powell, J.); id., at 348-350 (opinion of Brennan, White, Marshall, and Blackmun, JJ.).

deep national belief that state-sanctioned benefits and burdens should bear some relationship to individual merit and responsibility.

We concluded, therefore, that because a racial classification ostensibly designed for remedial purposes is susceptible to misuse, it may be justified only by showing "an important and articulated purpose for its use." [438 U.S.] at 361. "In addition, any statute must be stricken that stigmatizes any group or that singles out those least well represented in the political process to bear the brunt of a benign program." Ibid. In our view, then, the proper inquiry is whether racial classifications designed to further remedial purposes serve important governmental objectives and are substantially related to achievement of those objectives.

Judged under this standard, the 10% minority set-aside provision at issue in this case is plainly constitutional. Indeed, the question is not even a close one, [since] it is indisputable that Congress' articulated purpose for enacting the set-aside provision was to remedy the present effects of past racial discrimination. Congress had a sound basis for concluding that minority-owned construction enterprises, though capable, qualified, and ready and willing to work, have received a disproportionately small amount of public contracting business because of the continuing effects of past discrimination. Here, as in *Bakke*, supra, at 362, "minority underrepresentation is substantial and chronic, and ... the handicap of past discrimination is impeding access of minorities to" the benefits of the governmental program. In these circumstances, remedying these present effects of past racial discrimination is a sufficiently important governmental interest to justify the use of racial classifications.

Because the means chosen by Congress to implement the set-aside provision are substantially related to the achievement of its remedial purpose, the provision also meets the second prong of our *Bakke* test. Congress reasonably determined that race-conscious means were necessary to break down the barriers confronting participation by minority enterprises in federally funded public works projects. That the set-aside creates a quota in favor of qualified and available minority business enterprises does not necessarily indicate that it stigmatizes. As our opinion stated in *Bakke*, "[f]or purposes of constitutional adjudication, there is no difference between" setting aside "a predetermined number of places for qualified minority applicants rather than using minority status as a positive factor to be considered in evaluating the applications of disadvantaged minority applicants." Id., at 378. The set-aside, as enacted by Congress and implemented by the Secretary of Commerce, is carefully tailored to remedy racial discrimination while at the same time avoiding stigmatization and penalizing those least able to protect themselves in the political process. Since under the set-aside provision a contract may be awarded to a minority enterprise only if it is qualified to do the work, the provision stigmatizes as inferior neither a minority firm that benefits from it nor a nonminority firm that is burdened by it. Nor does the set-aside "establish a quota in the invidious sense of a ceiling," *Bakke*, supra, at 375, on the number of minority firms that can be awarded public works contracts. In addition, the set-aside affects only a miniscule amount of the funds annually expended in the United States for construction work.

In sum, it is clear to me that the racial classifications employed in the set-aside provision are substantially related to the achievement of the important and congressionally articulated goal of remedying the present effects of past racial discrimination. The provision, therefore, passes muster under the equal protection standard I adopted in *Bakke*.

Congress recognized these realities [of pervasive racial discrimination that could not be eradicated without "race-conscious remedies"] when it enacted the minority set-aside provision at issue in this case. Today, by upholding this race-conscious remedy, the Court accords Congress the authority necessary to undertake the task of moving our society toward a state of meaningful equality of opportunity, not an abstract version of equality in which the effects of past discrimination would be forever frozen into our social fabric. I applaud this result. . . .

Mr. Justice STEWART, with whom Mr. Justice REHNQUIST joins, dissenting. . . .

[Stating initially that "today's decision is wrong for the same reason that Plessy v. Ferguson was wrong," Justice Stewart quoted the "color-blindness" language from the first Justice Harlan's dissenting opinion in that case. Continuing, he stated:]

The equal protection standard of the Constitution has one clear and central meaning — it absolutely prohibits invidious discrimination by government. That standard must be met by every State under the Equal Protection Clause of the Fourteenth Amendment, [citing cases]. And that standard must be met by the United States itself under the Due Process Clause of the Fifth Amendment. Under our Constitution, any official action that treats a person differently on account of his race or ethnic origin is inherently suspect and presumptively invalid.

The hostility of the Constitution to racial classifications by government has been manifested in many cases decided by this Court, [citing cases]. And our cases have made clear that the Constitution is wholly neutral in forbidding such racial discrimination, whatever the race may be of those who are its victims. . . .

This history contains one clear lesson. Under our Constitution, the government may never act to the detriment of a person solely because of that person's race. The color of a person's skin and the country of his origin are immutable facts that bear no relation to ability, disadvantage, moral culpability, or any other characteristics of constitutionally permissible interest to government. . . . In short, racial discrimination is by definition invidious discrimination.

The rule cannot be any different when the persons injured by a racially biased law are not members of a racial minority. The guarantee of equal protection is universal in [its] application, to all persons ... without regard to any differences of race, of color, or of nationality. Yick Wo v. Hopkins, 118 U.S. 356, 369. The command of the equal protection guarantee is simple but unequivocal: In the words of the Fourteenth Amendment, "No State shall ... deny to *any* person ... the equal protection of the laws." Nothing in this language singles out some "persons" for more "equal" treatment than others.... From the perspective of a person detrimentally affected by a racially discriminatory law, the arbitrariness and unfairness is entirely the same, whatever his skin color and whatever the law's purpose, be it purportedly "for the promotion of the public good" or otherwise.

No one disputes the self-evident proposition that Congress has broad discretion under its Spending Power to disburse the revenues of the United States as it deems best and to set conditions on the receipt of the funds disbursed. No one disputes that Congress has the authority under the Commerce Clause to regulate contracting practices on federally funded public works projects, or that it enjoys broad powers under §5 of the Fourteenth Amendment "to enforce by appropriate legislation" the provisions of that Amendment. But these self-evident truisms do not begin to answer the question before us in this case. For in the exercise of its powers, Congress must obey the Constitution just as the legislatures of all the States must obey the Constitution in the exercise of their powers. If a law is unconstitutional, it is no less unconstitutional just because it is a product of the Congress of the United States.

On its face, the minority business enterprise (MBE) provision at issue in this case denies the equal protection of the law. The Public Works Employment Act of 1977 directs that all project construction shall be performed by those private contractors who submit the lowest competitive bids and who meet established criteria of responsibility. 42 U.S.C. §6705(e)(1) (1976 ed. Supp. I). One class of contracting firms — defined solely according to the racial and ethnic attributes of their owners — is, however, excepted from the full rigor of these requirements with respect to a percentage of each federal grant. The statute, on its face and in effect, thus bars a class to which the petitioners belong from having the opportunity to receive a government benefit, and bars the members of that class solely on the basis of their race or ethnic background. This is precisely the kind of law that the guarantee of equal protection forbids.

The Court's attempt to characterize the law as a proper remedial measure to counteract the effects of past or present racial discrimination is remarkably unconvincing. The Legislative Branch of government is not a court of equity. It has neither the dispassionate objectivity nor the flexibility that are needed to mold a race-conscious remedy around the single objective of eliminating the effects of past or present discrimination.

But even assuming that Congress has the power, under §5 of the Fourteenth Amendment or some other constitutional provision, to remedy previous illegal racial discrimination, there is no evidence that Congress has in the past engaged in racial discrimination in its disbursement of federal contracting funds. The MBE provision thus pushes the limits of any such justification far beyond the equal protection standard of the Constitution. Certainly, nothing in the Constitution gives Congress any greater authority to impose detriments on the basis of race than is afforded the Judicial Branch. And a judicial decree that imposes burdens on the basis of race can be upheld only where its sole purpose is to eradicate the actual effects of illegal race discrimination.

The provision at issue here does not satisfy this condition. Its legislative history suggests that it had at least two other objectives in addition to that of counteracting the effects of past or present racial discrimination in the public works construction industry. One such purpose appears to have been to assure to minority contractors a certain percentage of federally funded public works contracts. But, since the guarantee of equal protection immunizes from capricious governmental treatment "persons" — not "races," it can never countenance laws that seek racial balance as a goal in and of itself. "Preferring members of any one group for no reason other than race or ethnic origin is discrimination for its own sake. This the Constitution forbids." Regents of the University of California v. Bakke, 438 U.S. 265, 307 (opinion of Powell, J.). Second, there are indications that the MBE provision may have been enacted to compensate for the effects of social, educational, and economic "disadvantage." "No race, however, has a monopoly on social, educational, or economic disadvantage," and any law that indulges in such a presumption clearly violates the constitutional guarantee of equal protection. Since the MBE provision was in whole or in part designed to effectuate objectives other than the elimination of the effects of racial discrimination, it cannot stand as a remedy that comports with the strictures of equal protection, even if it otherwise could.

The Fourteenth Amendment was adopted to ensure that every person must be treated equally by each State regardless of the color of his skin. The Amendment promised to carry to its necessary conclusion a fundamental principle upon which this Nation had been founded — that the law would honor no preference based on lineage. Tragically, the promise of 1868 was not immediately fulfilled, and decades passed before the States and the Federal Government were finally directed to eliminate detrimental classifications based on race. Today, the Court derails this achievement and places its imprimatur on the creation once again by government of privileges based on birth.

The Court, moreover, takes this drastic step without, in my opinion, seriously considering the ramifications of its decision. Laws that operate on the basis of race require definitions of race. Because of the Court's decision today, our statute books will once again have to contain laws that reflect the odious practice of delineating the qualities that make one person a Negro and make another white. Moreover, racial discrimination, even "good faith" racial discrimination, is inevitably a two-edged sword.... Most importantly, by making race a relevant criterion once again in its own affairs, the Government implicitly teaches the public that the apportionment of rewards and penalties can legitimately be made according to race — rather than according to merit or ability — and that people can, and perhaps should, view themselves and others in terms of their racial characteristics. Notions of "racial entitlement" will be fostered, and private discrimination will necessarily be encouraged....

There are those who think that we need a new Constitution, and their views may someday prevail. But under the Constitution we have, one practice in which government may never engage is the practice of racism — not even "temporarily" and not even as an "experiment."

Mr. Justice STEVENS, dissenting....

The statutory definition of the preferred class includes "citizens of the United States who are Negroes, Spanish-speaking, Orientals, Indians, Eskimos, and Aleuts." All aliens and all nonmembers of the racial class are excluded. No economic, social, geographical or historical criteria are relevant for exclusion or inclusion. There is not one word in the remainder of the Act or in the legislative history that explains why any Congressman or Senator favored this particular definition over any other or that identifies the common characteristics that every member of the preferred class was believed to share. Nor does the Act or its history explain why 10% of the total appropriation was the proper amount to set aside for investors in each of the six racial subclasses.

Four different, though somewhat interrelated, justifications for the racial classification in this Act have been advanced: first, that the 10% set aside is a form of reparation for past injuries to the entire membership of the class; second, that it is an appropriate remedy for past discrimination against minority business enterprises that have been denied access to public contracts; third, that the members of the favored class have a special entitlement to "a piece of the action" when government is distributing benefits; and, fourth, that the program is an appropriate method of fostering greater minority participation in a competitive economy. Each of these asserted justifications merits separate scrutiny.

[Justice Stevens conceded that] [r]acial characteristics may serve to define a group of persons who have suffered a special wrong and, who, therefore, are entitled to special reparations.... [But] [r]acial classifications are simply too pernicious to permit any but the most exact connection between justification and classification....

Even if we assume that each of the six racial subclasses has suffered its own special injury at some time in our history, surely it does not necessarily follow that each of those subclasses suffered harm of identical magnitude. Although "the Negro was dragged to this country in chains to be sold in slavery," *Bakke*, opinion of Marshall, J., supra, 438 U.S., at 387, the "Spanish-speaking" subclass came voluntarily, frequently without invitation, and the Indians, the Eskimos and the Aleuts had an opportunity to exploit America's resources before most American citizens arrived. There is no reason to assume, and nothing in the legislative history suggests, much less demonstrates, that each of these subclasses is equally entitled to reparations from the United States Government.

At best, the statutory preference is a somewhat perverse form of reparation for the members of the injured classes. For those who are the most disadvantaged within each class are the least likely to receive any benefit from the special privilege even though they are the persons most likely still to be suffering the consequences of the past wrong. A random distribution to a favored few is a poor form of compensation for an injury shared by many.

My principal objection to the reparation justification for this legislation, however, cuts more deeply than my concern about its inequitable character. We can never either erase or ignore the history that Mr. Justice Marshall has recounted. But if that history can justify such a random distribution of benefits on racial lines as that embodied in this statutory scheme, it will serve not merely as a basis for remedial legislation, but rather as a permanent source of justification for grants of special privileges. For if there is no duty to attempt either to measure the recovery by the wrong or to distribute that recovery within the injured class in an evenhanded way, our history will adequately support a legislative preference for almost any ethnic, religious, or racial group with the political strength to negotiate "a piece of the action" for its members.

Although I do not dispute the validity of the assumption that each of the subclasses identified in the Act has suffered a severe wrong at some time in the past, I cannot accept this slapdash statute as a legitimate method of providing classwide relief. . . .

The argument that our history of discrimination has left the entire membership of each of the six racial classes identified in the Act less able to compete in a free market than others is more easily stated than proved. The reduction in prejudice that has occurred during the last generation has accomplished much less than was anticipated; it nevertheless remains true that increased opportunities have produced an ever increasing number of demonstrations that members of disadvantaged races are entirely capable not merely of competing on an equal basis, but also of excelling in the most demanding professions. But, even though it is not the actual predicate for this legislation, a statute of this kind inevitably is perceived by many as resting on an assumption that those who are granted this special preference are less qualified in some respect that is identified purely by their race. Because that perception — especially when fostered by the Congress of the United States — can only exacerbate rather than reduce racial prejudice, it will delay the time when race will become a truly irrelevant, or at least insignificant, factor. Unless Congress clearly articulates the need and basis for a racial classification, and also tailors the classification to its justification, the Court should not uphold this kind of statute. . . .

A comparable approach in the electoral context would support a rule requiring that at least 10% of the candidates elected to the legislature be members of specified racial minorities. Surely that would be an effective way of ensuring black citizens the representation that has long been their due. Quite obviously, however, such a measure would merely create the kind of inequality that an impartial sovereign cannot tolerate. Yet that is precisely the kind of "remedy" that this Act authorizes. In both political and economic contexts, we have a legitimate interest in seeing that those who were disadvantaged in the past may succeed in the future. But neither an election nor a market can be equally accessible to all if race provides a basis for placing a special value on votes or dollars.

The ultimate goal must be to eliminate entirely from governmental decisionmaking such irrelevant factors as a human being's race. The removal of barriers to access to political and economic processes serves that goal. But the creation of new barriers can only frustrate true progress. For . . . such protective barriers reinforce habitual ways of thinking in terms of classes instead of individuals. Preferences based on characteristics acquired at birth foster intolerance and antagonism against the entire membership of the favored classes. For this reason, I am firmly convinced that this "temporary measure" will disserve the goal of equal opportunity. . . .

Unlike Mr. Justice Stewart and Mr. Justice Rehnquist, however, I am not convinced that the [Constitution] contains an absolute prohibition against any statutory classification based on race. I am nonetheless persuaded that it does impose a special obligation to scrutinize any governmental decisionmaking process that draws nationwide distinctions between citizens on the basis of their race and incidentally also discriminates against noncitizens in the preferred racial classes. For just as procedural safeguards are necessary to guarantee impartial decisionmaking in the judicial process, so can they play a vital part in preserving the impartial character of the legislative process.

In both its substantive and procedural aspects this Act is markedly different from the normal product of the legislative decisionmaking process. The very fact that Congress for the first time in the Nation's history has created a broad legislative classification for entitlement to benefits based solely on racial characteristics identifies a dramatic difference between this Act and the thousands of statutes that preceded it. . . .

Although it is traditional for judges to accord the same presumption of regularity to the legislative process no matter how obvious it may be that a busy Congress has acted precipitately, I see no reason why the character of their procedures may not be considered relevant to the decision whether the legislative product has caused a deprivation of liberty or property without due process of law. Whenever Congress creates a classification that would be subject to strict scrutiny under the Equal Protection Clause of the Fourteenth Amendment if it had been fashioned by a state legislature, it seems to me that judicial review should include a consideration of the procedural character of the decisionmaking process. A holding that the classification was not adequately preceded by a consideration of less drastic alternatives or adequately explained by a statement of legislative purpose would be far less intrusive than a final determination that the substance of the decision is not "narrowly tailored to the achievement of that goal," [quoting from Chief Justice Burger's plurality opinion]. If the general language of the Due Process Clause of the Fifth Amendment authorizes this Court to review acts of Congress under the standards of the Equal Protection Clause of the Fourteenth Amendment — a clause that cannot be found in the Fifth Amendment — there can be no separation of powers objection to a more tentative holding of unconstitutionality based on a failure to follow procedures that guarantee the kind of deliberation that a fundamental constitutional issue of this kind obviously merits.

In all events, rather than take the substantive position expressed in Mr. Justice Stewart's dissenting opinion, I would hold this statute unconstitutional on a narrower ground. It cannot fairly be characterized as a "narrowly tailored" racial classification because it simply raises too many serious questions that Congress failed to answer or even to address in a responsible way. The risk that habitual attitudes toward classes of persons, rather than analysis of the relevant characteristics of the class, will serve as a basis for a legislative classification is present when benefits are distributed as well as when burdens are imposed. In the past, traditional attitudes too often provided the only explanation for discrimination against women, aliens, illegitimates, and black citizens. Today there is a danger that awareness of past injustice will lead to automatic acceptance of new classifications that are not in fact justified by attributes characteristic of the class as a whole.

When Congress creates a special preference, or a special disability, for a class of persons, it should identify the characteristic that justifies the special treatment. When the classification is defined in racial terms, I believe that such particular identification is imperative.

In this case, only two conceivable bases for differentiating the preferred classes from society as a whole have occurred to me: (1) that they were the victims of unfair treatment in the past and (2) that they are less able to compete in the future. Although the first of these factors would justify an appropriate remedy for past wrongs, for reasons that I have already stated, this statute is not such a remedial measure. The second factor is simply not true. Nothing in the record of this case, the legislative history of the Act, or experience that we may notice judicially provides any support for such a proposition. It is up to Congress to demonstrate that its unique statutory prefcrence is justified by a relevant characteristic that is shared by the members of the preferred class. In my opinion, because it has failed to make that demonstration, it has also failed to discharge its duty to govern impartially embodied in the Fifth Amendment to the United States Constitution.

NOTES

1. What was the *holding* in *Fullilove*? Which opinion should be regarded as controlling? Is the decision consistent with *Bakke*? How important is the fact that a congressional enactment was involved in *Fullilove*, unlike in *Bakke*? Is Justice Powell's reconciliation of the two cases persuasive? In what significant respects do the Stewart and Stevens dissents differ? More generally, what are the implications of *Fullilove* for other situations involving race-based, quota-oriented preferential treatment? By state legislatures instead of Congress, or by local governmental bodies? Does it follow from *Fullilove* that statutes such as Title VII (and so-called affirmative action in the employment context generally) are *a fortiori* constitutional?

2. For post-*Bakke* discussion of the so-called reverse discrimination question, see, e.g., Van Alstyne, Rites of Passage: Race, the Supreme Court, and the Constitution, 46 U. Chi. L. Rev. 775 (1979); Tribe Perspectives on *Bakke:* Equal Protection, Procedural Fairness or Structural Justice? 92 Harv. L. Rev. 864 (1979); Kitch, The Return of Color Consciousness to the Constitution: *Weber, Dayton* and *Columbus,* 1979 Sup. Ct. Rev. 1; Stone, Equal Protection in Special Admissions Programs: Forward from *Bakke,* 6 Hastings Const. L.Q. 719 (1979); Neuborne, Observations on *Weber,* 54 N.Y.U.L. Rev. 546 (1979); McCormack, Race and Politics in the Supreme Court: *Bakke* to Basics, 1979 Utah L. Rev. 491; Edwards, Affirmative Action or Reverse Discrimination: The Head and Tail of *Weber,* 13 Creighton L. Rev. 713 (1980). See generally *Bakke* Symposium: Civil Rights Perspectives, 14 Harv. Civ. Rights-Civ. Lib. L. Rev. 1 (1979); Regents of the University of California v. Bakke: A Symposium, 67 Calif. L. Rev. 1 (1979).

Page 986. At the end of Note 1 add:

Sellers, The Impact of Intent on Equal Protection Jurisprudence, 84 Dick. L. Rev. 363 (1980).

For a case applying the rationale of Washington v. Davis in the voting context to uphold an at-large election scheme, where there was not a sufficient showing of discriminatory purpose, although discriminatory effect was conceded, see City of Mobile v. Bolden, 446 U.S. 55, 100 S. Ct. 1490, 64 L. Ed. 2d 47 (1980), infra in this Supplement, addition to Casebook p.1018.

Page 986. Add as a new Note 3:

3. In City of Memphis v. Greene, 451 U.S. 100, 101 S. Ct. 1584, 67 L. Ed. 2d 769 (1981), city officials voted to close down the north end of a street that bordered a predominantly black residential area. The stated reasons for the closing were to reduce the flow of traffic, to increase safety to children, and to reduce the traffic pollution in that area of the city. The residents of the predominantly black area brought a class action in federal court against the city, alleging that the street closing violated both 42 U.S.C. 1982 and the Thirteenth Amendment. The district court found for the defendant, but the court of appeals reversed and remanded, holding that the street closing was invalid because it adversely affected the respondents' ability to hold and enjoy property.

In a passage written by Justice Stevens, which seems more conclusory than it is analytical, he summed up the critical facts, as established by the record, as these: "The city's decision to close West Drive was motivated by its interest in protecting the safety and tranquility of the residential neighborhood. The procedures followed in making the decision were fair and not affected by any racial or other impermissible factors. The city has conferred a benefit on certain white property owners but there is no reason to believe it would refuse to confer a comparable benefit on black property owners. [Finally,] the closing has not affected the value of property owned by black citizens, but it has caused some slight inconvenience on black motorists outside the scope of protected rights by way of §1982."

Addressing the Thirteenth Amendment arguments advanced by the respondents, Stevens emphasized that the record failed to disclose a racially discriminatory motive on the part of the city. The Court accepted the city's argument that the reasons underlying the street closing were based on legitimate health and safety concerns. By classifying such interests as legitimate, the Court expressed an unwillingness to review the wisdom of the city's policy decision. Accordingly, Stevens described the "slight inconvenience" experienced by the black citizens of the area as "a routine burden of citizenship, and not as a violation of the Thirteenth Amendment."

Justice Marshall, joined by Justices Brennan and Blackmun, dissented from the Court's holding. After examining the transcript from the district court, Marshall concluded: "Until today I would have thought that the city's erection of a barrier, at the behest of a historically all-white community, to keep out predominantly Negro traffic, would have been among the least of the statute's [§1982] prohibitions. Certainly I suspect that the Congress that enacted §1982 would be surprised to learn that it has no application in such a case. . . . The major concern of the statute's supporters was the elimination of the effects of local prejudice on Negro residents. In my view, the evidence before us supports a strong inference that the operation of such prejudices is precisely what has led to the closing of

West Drive. And against this record, the government should be able to do far more than it has here to justify an action that so obviously damages and stigmatizes a racially identifiable group of its citizens. In short, I conclude that the plain language of §1982 and its legislative history show that the harm established by a fair reading of the record falls within the prohibition of the statute."

In a footnote, Justice Marshall also discussed the Thirteenth Amendment arguments, stating: "I would conclude that official action causing harm of the magnitude suffered here plainly qualifies as a 'badge or incident' of slavery, at least as those terms were understood by the reconstruction Congress.... I would [further] hold that because of the closing of West Drive is forbidden on these facts by §1982, it is *a fortiori* a violation of the Thirteenth Amendment as well." (n.18.)

Page 1006. Add to the asterisked material:

Bickerstaff, Reapportionment by State Legislature: A Guide for the 1980's, 34 Sw. L.J. 607 (1980).

Page 1016. At the end of Note 2 add:

In Ball v. James, 451 U.S. 355, 101 S. Ct. 1811, 68 L. Ed. 2d 150 (1981), Justice Stewart, joined by Chief Justice Burger and Justices Powell, Rehnquist, and Stevens, delivered the Court's opinion concerning the constitutionality of a system for electing the directors of a large water reclamation district in Arizona, a scheme which limits voting eligibility to landowners and apportions voting power according to the amount of land owned. Justice Stewart framed the questions presented as follows: "[W]hether the peculiar narrow function of the local governmental body and the special relationship of one class of citizens to that body releases it from the strict demands of the one-person-one-vote principle of the Equal Protection Clause of the Fourteenth Amendment." Stewart continued: "This lawsuit was brought by a class of registered voters who live within the geographic boundaries of the district, and who own either no land or less than an acre of land within the district. The complaint alleged that the district enjoys such governmental powers as the power to condemn land, to sell tax-exempt bonds, to levy taxes on real property. It also alleged that because the district sells electricity to virtually half the population of Arizona, and because, through its water operations, it can exercise significant influence on flood control and environmental management within its boundaries, the district's policies and actions have a substantial effect on all people who live within the district, regardless of property ownership."

The district court had found the voting scheme constitutional and dismissed the complaint. A divided panel of the Ninth Circuit reversed, concluding that the "Salt River District does not serve the sort of special narrow purpose that proved decisive in [the] *Salyer* [case]."

The Supreme Court rejected the court of appeals' attempt to distinguish *Salyer* as inappropriate. Although acknowledging the fact that services provided by the district are more diverse and affect far more people than the Tulare Lake Basin District in *Salyer*, the Court noted that these distinctions "do not amount to a constitutional difference."

Continuing, Justice Stewart stated: "The [Salt River] District simply does not exercise the sort of governmental powers that invoke the strict demands of *Reynolds*. The district cannot impose *ad valorem* property taxes or sales taxes. It cannot enact any law governing the conduct of citizens, nor does it administer such normal functions of government as the maintenance of streets, the operation of schools, or sanitation, health or welfare services."

Stewart next characterized the functions of the Salt River District as consisting of a "narrow, special sort which justifies a departure from the popular election requirement of the *Reynolds* case.... [A]s in *Salyer*, an aspect of that limited purpose is the disproportionate relationship the District's functions bear to the specific class of people whom the system makes eligible to vote. The voting landowners are the only residents of the District whose lands are subject to liens to secure District bonds. Only these landowners are subject to the acreage-based taxing power of the District, and voting landowners are the only residents who have ever committed capital to the District through stock assessments charged by the Association. The *Salyer* opinion did not say that the selected class of voters for a special public entity must be the only parties at all affected by the operations of the entity, or that their entire economic well-being must depend on that entity. Rather, the question was whether the effect of the entity's operations on them was disproportionately greater than the effect on those seeking the vote."

Concluding, he wrote: "As in the *Salyer* case, we conclude that the voting scheme for the District is constitutional because it bears a reasonable relationship to its statutory objectives. Here, according to the stipulation of the parties, the subscription of land which made the Association and then the District possible might well have never occurred had not the subscribing landowners been assured a special voice in the conduct of the District's business. Therefore, as in *Salyer*, the State could rationally limit the vote to landowners. Moreover, Arizona could rationally make the weight of their vote dependent upon the number of acres they own, since that number reasonably reflects the relative risks they incurred as landowners and the distribution of the benefits and the burdens of the District's water operations."

Justice Powell filed a separate concurrence.

Justice White, joined by Justices Brennan, Marshall, and Blackmun, criticized the majority in a dissent that, in pertinent part, stated: "[B]y concluding that the District's 'one-acre, one-vote' scheme is constitutional, the Court misapplies the limited exception recognized in *Salyer* on the strained logic that the provision of water and electricity to several hundred thousand citizens is a 'peculiarly narrow function.' Because the Court misreads our prior cases and its opinion is conceptually unsound, I dissent." Continuing, he stated: "To be sure, the Court approved limiting the vote to landowners in electing the board of directors of a water storage district in *Salyer*. . . . But nothing in *Salyer* changed the relevant constitutional inquiry. Rather, the Court held the *Reynolds-Avery-Kramer* line of cases inapplicable to the water district because of its 'special limited purpose and the disproportionate effects of its activities on land owners as a group. . . .' An analysis of [those] two relevant factors demonstrates that the Salt River District possesses significant governmental authority and has a sufficiently wide effect on nonvoters to require application of the strict scrutiny mandated by *Kramer*."

In summation Justice White wrote: "The purpose and authority of the Salt River District are of extreme public importance. The District affects the daily lives of thousands of citizens who because of the present voting scheme and the powers vested in the District by the State are unable to participate in any meaningful way in the conduct of the District's operation. In my view, the court of appeals properly reasoned that the limited exception recognized in *Salyer* does not save this voting arrangement. I cannot agree with the Court's extension of *Salyer* to the facts of [this] case, and its unwise suggestion that the provision of electrical and water services are somehow too private to warrant the Fourteenth Amendment's safeguards."

Page 1017:

In lines 2 and 3 of Note 4, place "principle" after instead of before "equal-population."

Page 1018. At the end of Note 6 add:

See also City of Mobile v. Bolden, 446 U.S. 55, 100 S. Ct. 1490, 64 L. Ed. 2d 47 (1980), which involved a challenge to Mobile's longstanding system of electing its city commission on an at-large basis, on the ground that this arrangement discriminated against Negro voters, in violation of the Fifteenth Amendment and the Fourteenth Amendment's equal protection clause. Justice Stewart's plurality opinion stated that "racially discriminatory motivation is a necessary ingredient of a Fifteenth Amendment violation," citing Gomillion v. Lightfoot and Wright v. Rockefeller. Since the record showed that Negroes in Mobile could "register and vote without hindrance," the lower courts had erred, Stewart stated, in finding that their Fifteenth Amendment rights had been transgressed. Turning to the equal protection claim, Stewart analogized to the several cases upholding the constitutionality of multimember districts absent a showing of purposeful discrimination, citing, e.g.,

Whitcomb v. Chavis and White v. Regester. And, he asserted, the burden of proof in this regard "is simply one aspect of the basic principle that only if there is purposeful discrimination can there be a violation of the Equal Protection Clause of the Fourteenth Amendment," citing and quoting from Washington v. Davis, Casebook p.981, and related cases. Referring to White v. Regester as the only case where the Court had "sustained a claim that multimember legislative districts unconstitutionally diluted the voting strength of a discrete group," he asserted that the holding there was consistent with the view that "only a purposeful dilution of the plaintiffs' vote would offend the Equal Protection Clause." But, relying on *Village of Arlington Heights*, Casebook p.985, Stewart stated that "where . . . an entire system of local governance is brought into question, disproportionate impact alone cannot be decisive, and courts must look to other evidence to support a finding of discriminatory purpose." Here, Stewart concluded, the evidence relied on by the lower courts "fell far short of showing" the requisite discriminatory purpose. Justice Marshall's lengthy dissent was unpersuasive, Stewart maintained, for the equal protection concept "does not require proportional representation [of every "political group"] as an imperative of political organization." While "the Equal Protection Clause confers a substantive right to participate in elections on an equal basis with other qualified voters," the right to vote in state and local elections does not derive from the federal Constitution. Thus, the "right to equal participation in the electoral process does not protect any 'political group,' however defined, from electoral defeat," distinguishing Reynolds v. Sims and its progeny as well as the voter-qualification cases on which Marshall relied. Justices Stevens and Blackmun concurred separately, while Justice White dissented. Justice Marshall, joined by Justice Brennan, disagreed entirely with the plurality's approach, suggesting that proof of a discriminatory purpose was not necessary where the fundamental right to vote was being diluted, relying extensively on Reynolds v. Sims and like cases as well as on the Court's voter-qualification cases (Casebook pp. 1018-1035). In the voting area, he asserted, proof of discriminatory effect is sufficient, as to both Fourteenth and Fifteenth Amendment claims. Washington v. Davis has application only where a suspect basis of classification is relied upon, not where a fundamental right is involved. "The plurality's requirement of proof of *intentional discrimination* . . . may represent an attempt to bury the legitimate concerns of the minority beneath the soil of a doctrine almost as impermeable as it is specious," he concluded.

Page 1039. At the end of the first paragraph add:

Cf. Cousins v. Wigoda, 419 U.S. 477, 95 S. Ct. 541, 42 L. Ed. 2d 595 (1975); Democratic Party of United States v. LaFollette, 450 U.S. 107, 101

S. Ct. 1010, 67 L. Ed. 2d 82 (1981), infra in this Supplement, addition to Casebook p.1269.

Page 1039. At the end of Note 4 add:

See also Kamenshine, The First Amendment's Implied Political Establishment Clause, 67 Calif. L. Rev. 1104 (1979).

Page 1039. Add to the asterisked material:

Barrett, The Rational Basis Standard for Equal Protection Review of Ordinary Legislative Classifications, 68 Ky. L.J. 845 (1979); Symposium: Equal Protection, The Standards of Review: The Path Taken and the Road Beyond, 57 U. Det. J. Urb. L. 701 (1980); Treiman, Equal Protection and Fundamental Rights — A Judicial Shell Game, 15 Tulsa L.J. 183 (1980).

Page 1046. At the end of Note 6 add:

See also Lewis v. United States, 445 U.S. 55, 100 S. Ct. 915, 63 L. Ed. 2d 198 (1980) (federal firearms statute does not violate equal protection by prohibiting the possession of firearms by convicted felons, even if conviction is subject to collateral attack on constitutional grounds.)

Page 1047. At the end of the carryover paragraph add:

Lassiter v. Department of Social Services of Durham County, 452 U.S. 18, 101 S. Ct. 2153, 68 L. Ed. 2d 640 (1981), supra in this Supplement, addition to Casebook p.785, where the Court held that indigent parents do not necessarily have a right to counsel at parental termination hearings. Interestingly enough, *Lassiter* was decided the same day as Little v. Streater, supra in this Supplement, addition to Casebook p.785, which sustained an indigent's due process argument that the state must pay for the costs of blood group tests in a paternity suit initiated primarily because of the state's involvement in the question.

Page 1053:

In line 14 of Note 6 change "handle" to "hurdle."

Page 1054. Add to the end of the first full paragraph:

See also Cabell v. Chavez-Salido, — U.S. — , 102 S. Ct. 735, — L. Ed. 2d — (1982), where the Court once again was called on to consider the constitutionality of a citizenship requirement imposed by a state on those seeking access to certain governmental jobs. After reviewing the long history of cases which the Court has dealt with state classifications of aliens, the Court concluded that the appropriate way to decide whether a particular restriction on aliens serves political and not economic goals is through use of the two-step test stated in *Sugarman*. "First, the specificity of the classification will be examined: a classification that is substantially over- or under-inclusive tends to undercut the governmental claim that the classification serves legitimate political ends. . . . Second, even if the classification is sufficiently tailored, it may be applied in a particular case only to 'persons holding state elective or important nonelective executive, legislative, and judicial positions,' those officers who 'participate directly in the formulation, operation, or review of broad public policy' and hence 'perform functions that go to the heart of representative government.' "

Turning next to the classification adopted by the State of California in the instant case, the Court held that the district court relied too heavily on a comparison of the characteristics and functions of probation officers (the position herein restricted to United States citizens) with those of state troopers at issue in *Foley* and teachers in *Ambach*. Justice White, delivering the Court's opinion stated: "*Foley* and *Ambach* did not describe the outer limits of permissible citizenship requirements. For example, although both of those cases emphasized the community-wide responsibilities of teachers and police, there was no suggestion that judges, who deal only with a narrow subclass of the community, cannot be subject to a citizenship requirement. . . . Similarly, although both *Foley* and *Ambach* emphasized the unsupervised discretion that must be exercised by the teacher and the police officer in the performance of their duties, neither case suggested that jurors, who act under a specific set of institutions, could not be required to be citizens. Definition of the important sovereign functions of the political community is necessarily the primary responsibility of the representative branches of Government, subject to limited [judicial] review. . . . Looking at the functions of California probation officers, we conclude that they, like the state troopers involved in *Foley*, sufficiently partake of the sovereign's power to exercise coercive force over the individual that they may be limited to citizens."

Justice Blackmun, joined by Justices Brennan, Marshall, and Stevens, dissented from the Court's decision, concluding that "California's exclusion of these appellees from the position of deputy probation officer stems solely from state parochialism and hostility toward foreigners who have come to this country lawfully, [finding] it ironic that the Court invokes the principles of democratic self-government to exclude from the law enforcement process individuals who have not only resided here lawfully, but who now desire merely to help the state enforce its laws. [The California law] violates appellees' right to equal treatment and an individual determination of fitness."

Page 1055. At the end of Morton v. Mancari add:

See also Merrion v. Jicarilla Apache Tribe, supra in this Supplement, addition to Casebook p.526, where the Court upheld the Tribe's power to tax the extraction of oil and gas on tribal lands as an essential attribute of Indian sovereignty.

Page 1064. At the end of Note 5 add:

See also United States v. Clark, 445 U.S. 23, 100 S. Ct. 895, 63 L. Ed. 2d 171 (1980).

Page 1065. Add as a new Note 7:

6. In Mills v. Habluetzel, — U.S. —, 102 S. Ct. 1549, — L. Ed. 2d — (1982), the Court held that a Texas statute, requiring that paternity suits to establish the natural father of an illegitimate child be brought before the child is one year old, denies equal protection. The Court's opinion focused upon the period of time provided by the statute to bring suit and reasoned that the period set by the state must be "sufficiently long in duration to present a reasonable opportunity for those with an interest in such children to assert claims on their behalf." The Court further stated that any time limitation placed on this opportunity must be substantially related to state's interest in avoiding the litigation of stale or fraudulent claims. Applying these requirements, the Court found the Texas statute unconstitutional as violative of the equal protection right of illegitimate children in Texas.

Page 1065. After the second full paragraph add:

With respect to the equal protection aspects of a woman's privacy-related right to terminate a pregnancy, see Casebook pp.1586-1590, and in particular Maher v. Roe, 432 U.S. 464, 97 S. Ct. 2376, 53 L. Ed. 2d 484 (1977), and Harris v. McRae, 448 U.S. 297, 100 S. Ct. 2671, 65 L. Ed. 2d 78 (1980), infra in this Supplement, addition to Casebook p.1591.

Page 1070. At the end of Note 2 add:

Comment, The Equal Rights Amendment and Article V: A Framework for Analysis of the Extension and Rescission Issues, 127 U. Pa. L. Rev. 494 (1978).

Page 1073. At the end of Note 2 add:

In County of Washington, Ore. v. Gunther, 452 U.S. 161, 101 S. Ct. 2242, 68 L. Ed. 2d 751 (1981), the Court held that Title VII's so-called Bennett Amendment does not require claimants alleging sex discrimination to show equal pay for "equal work" as long as the wage differential is not supported by any of the Equal Pay Act's affirmative defenses.

Page 1074. At the end of Note 3 add:

Cf. Kirchberg v. Feenstra, 450 U.S. 455, 101 S. Ct. 1195, 67 L. Ed 2d 428 (1981), where the Court struck down a Louisiana statute that gave a husband, as "head and master" of property jointly owned with his wife, the unilateral right to dispose of such property without his spouse's consent.

Justice Marshall wrote for the Court: "Because this provision explicitly discriminated on the basis of gender, the Court of Appeals properly inquired whether the statutory grant to the husband of exclusive control over disposition of community property was substantially related to the achievement of an important governmental objective. . . . The court noted that the State has advanced only one justification for this provision — that '[o]ne of the two spouses has to be designated as manager of the property.' The court agreed that the State had an interest in defining the manner in which the community property was to be managed, but found that the statute had failed to show why this mandatory designation of the husband . . . was necessary to further that interest."

Page 1078. At the end of Note 3 add:

Missouri's worker's compensation statute was held to violate equal protection by denying a widower benefits from his wife's work-related death unless he either was mentally or physically incapacitated or proved dependence on her earnings, while granting similar benefits automatically to widows. Wengler v. Druggists Mutual Insurance Co., 446 U.S. 142, 100 S. Ct. 1540, 64 L. Ed. 2d 107 (1980). Applying the Reed v. Reed standard, to the effect that gender-based discrimination must satisfy important governmental objectives and that the discriminatory means employed must be substantially related to those objectives, the Court concluded that the state's claim of administrative convenience failed to meet the applicable constitutional test. Cases from the Social Security Act context, as well as *Frontiero* and Craig v. Boren, were cited and relied upon. Justice Rehnquist dissented.

Page 1081. At the end of Note 2 add:

Cf. Michael M. v. Superior Court of Sonoma County, 450 U.S. 464, 101 S. Ct. 1200, 67 L. Ed. 2d 437 (1981), upholding California's statutory rape law, which defines unlawful sexual intercourse as "an act of sexual intercourse accomplished with a female not the wife of the perpetrator, where the female is under the age of 18 years," despite petitioner's equal protection challenge that the statute on its face and as applied makes men alone criminally liable for the act of sexual intercourse.

Justice Rehnquist, writing for the Court, stated: "The justification for the statute offered by the State, and accepted by the Supreme Court of California, is that the legislature sought to prevent illegitimate teenage pregnancies. That finding, of course, is entitled to great deference. . . . And although our cases establish that a State's asserted reason for the enactment of a statute may be rejected, 'if it could not have been a goal of the legislation'. . . , this is not such a case. We are satisfied not only that the prevention of illegitimate pregnancy is at least one of the 'purposes' of the statute, but that the State has a strong interest in preventing such pregnancy. . . . The question thus boils down to whether a State may attack the problem of sexual intercourse and teenage pregnancy directly by prohibiting a male from having sexual intercourse with a minor female. We hold that such a statute is sufficiently related to the State's objectives to pass constitutional muster." Justice Brennan, joined by Justices White and Marshall, dissented from the Court's holding, stating essentially that the state had not met its burden of proving that the statutory classification was substantially related to the achievement of its asserted goals. Justice Stevens, dissenting separately, stated that the inequity resulting from a less than evenhanded enforcement of the statute on a neutral basis violated the essence of the constitutional requirement that the sovereign must govern impartially.

Cf. Northwest Airlines, Inc. v. Transport Workers Union of America, infra in this Supplement, addition to Casebook p.1149.

Page 1082. After Note 4 add:

ROSTKER v. GOLDBERG, 453 U.S. 57, 101 S. Ct. 2646, 69 L. Ed. 2d 478 (1981). At issue was the constitutionality of that provision of the Military Selective Service Act requiring the registration for possible military service of males but not females, so as to facilitate any eventual conscription under the act. Several males challenged the act's constitutionality on equal protection grounds. A lower federal court held that the act's gender-based discrimination violated the equal protection component of the Fifth Amendment's due process clause and enjoined registration pursuant to its requirement. On appeal, the Supreme Court reversed. In pertinent part Justice Rehnquist's majority opinion stated:

"This is not ... merely a case involving the customary deference accorded [by the judiciary to] congressional decisions. The case arises in the context of Congress' authority over national defense and military affairs, and perhaps in no other area has the Court accorded Congress greater deference. In rejecting the registration of women, Congress explicitly relied upon its constitutional powers under Art. I, §8, cls. 12-14, [discussing the pertinent legislative history]. This Court has consistently recognized Congress' 'broad constitutional power' to raise and regulate armies and navies, Schlesinger v. Ballard, 419 U.S. 498, 510 (1975). As the Court noted in considering a challenge to the selective service laws, 'The constitutional power of Congress to raise and support armies and to make all laws necessary and proper to that end is broad and sweeping.' United States v. O'Brien, 391 U.S. 367, 377 (1968). ...

"Not only is the scope of Congress' constitutional power in this area broad, but the lack of competence on the part of the courts is marked. ... [It is not surprising that the] operation of a healthy deference to legislative and executive judgments in the area of military affairs is evident in several recent decisions of this Court. ...

"In Schlesinger v. Ballard, 419 U.S. 498 (1975), the Court considered a due process challenge, brought by males, to the Navy policy of according females a longer period than males in which to attain promotions necessary to continued service. The Court distinguished previous gender-based discriminations held unlawful in Reed v. Reed, 404 U.S. 71 (1971) and Frontiero v. Richardson, 411 U.S. 677 (1973). In those cases, the classifications were based on overbroad generalizations. See 419 U.S., at 506-507.... In light of the combat restrictions, women did not have the same opportunities for promotion as men, and therefore it was not unconstitutional for Congress to distinguish between them.

"None of this is to say that Congress is free to disregard the Constitution when it acts in the area of military affairs. In that area as any other Congress remains subject to the limitations of the Due Process Clause, see Ex parte Milligan, 4 Wall. 2 (1866)..., but the tests and limitations to be applied may differ because of the military context. We of course do not abdicate our ultimate responsibility to decide the constitutional question, but simply recognize that the Constitution itself requires such deference to congressional choice.... In deciding the question before us we must be particularly careful not to substitute our judgment of what is desirable for that of Congress, or our own evaluation of evidence for a reasonable evaluation by the Legislative Branch....

"... We find ... efforts to divorce registration from the military and national defense context, with all the deference called for in that context, singularly unpersuasive. United States v. O'Brien, supra, recognized the broad deference due Congress in the selective service area before us in this case. Registration is not an end in itself in the civilian world but rather the first step in the induction process into the military one, and Congress specifically linked its consideration of registration to induction.... Congressional judgments concerning registration and the draft are based on judgments concerning military operations and needs,... and the deference unquestionably due the latter judgments is necessarily required in assessing the former as well.... It would be blinking reality to say that our precedents requiring deference to Congress in military affairs are not implicated by the present case.

"The Solicitor General argues, largely on the basis of the foregoing cases emphasizing the deference due Congress in the area of military affairs and national security, that this Court should scrutinize the MSSA only to determine if the distinction drawn between men and women bears a rational relation to some legitimate government purpose,... and should not examine the Act under the heightened scrutiny with which we have approached gender-based discrimination, [citing, e.g., Craig v. Boren and Reed v. Reed]. We do not think that the substantive guarantee of due process or certainty in the law will be advanced by any further 'refinement' in the applicable tests as suggested by the Government. Announced degrees of 'deference' to legislative judgments, just as levels of 'scrutiny' which this Court announces that it applies to particular classifications made by a legislative body, may all too readily become facile abstractions used to justify a result. In this case the courts are called upon to decide whether Congress, acting under an explicit constitutional grant of authority, has by that action transgressed an explicit guarantee of individual rights which limits the authority so conferred. Simply labelling the legislative decision 'military' on the one hand or 'gender-based' on the other does not automatically guide a court to the correct constitutional result.

"No one could deny that under the test of Craig v. Boren, supra, the Government's interest in raising and supporting armies is an 'important governmental interest.' Congress and its committees carefully considered and debated two alternative means of furthering that interest: the first was to register only males for potential conscription, and the other was to register both sexes. Congress chose the former alternative. When that decision is challenged on equal protection grounds, the question a court must decide is not which alternative it would have chosen, had it been the primary decisionmaker, but whether that chosen by Congress denies equal protection of the laws. . . .

"This case is quite different from several of the gender-based discrimination cases we have considered in that, despite appellees' assertions, Congress did not act 'unthinkingly' or 'reflexively and not for any considered reason.' . . . The question of registering women for the draft not only received considerable national attention and was the subject of wide-ranging public debate, but also was extensively considered by Congress in hearings, floor debate, and in committee. Hearings held by both Houses of Congress in response to the President's request for authorization to register women adduced extensive testimony and evidence concerning the issue. . . . These hearings built on other hearings held the previous year addressed to the same question."

Justice Rehnquist's extensive discussion of the act's legislative history, showing that "the decision to exempt women from registration was not the 'accidental by-product of a traditional way of thinking about women,' " but rather "to prepare for a draft of *combat troops*," is omitted. He continued:

"Women as a group, however, unlike men as a group, are not eligible for combat. The restrictions on the participation of women in combat in the Navy and Air Force are statutory. Under 10 U.S.C. §6015 'women may not be assigned to duty on vessels or in aircraft that are engaged in combat missions,' and under 10 U.S.C. §8549 female members of the Air Force 'may not be assigned to duty in aircraft engaged in combat missions.' The Army and Marine Corps preclude the use of women in combat as a matter of established policy. . . . Congress specifically recognized and endorsed the exclusion of women from combat in exempting women from registration [and the] President expressed his intent to continue the current military policy precluding women from combat. . . .

"The existence of the combat restrictions clearly indicates the basis for Congress' decision to exempt women from registration. The purpose of registration was to prepare for a draft of combat troops. Since women are excluded from combat, Congress concluded that they would not be needed in the event of a draft, and therefore decided not to register them. . . .

"The District Court stressed that the military need for women was irrelevant to the issue of their registration. As that court put it: 'Congress could not constitutionally require registration under MSSA of only black citizens or only white citizens, or single out any political or religious group simply because those groups contained sufficient persons to fill the needs of the Selective Service System.' 509 F. Supp., at 596. This reasoning is beside the point. The reason women are exempt from registration is not because military needs can be met by drafting men. This is not a case of Congress arbitrarily choosing to burden one of two similarly situated groups, such as would be the case with an all-black or all-white, or an all-Catholic or all-Lutheran, or an all-Republican or all-Democratic registration. Men and women, because of the combat restrictions on women, are simply not similarly situated for purposes of a draft or registration for a draft."

Concluding, Justice Rehnquist wrote:

"Congress' decision to authorize the registration of only men, therefore, does not violate the Due Process Clause. The exemption of women from registration is not only sufficiently but closely related to Congress' purpose in authorizing registration, [citing cases]. The fact that Congress and the Executive have decided that women should not serve in combat fully justifies Congress in not authorizing their registration, since the purpose of registration is to develop a pool of potential combat troops. As was the case in Schlesinger v. Ballard, supra, 'the gender classification is not invidious, but rather realistically reflects the fact that the sexes are not similarly situated' in this case. . . . The Constitution requires that Congress treat similarly situated persons similarly, not that it engage in gestures of superficial equality."

Justice White, joined by Justice Brennan, wrote a short dissenting opinion that took issue with the majority's assumption that Congress in fact "concluded that every position in the military, no matter how far removed from combat, must be filled with combat-ready men." Nor, White stated, could he agree with the majority's apparent view that "all the women who could serve in wartime without adversely affecting combat readiness could predictably be obtained through volunteers. In that event, the equal protection component of the Fifth Amendment would not require the United States to go through, and a large segment of the population to be involved with, the experience and essentially useless procedure of registering women." Indicating that he basically disagreed with the majority's reading of the legislative record, Justice White concluded that "the number of women who could be used in the military without sacrificing combat-readiness is not at all small or unsubstantial, and administrative convenience has not been sufficient justification for the kind of outright gender-based discrimination involved in registering and conscripting men but no women at all."

Justice Marshall, joined by Justice Brennan, also dissented. In substance, he concluded that the Court was acting inconsistently with "the Constitution's guarantee of equal protection of the laws" by "uphold[ing] a statute that required males but not females to register for the draft, and which thereby categorically excludes women from a fundamental civic obligation." Stressing that the case involved only whether sex-based discrimination was permissible in the context of registering persons for possible military service, he concluded that "the 'heightened' scrutiny mandated by Craig v. Boren" should be applied, and that under this intermediate test the congressional act failed to pass constitutional muster. While an "important governmental interest" was involved, Marshall mentioned that "the discriminatory means employed [does not serve] the statutory end," for "there simply is no basis for concluding ... that excluding women from registration is substantially related to the achievement of a considerably important governmental interest in maintaining an effective defense."

Page 1084. At the end of the second full paragraph add:

Cf. Schweiker v. Gray Panthers, 453 U.S. 34, 101 S. Ct. 2633, 69 L. Ed. 2d 460 (1981), holding that federal regulations permitting states to determine an applicant's entitlement to Medicaid benefits by assuming that a portion of his or her spouse's income is "available" to the applicant, even if that person is institutionalized, are consistent with the Social Security Act and constitute a reasonable exercise of the powers delegated by Congress to the Secretary of Health and Human Services to define Medicaid eligibility requirements.

The Supreme Court also recently ruled that the Age Discrimination in Employment Act of 1967, as amended in 1974 to include federal employees, does not grant those *federal* employees who bring suit against the government the right to a jury trial. The Court stated that when Congress waives a governmental immunity, the plaintiff has a right to a jury trial only where Congress has affirmatively and unambiguously granted that right by statute. The Court went on to find that Congress had not granted that right to federal employees in the 1974 amendment to the ADEA. Lehman v. Nakshian, 453 U.S. 156, 101 S. Ct. 2698, 69 L. Ed. 2d 548 (1981).

Page 1084. At the end of the footnoted material add:

See Pennhurst State School and Hospital v. Halderman, 451 U.S. 1, 101 S. Ct. 1531, 69 L. Ed. 2d 694 (1981), where the Court held that the Developmentally Disabled Assistance and Bill of Rights Act of 1975, which established a federal-state grant program providing financial assistance to participating states to aid them in the care and treatment of the developmentally disabled, does not create in favor of the mentally retarded substantive rights to "appropriate treatment" in a "least restrictive environment." The Court held that §6010 of the act "does no more than express a congressional preference for certain kinds of treatment."

Page 1085. At the end of the carryover paragraph add:

Cook & Laski, Beyond *Davis*: Equality of Opportunity for Higher Education for Disabled Students Under the Rehabilitation Act of 1973, 15 Harv. Civ. Rights-Civ. Lib. L. Rev. 415 (1980); Schoenfeld, Constitutional Rights of the Mentally Retarded, 32 Sw. L.J. 605 (1978).

Page 1096. At the end of Note 9 add:

In Jones v. Helms, 452 U.S. 412, 101 S. Ct. 2434, 69 L. Ed. 2d 118 (1981), the appellee challenged Georgia's system of classification, which differentiates between a parent who willfully and voluntarily abandons his or her dependent child and remains in Georgia, and those parents who commit the same offense and leave the state. The former constitutes a misdemeanor, while the later is a felony. The court of appeals applied a strict scrutiny analysis, justifying this standard upon an infringement of the fundamental right to travel. The Supreme Court reversed. Justice Stevens delivered the opinion of the Court. After discarding the appellee's right-to-travel argument (infra in this Supplement, addition to Casebook p.1595), Stevens examined the equal protection challenge, stating: "The portion of the Georgia statute at issue in this case applies equally to all parents residing in Georgia; nothing in appellee's argument or in the record suggests that the statute has been enacted against appellee any differently than it would be enforced against anyone else who engaged in the same conduct." Accordingly, Stevens concluded that the appellee's equal protection challenge was not well founded.

Chapter Nine

The Power of Congress to Enforce the Civil War Amendments

Page 1106. At the end of the last full paragraph add:

With respect to the meaning of the phrase "prevailing party" in the Civil Rights Attorney's Fees Awards Act of 1976, 42 U.S.C. 1988, see Hanrahan v. Hampton, 446 U.S. 754, 100 S. Ct. 1987, 64 L. Ed. 2d 670 (1980), concluding that "Congress intended to permit the interim award of counsel fees only when a party has prevailed on the merits of at least some of his claims."

The Equal Access to Justice Act (P.L. 96-481) provides in pertinent part for the award of attorneys fees against the United States incurred by a class of individuals, partnerships, corporations, and labor and other organizations described therein, in an attempt to diminish the deterrent effect of seeking review of, or defending against, governmental action in civil and administrative proceedings.

See also Hughes v. Rowe, 449 U.S. 5, 101 S. Ct. 173, 66 L. Ed. 2d 163 (1980).

Page 1108. At the end of the carryover paragraph add:

See Pennhurst State School and Hospital v. Halderman, 451 U.S. 1, 101 S. Ct. 1531, 67 L. Ed. 2d 694 (1981).

Page 1113. At the end of Note 2 add:

See also City of Rome v. United States, 446 U.S. 156, 100 S. Ct. 1548, 64 L. Ed. 2d 119 (1980), holding §5 of the Voting Rights Act applicable to certain electoral changes and annexations made by the city and upholding its constitutionality as applied in the instant circumstances. As part of a state within §4's coverage formula, the city was required to obtain preclearance from the Attorney General or the District of Columbia District Court before changing any voting standards, practices, or procedures from those in effect in 1964, and the city had failed to do so. As a political subdivision within a covered state, Rome could not invoke the "bail out" procedure of §4 on its own accord to avoid compliance with §5. With specific regard to §5 the Court, speaking through Justice Marshall, stated that "[b]y describing the elements of discriminatory purpose and effect in the conjunctive, Congress plainly intended that a voting practice not be precleared unless *both* discriminatory purpose and effect are absent," citing, e.g., the *Beer* case. Moreover, the Court continued, "even if §1 of the [Fifteenth] Amendment prohibits only purposeful discrimination, the prior decisions of this Court foreclose any argument that Congress may not, pursuant to §2, outlaw voting practices that are discriminatory in effect. Congress could rationally have concluded that, because electoral changes by jurisdictions with a demonstrable history of intentional racial discrimination in voting create the risk of purposeful discrimination, it was proper to prohibit changes that have a discriminatory impact." In addition, the Court rejected arguments that §5 violates principles of federalism, stating that appellants' reliance on National League of Cities v. Usery, Casebook p.218, in this regard was misplaced; and it rejected arguments to the effect that the Act and its preclearance requirement had outlived its usefulness by 1975, when Congress had last extended its provisions. Justices Blackmun and Stevens wrote concurring opinions, while Justices Powell, Rehnquist, and Stewart dissented.

Cf. McDaniel v. Sanchez, 452 U.S. 130, 101 S. Ct. 2224, 68 L. Ed. 2d 724 (1981), where the Court held that a reapportionment plan submitted to and approved by a federal district court after an initial judicial determination that the existing apportionment plan was unconstitutional, is a legislative rather than a judicial plan, and, as such, is subject to §5 of the Voting Rights Act of 1965, which requires preclearance by either the Attorney General or the District Court for the District of Columbia before the plan may be put into effect.

Page 1137. At the end of the carryover paragraph add:

Cf. Polk County v. Dodson, — U.S. —, 102 S. Ct. 445, — L. Ed. 2d — (1981), where the Court held that public defenders are not acting "under color of state law" when they perform a lawyer's traditional function as counsel to an indigent defendant in a criminal proceeding.

Page 1137. At the end of Note 3 add:

See Parratt v. Taylor, 451 U.S. 527, 101 S. Ct. 1908, 68 L. Ed. 2d 420 (1981), where the Court held that a Nebraska inmate, who filed a §1983 action against certain prison officials for the negligent loss of hobby materials, was not denied due process of law. The Court categorized the petitioner's loss as "not the result of some established state procedure." Moreover, the petitioner had failed to avail himself of Nebraska's own tort claims procedure, which provides a remedy to persons who have suffered a tortious loss at the hands of the state.

Such a procedure was held by the Court to satisfy the requirements of due process.

In Fair Assessment in Real Estate Assn., Inc. v. McNary, — U.S. —, 102 S. Ct. 177, — L. Ed. 2d — (1981), the Court held that principles of comity bar a taxpayer damage suit in federal court, based on 42 U.S.C. 1983, to redres the alleged unconstitutional administration of a state tax system. The Court, per Justice Rehnquist, wrote: "This case is ... controlled by principles articulated even before enactment of §1983 and followed in later decisions. . . . The recovery of damages under the Civil Rights Act first required a declaration or determination of the unconstitutionality of a state tax scheme that would halt its operation. And damage actions, no less than actions for an injunction, would hale state officers into federal court every time a taxpayer alleged the requisite elements of a §1983 claim. We consider such an interference to be contrary to 'the scrupulous regard for the rightful independence of state governments which should at all times actuate the federal courts.'. . . Such taxpayers must seek protection of their federal rights by state remedies, provided of course that those remedies are plain, adequate, and complete, and may ultimately seek review of the state decision in this Court."

Justice Brennan, with whom Justices Marshall, Stevens, and O'Connor joined, concurring in the judgment, disagreed with the majority's approach of dismissing the petitioner's complaint by " 'applying a principle of comity' grounded solely on this Court's notion of an appropriate division of responsibility between the federal and state judicial systems." Rather, the minority opinion's rationale for concurring in the judgment was based on the petitioner's apparent failure to exhaust state administrative remedies in each tax year for which they sought damages.

Page 1137. At the end of Note 4 add:

See also Carlson v. Green, 446 U.S. 14, 100 S. Ct. 1468, 64 L. Ed. 2d 15 (1980), where the Court concluded that a damage action against federal prison officials was available, under the rationale of *Bivens*, for violation of the Eighth Amendment, resulting from failure to provide proper medical attention, even though suit could be brought against the government itself under the Federal Tort Claims Act. The Court ruled that the *Bivens* remedy was preempted only where "Congress has provided an alternative remedy which it explicitly declared to be a *substitute* for recovery directly under the Constitution and viewed as equally effective," citing Davis v. Passman, Casebook p.1081. Consideration of pertinent legislative history "made it crystal clear that Congress views the FTCA and *Bivens* as [providing] parallel, complementary causes of action," the Court stated.

Page 1144. At the end of the carryover paragraph add:

Accord, Havens Realty Corp. v. Coleman, supra in this Supplement, addition to Casebook p.86.

Page 1146. At the end of Note 1 add:

But see Delaware State College v. Ricks, 449 U.S. 250, 101 S. Ct. 498, 66 L. Ed. 2d 431 (1980) (infra in this Supplement, addition to Casebook p.1148), where the Court held the respondent's Title VII and §1981 claims untimely. See also Allen v. McCurry, 449 U.S. 90, 101 S. Ct. 411, 66 L. Ed. 2d 308 (1980), supra in this Supplement, addition to Casebook p.137.

Page 1146. Add as a new Note 3:

3. In City of Memphis v. Greene, 451 U.S. 100, 101 S. Ct. 1584, 67 L. Ed. 2d 769 (1981), the Court was confronted with a challenge to the city's decision to close down a street at a point which divided an all-white neighborhood from one which is predominantly black. The affected black citizens of the community attacked the city's decision, alleging violations of both 42 U.S.C. 1982 and the Thirteenth Amendment.

Turning first to the §1982 claim, the Court, through Justice Stevens, indicated that cases interpreting §1982 have broadly defined the property rights of black citizens. Today §1982 is read to protect the right of black persons to hold and acquire property on an equal basis with white persons. After noting the broad coverage of §1982, Justice Stevens examined the relationship between the street closing and the property rights of the black citizens, concluding that their property rights had not been impaired. Stevens suggested three findings which would support a §1982 violation: First, "A municipal action benefiting white property owners that would be refused to similarly situated black property owners, for official action of that kind would prevent blacks from exercising the same property rights as whites. But respondents' evidence failed to support the legal theory. Alternatively . . ., the statute might be violated by official action that depreciated the value of the property owned by black citizens. But the record discloses no effect on the value of the property owned by any member of the respondent class. Finally, the statute may be violated if the street closing severely restricted access to black homes, because blacks would then be hampered in their use of their property. Again the record discloses no such restriction."

Justice Marshall, joined by Justices Brennan and Blackmun, dissented from the Court's holding, finding that the record indicated that the effect of closing the street would do more than "slightly inconvenience" black motorists, and would surely depreciate the property values of black residents of the affected area. Marshall summed up the dissenters' analysis of the statutory challenge, stating: "[B]ecause of our nation's sad legacy of discrimination and the broad remedial purpose of §1982 . . ., I believe that when [the government] takes action with full knowledge of its enormously disproportionate racial impact . . . §1982 requires that the government carry a heavy burden in order to justify its action. Absent such a justification, the injured property owners are entitled to relief. There is no need to suggest here just how great the government's burden should be, because the reasons set forth by the city for the closing of West Drive [reduce the flow of traffic and noise and air pollution] could not, on the facts of the case, survive any but the most minimal scrutiny."

Page 1147. At the end of the first full paragraph add:

But see Weinberger v. Rossi, supra in this Supplement, addition to Casebook p.874, upholding an executive agreement providing for preferential treatment of foreign nationals on military bases abroad.

Page 1148. At the end of the carryover paragraph add:

Cf. New York Gaslight Club, Inc. v. Carey, 447 U.S. 54, 100 S. Ct. 2024, 64 L. Ed. 2d 723 (1980) (under Title VII the prevailing party may be awarded attorneys' fees for legal services performed in prosecuting an employment discrimination claim in state administrative proceedings that federal claimants are required to invoke).

See also General Telephone Co. of the Northwest, Inc. v. Equal Employment Opportunity Commn., 446 U.S. 318, 100 S. Ct. 1698, 64 L. Ed. 2d 319 (1980), holding that the EEOC may seek classwide relief under Title VII without being certified as a class representative under Rule 23 of the Federal Rules of Civil Procedure. See also California Brewers Assn. v. Bryant, 444 U.S. 598, 100 S. Ct. 814, 63 L. Ed. 2d 55 (1980).

In Delaware State College v. Ricks, 449 U.S. 250, 101 S. Ct. 498, 66 L. Ed. 2d 431 (1980), the respondent was denied tenure by the Board of Trustees of Delaware State College and immediately complained to the Board's grievance committee. The respondent was then offered a one-year "terminal" contract for the following year, which he accepted. Subsequently, the Board notified the respondent that his grievance had been denied; the respondent reacted by filing a Title VII complaint with the Equal Employment Opportunity Commission. Two years later the EEOC issued a "right to sue letter" and the respondent filed both a Title VII and a §1981 action in the district court. Title VII requires that a complaint be filed with the EEOC within 180 days "after the alleged unlawful employment practice occurred," and under the applicable Delaware statute of limitations, a §1981 action must be filed within three years of the alleged discriminatory practice. The Court was thus faced with the question of when the alleged discriminatory actions occurred — at the time the respondent was first notified of his denial of tenure, at the time the grievance committee rejected the respondent's grievance, or at the expiration of the terminal contract.

In a five-to-four decision, the Court held that the "limitations periods commenced to run when the tenure decision was [first] made and Ricks was notified." The Court specifically rejected a "continuing violation" argument, stating that "[i]t is simply insufficient for Ricks to allege that his termination gives present effect to the past illegal act and therefore perpetuates the consequences of the forbidden discrimination."

Justice Stewart, joined by Justices Brennan and Marshall, dissented, stating that for purposes of Title VII and §1981 statute of limitations requirements, he would hold that the limitations period did not begin to run until Ricks was notified of the outcome of his grievance proceeding.

Justice Stevens dissented separately.

In Zipes v. Transworld Airlines, Inc., — U.S. — , 102 S. Ct. 1127, — L. Ed. 2d — (1982), the Court held that the filing of a timely charge of employment discrimination with the EEOC is *not* a jurisdictional prerequisite to a suit in federal court. The Court went on to hold that a timely charge requirement is more like a statute of limitations which is subject to waiver, estoppel and equitable tolling.

In American Tobacco Co. v. Patterson, — U.S. — , 102 S. Ct. 1534, — L. Ed. 2d — (1982), the Court held that §703(h) of the Civil Rights Act of 1964, which exempts unintentional discrimination caused by the use of a bona fide seniority system from Title VII challenge, is applicable to seniority systems adopted *after* the effective date of the Act. Cf. Pullman-Standard v. Swint, — U.S. — , 102 S. Ct. 1781, — L. Ed. 2d — (1982), also interpreting §703(h)'s requirement of discriminatory intent. See also Chardon v. Fernandez, infra this Supplement, addition to Casebook p.1184.

Page 1148. At the end of the first full paragraph add:

Cf. Texas Department of Community Affairs v. Burdine, 450 U.S. 248, 101 S. Ct. 1089, 67 L. Ed. 2d 207 (1981), the Court specifically rejected application of the preponderence of evidence standard in Title VII cases, holding that when a plaintiff has proven a prima facie case of discrimination, the defendant only bears the burden of "explaining clearly" the nondiscriminatory reasons for its actions.

Page 1148. At the end of the second paragraph add:

Cf. Equal Employment Opportunity Commn. v. Associated Dry Goods Corp., 449 U.S. 590, 101 S. Ct. 817, 66 L. Ed. 2d 762 (1981). The Court interpreted §§706(b) and 709(e) of Title VII to permit the disclosure of charges and other information to the immediate parties to an informal commission hearing despite the prohibitions in these sections against the "public" disclosure of anything "said or done" during such hearings.

Page 1149. At the end of the carryover paragraph add:

See County of Washington, Ore. v. Gunther, 452 U.S. 161, 101 S. Ct. 2242, 68 L. Ed. 2d 751 (1981), where the Court held that §703(h) of Title VII (the "Bennett Amendment"), which provides that it shall not be an unlawful employment practice for an employer to differentiate on the basis of sex in determining the amount of its employees' wages if such differentiation is "authorized by the Equal Pay Act," does not restrict Title VII's prohibition of sex-based discrimination to claims for equal pay for "equal work." Rather, claims may be brought under Title VII even where no member of the opposite sex holds an equal but higher paying job, provided that the challenged wage rate is not exempted under the Equal Pay Act's affirmative defenses.

Page 1149. At the end of the second full paragraph add:

See also Northwest Airlines, Inc. v. Transport Workers Union of America, 451 U.S. 77, 101 S. Ct. 1571, 67 L. Ed. 2d 750 (1981), where the petitioner was held liable to a class of female cabin attendants for back pay based upon the use of illegitimate wage differentials between men and women cabin attendants. The petitioner, in turn, claimed both a statutory and a common-law right to contribution from the respondent union, which had entered into the collective bargaining agreement which provided for these wage differentials. The Court held: "Neither the Equal Pay Act nor Title VII expressly [or impliedly] creates a right to contribution in favor of employers. . . . [I]t cannot possibly be said that employers are members of the class for whose benefit either the Equal Pay Act or Title VII was enacted. . . . To the contrary, both statutes are expressly directed against employers; Congress intended in these statutes to regulate their conduct for the benefit of the employee." The Court went on to reject the petitioner's common-law argument, essentially stating that when Congress has enacted a "comprehensive legislative scheme including an integrated system of procedures for enforcement," the judiciary should not attempt to "fashion new remedies that might upset carefully considered legislative programs."

Page 1149. At the end of the last full paragraph add:

Comment, Continuing Violation Theory Under Title VII, 32 Ark. L. Rev. 381 (1978); Comment, Title VII's Reasonable Accommodation Standard, 44 Brooklyn L. Rev. 598 (1978).

Chapter Ten

The First Amendment — Freedom of Expression, Association, and the Press

Page 1154. Add to the footnoted material:

Emerson, First Amendment Doctrine and the Burger Court, 68 Calif. L. Rev. 422 (1980); Kurland, The Irrelevance of the Constitution: The First Amendment's Freedom of Speech and Freedom of Press Clauses, 29 Drake L. Rev. 1 (1980); O'Brien, The First Amendment and the Public's Right to Know, 7 Hastings Const. L.Q. 759 (1980).

Page 1184. At the end of the carryover paragraph add:

In Chardon v. Fernandez, — U.S. — , 102 S. Ct. 28, — L. Ed. 2d — (1981), the Court followed the reasoning adopted the previous term in Delaware State College v. Ricks. The court of appeals distinguished *Ricks* on the grounds that "Ricks had alleged that [the] *denial of tenure* was the 'unlawful employment practice,' whereas here respondents allege that *termination of their employment* as administrators was the 'unlawful employment practice.' " The Supreme Court rejected this holding, concluding that *Ricks* was indistinguishable. "[I]n each case, the operative decision was made — and notice given — in advance of a designed date on which employment terminated." The Court held in *Ricks* that "the proper focus [for statute of limitation purposes] is on the time of the *discriminatory act*, not the point at which the *consequences* of the act become painful."

Page 1192. At the end of the first paragraph add:

Shaman, The First Amendment Rule Against Overbreadth, 52 Temple L.Q. 259 (1979).

Page 1196. At the end of Note 1 add:

See also Schad v. Borough of Mount Ephraim, 452 U.S. 61, 101 S. Ct. 2176, 68 L. Ed. 2d 671 (1981), infra in this Supplement, addition to

Casebook p.1402, where the Court held that a zoning ordinance which excluded from an otherwise broad range of commercial uses all forms of live entertainment, including non-obscene nude dancing, violated the First Amendment. The Court relied heavily upon the ordinance's constitutional defect of overbreadth.

Page 1197. At the end of Note 3 add:

See also Village of Hoffman Estates v. Flipside, Hoffman Estates, Inc., — U.S. — , 102 S. Ct. 1186, — L. Ed. 2d — (1982), rejecting vagueness and overbreadth challenges to a municipal ordinance which required a business to obtain a license if it sells any items that are "designed or marketed" for use with illegal cannabis or drugs. Writing for a unanimous Court, Justice Marshall added: "In a facial challenge to the overbreadth and vagueness of a law, a court's first task is to determine whether the enactment reaches a substantial amount of constitutionally protected conduct. If it does not, then the overbreadth challenge must fail. The Court should then examine the facial vagueness challenge and, assuming the enactment implicates no constitutionally protected conduct, should uphold the challenge only if the enactment is impermissibly vague in all of its applications." Here the ordinance was not facially invalid, the Court held, since it neither directly infringed upon any noncommercial speech nor impinged on commercial speech, except to the extent that it "propos[ed] an illegal transaction which a government may regulate or ban entirely." In any event, Marshall wrote, "the overbreadth doctrine does not apply to commercial speech," citing the *Central Hudson* case. Finally, the Court rejected the vagueness challenge on the ground that the appellee had not demonstrated "that the law is impermissibly vague in all of its applications," relying on Grayned v. City of Rockford. Here the "ordinance simply regulates business behavior and contains a *scienter* requirement with respect to the 'marketed for use' standard." Thus, the "facial challenge fails because, under the test applicable to either a quasi-criminal or a criminal law, the ordinance is sufficiently clear as applied" to the appellee and, in addition, "affords fair warning of what is proscribed." The Court postponed consideration of the potential the law posed for "discriminatory enforcement," finding that issue not to be properly presented in a pre-enforcement challenge such as was there involved.

Justice White concurred separately, while Justice Stevens did not participate.

In City of Mesquite v. Alladin's Castle, Inc., — U.S. — , 102 S. Ct. 1070, — L. Ed. 2d — (1982), the Court assumed that the definition of the phrase "connection with criminal elements" as used in a city ordinance was so vague that a defendant could not be convicted of the offense of having such a connection. Despite this finding the Court held that, because the phrase was not used as the standard for approval or disapproval of a license application, but was rather a vague and ambiguous direction to an official to consider in making a recommendation to grant a license, such language did not violate the notion of due process.

Page 1200. At the end of the carryover paragraph add:

See Heffron v. International Society for Krishna Consciousness, Inc., 452 U.S. 640, 101 S. Ct. 2559, 69 L. Ed. 2d 298 (1981), where the Court was presented with a First and Fourteenth Amendment challenge to a state rule which may require a religious organization desiring to distribute and sell religious literature and to solicit donations at a state fair to conduct those activities at assigned locations. Justice White delivered the opinion of the Court, saying: "The issue here . . . is whether Rule 6.05 is a permissible restriction on the place and manner of communicating the views of the Krishna religion. . . . A major criterion for a valid time, place and manner restriction is that the restriction 'may not be based upon either the content or the subject matter of the speech.' . . . Rule 6.05 qualifies in this respect, since . . . the Rule applies evenhandedly to all who wish to distribute and sell written materials or solicit funds. No person or organization, whether commercial or charitable, is permitted to engage in such activities except from a booth rented for those purposes. . . . Nor does Rule 6.05 suffer from the more covert form of discrimination that may result when arbitrary discretion is invested in some governmental authority. The method of allocating is a straightforward first-come, first-served system. . . . [Also,] a valid time, place and manner regulation must . . . 'serve a significant governmental interest.' . . . Here the principal justification asserted by the State in support of Rule 6.05 is the need to maintain the orderly movement of the crowd given the large number of exhibitors and persons attending the fair."

The Court next rejected the society's claim that because its church ritualizes face-to-face solicitation, this entitles its members to a solicitation right in a public forum superior to those of members of other religious groups which do not ritualize the process. Justice White continued: "ISKCON desires to proselytize at the fair because it believes it can successfully communicate and raise funds. In its view, this can be done only by intercepting fair patrons as they move about, and if success is achieved, stopping them momentarily or for longer periods as money is given or exchanged for literature. This consequence would be multiplied many times over if Rule 6.05 could not be applied to confine such transactions by ISKCON and others to fixed locations. Indeed, the court below agreed that without Rule 6.05 there would be widespread disorder at the fairgrounds. . . . Given these considerations, we hold that the state's interest in confining distribution, selling, and fund solicitation activities to fixed locations is sufficient to satisfy the requirement that a place or manner restriction must serve a substantial state interest. . . ."

Justice Brennan, joined by Justices Marshall and Stevens, concurred in part and dissented in part, essentially stating that Rule 6.05's restriction, as applied to sales and solicitation, is validly based on the state's strong interest in protecting fairgoers from deceptive solicitation practices. Justice Brennan departed from the Court's approval of Rule 6.05 as it applied to the distribution of literature, however. Brennan stated: "Because I believe that the state could have drafted a more narrowly-drawn restriction on the right to distribute literature without undermining its interests in maintaining crowd control on the fair grounds, I would affirm the part of the judgement below that strikes down Rule 6.05 as it applies to the distribution of literature."

Justice Blackmun also concurred in part and dissented in part. Blackmun would also hold that Rule 6.05's restrictions on the distribution of literature is an unconstitutional infringement on the First Amendment rights, but on differing grounds, stating: "The distribution of literature does not require that a recipient stop in order to receive the message the speaker wishes to convey; instead, the recipient is free to read the message at a later time. For this reason, literature distribution may present even fewer crowd control problems than the oral proselytizing that the statute allows upon the fairgrounds [at designated and limited locations]." Justice Blackmun concurred with the Court's reasoning in upholding Rule 6.05 insofar as it applies to solicitation and sales.

Page 1204. At the end of Note 7 add:

A village ordinance prohibiting door-to-door or on-street solicitation of contributions by charitable organizations not using at least 75 percent of their receipts (exclusive of legitimate operating expenses) for "charitable purposes" was invalidated on First Amendment grounds in Village of Schaumburg v. Citizens for a Better Environment, 444 U.S. 620, 100 S. Ct. 826, 63 L. Ed. 2d 73 (1980). Speaking through Justice White, the Court concluded that the 75-percent requirement only peripherally promoted the governmental interest in "protecting the public from fraud, crime and undue annoyances." A canvass of prior cases "clearly establish[ed] that charitable appeals for funds, on the street or door to door, involve a variety of speech interests — communication of information, the dissemination and propagation of views and ideas, and the advocacy of causes — that are within the protection of the First Amendment." While the "soliciting [of] financial support is undoubtedly subject to reasonable regulation," here the municipality had not proceeded "in such a manner as not unduly to intrude upon the rights of free speech." Essentially, the Court concluded, the ordinance was excessively overbroad. Finding that a less restrictive means was available to protect against fraudulent misrepresentations and to promote financial disclosures, and that there was not a substantial relationship between the 75-percent requirement and privacy interests, the Court continued its generally negative policy toward such restrictions by municipalities. Only Justice Rehnquist dissented, asserting that the Court overestimated the value, for constitutional purposes, of door-to-door solicitation for financial contributions and simultaneously underestimated the reasons why a municipality might validly conclude that regulation of such activity was necessary.

Page 1207. Add to the footnoted material:

Farber, Content Regulation and the First Amendment: A Revisionist View, 68 Geo. L.J. 727 (1980).

Page 1210. At the end of the full paragraph add:

See Farber, Civilizing Public Discourse: An Essay on Professor Bickel, Justice Harlan, and the Enduring Significance of Cohen v. California, 1980 Duke L.J. 283.

Page 1216. At the end of Note 1 add:

Cf. Widmar v. Vincent, — U.S. — , 102 S. Ct. 269, — L. Ed. 2d — (1981), which presented the question of "whether a state university which made its facilities generally available for the activities of registered student groups, may close its facilities to a registered student group desiring to use the facilities for religious worship and discussion." Justice Powell delivered the Court's opinion:

"Through its policy of accommodating their meetings, the University [of Missouri] has created a forum generally open for use by student groups. Having done so, the University has assumed an obligation to justify its discriminations and exclusions under applicable constitutional norms. The Constitution forbids a State to enforce certain exclusions from a forum generally open to the public, even if it were not required to create for forum in the first place. . . . Here the University of Missouri has discriminated against student groups and speakers based on their desire to use a generally open forum to engage in religious worship and discussion. Those are forms of speech and association protected by the First Amendment. . . . In order to justify discriminatory exclusion from a public forum based on the religious content of a group's intended speech, the University must therefore satisfy the standard of review appropriate to content-based exclusions. It must show that its regulation is necessary to serve a compelling state interest and that it is narrowly drawn to achieve that end."

The Court then turned to the University's claimed compelling interest in maintaining strict separation of church and state based upon the establishment clauses of both the United States and Missouri constitutions. The Court rejected this argument, stating: "In this context we are unpersuaded that the primary effect of the public forum, open to all forms of discourse, would be to advance religion. . . . We are not oblivious to the range of an open forum's likely effects. It is possible — perhaps even foreseeable — that religious groups will benefit from access to University facilities. But this Court has explained that a religious organization's enjoyment of merely 'incidental' benefits does not violate the prohibition against the 'primary advancement' of religion," citing *Nyquist.*

Continuing, Powell wrote: "Our holding in this case in no way undermines the capacity of the University to establish reasonable time, place, and manner regulations. . . . The basis for our decision is narrow. Having created a forum generally open to student groups, the University seeks to enforce a content-based exclusion of religious speech. Its exclusionary policy violates the fundamental principles that a state regulation of speech should be content-neutral and the University is unable to justify this violation under applicable constitutional standards."

Justice Stevens concurred separately. Justice White entered a dissent, essentially finding the Court's acceptance of the group's argument that "because a religious worship uses speech, it is protected by the free speech clause of the First Amendment . . . [as] plainly wrong. Were it right, the Religion Clauses would be emptied of any independent meaning in circumstances in which religious practices took the form of speech."

Page 1217. At the end of the first full paragraph add:

Compare U.S. Postal Service v. Council of Greenburgh Civic Assns., 453 U.S. 114, 101 S. Ct. 2676, 69 L. Ed. 2d 517 (1981), upholding the constitutionality of a federal law (18 U.S.C. 1725) that prohibits the deposit of unstamped "mailable matter" in a letter box approved by the Postal Service. Appellees' First Amendment rights were not abridged by this statute, the Court determined, because it was not geared in any way to the content of the message sought to be placed in such letter boxes. Such an "authorized depository" becomes an essential part of the Postal Service's national system for the delivery and receipt of mail, and is in no respect a "public forum" of some sort to which the First Amendment guarantees access. Such letter boxes cannot properly be analogized to streets and parks; thus, a traditional "time, place, and manner" analysis was inappropriate. *Lehman,* together with Greer v. Spock and Adderley v. Florida (Casebook pp. 1229 and 1279, respectively) were relied on, and cases relating to the "public forum" were distinguished. Justice Brennan concurred separately, asserting that §1725 was "a reasonable time, place, and manner restriction on . . . First Amendment rights," while disagreeing with the majority's "resting its judgment instead on the conclusion that a letter box is not a public forum." Justice White concurred in the judgment; Justice Marshall dissented, "tak[ing] exception to the [Court's] result, the analysis, and the premise that private persons lose their prerogatives over the letter boxes they own and supply for mail service." Letter boxes should be regarded as part of the public forum, he asserted; even if they are not, and even though the restriction is not "content-based," since it affected First Amendment rights it should be sustained only if "justified by a significant governmental interest substantially advanced by [§1725]." Justice Stevens also dissented, but disagreed with Marshall's view that private mail boxes "are the functional equivalent of public fora."

Page 1232. At the end of the first paragraph of Note 2 add:

Relying on *Mosley*, the Court in Carey v. Brown, 447 U.S. 455, 100 S. Ct. 2286, 65 L. Ed. 2d 263 (1980), held invalid an Illinois statute prohibiting residential picketing, but exempting from its prohibition the "peaceful picketing of a place of employment involved in a labor dispute," as impermissibly discriminating between various forms of peaceful picketing. In "regulat[ing] expressive conduct that falls within the First Amendment's preserve ... , the Illinois statute discriminates between lawful and unlawful conduct based upon the content of the demonstrator's communication," and thus makes "[t]he permissibility of residential picketing ... dependent solely on the nature of the message being conveyed." Continuing, the Court stated: "When government regulation discriminates among speech-related activities in a public forum, the Equal Protection Clause mandates that the legislation be finely tailored to serve substantial state interests, and the justification offered for any distinctions it draws must be carefully scrutinized." Moreover, the Court noted, since "[t]he State's interest in protecting the well-being, tranquility, and privacy of the home is certainly of the highest order in a free and civilized society," time, place, and manner restrictions applicable to all speech regardless of content are permissible in certain circumstances. Justice Rehnquist, joined by Chief Justice Burger and Justice Blackmun, dissented, distinguishing *Mosley* and urging that the Illinois law was a narrowly tailored time, place, and manner regulation that protected substantial governmental interests unrelated to suppressing free speech, and thus comported with both the First Amendment and equal protection principles.

Page 1235. At the end of the last paragraph of the carryover Note add:

In PruneYard Shopping Center v. Robins, 447 U.S. 74, 100 S. Ct. 2035, 64 L. Ed. 2d 741 (1980), the Court ruled that neither the federally recognized property rights of shopping-center owners nor their First Amendment rights were infringed by the California Supreme Court's decision that members of the public could exercise state-protected rights of free expression and petition on such private property. Noting that "the shopping center by choice of its owner is not limited to [his] personal use," but "is instead a business establishment that is open to the public to come and go as they please," the Court pointed out that the views expressed by members of the public are unlikely to be identified with those of the owner. Moreover, "no specific message is dictated by the State to be displayed on" the property in question, and property owners are not "compelled to affirm their belief in any governmentally prescribed view" under the California law. Finally, the Court stated, the owner "can expressly disavow any connection with the message by simply posting signs in the area where the speakers or handbillers stand." While the owner sought to enforce his antispeech policy in a nondiscriminatory manner, the California Constitution protects "speech and petitioning reasonably exercised in shopping centers even when the centers are privately owned." The Court distinguished the *Tornillo* case as well as *Lloyd* and related shopping-center and mall picketing cases as inapposite, and also rejected appellants' taking clause argument (see supra in this Supplement, additions to Casebook pp.847 and 670). Justice Marshall concurred, urging a return to *Logan Valley Plaza,* and suggesting further that *Lloyd* and *Hudgens* be abandoned. Justices White and Powell concurred separately. See Note, Robins v. PruneYard Shopping Center: Free Speech Access to Shopping Centers Under the California Constitution, 68 Calif. L. Rev. 641 (1980).

Page 1235. After the heading and citation of United States v. O'Brien, add:

Mr. Chief Justice WARREN delivered the opinion of the Court.

Page 1262. At the end of Note 3 add:

See also In re R.M.J., — U.S. — , 102 S. Ct. 929, — L. Ed. 2d — (1982), where a unanimous Court, per Justice Powell, held that, although the states retain the ability to regulate commercial speech in general and lawyer advertising in particular, they must do so with care and in a manner which is the least restrictive of First Amendment rights.

In this case a Missouri attorney announced the opening of his law office in St. Louis by mailing professional announcement cards, as well as by placing several advertisements in the local newspapers and telephone directories. These advertisements contained information which was not specifically permitted by Rule 4 of the State Supreme Court. The Missouri state court advisory committee filed an information in the supreme court charging the appellant with unprofessional conduct. In a subsequent disbarment proceeding, the Supreme Court of Missouri upheld the constitutionality of Rule 4 and issued a private reprimand. The U.S. Supreme Court granted plenary consideration and, after reviewing *Bates* and the line of cases following it, concluded that "truthful advertising related to lawful activities is entitled to the protections of the First Amendment. But when the particular content or method of the advertising is subject to abuse, the states may impose appropriate restrictions. Misleading advertising may be prohibited entirely. But the states may not place an absolute prohibition on certain types of potentially misleading advertising ... if the information also may be presented in a way that is not deceptive. [E]ven when a communication is not misleading, the state retains some authority to regulate. But the state must assert a substantial interest and the interference with speech must be in proportion to the interest served.... Restrictions must be narrowly drawn, and the state lawfully may regulate only to the extent regulation furthers the state's substantial interest...."

Turning to the lawyer advertising challenged here, the Court found the advertising of arcas of the law (such as real estate and contracts) not to be misleading and that there are no substantial interests promoted by the restriction. Similarly, the Court found that the restriction prohibiting a lawyer from identifying the jurisdictions in which he is licensed to practice is not misleading on its face and does not serve to foster a substantial state interest. The Court did find the appellant's mention (in bold-face type) that he was a member of the Supreme Court of the United States to be relatively uninformative and in bad taste, but it also concluded that it was not misleading. Finally, the Court found the restriction on mailing announcement cards to be too restrictive, stating that there is no indication in the record that an inability to supervise is the reason the state restricts the potential audience of the cards.

Page 1269. At the end of Note 1 add:

See also Brown v. Hartlage, — U.S. —, 102 S. Ct. 1523, — L. Ed. 2d — (1982), where the Court held that a Kentucky statute prohibiting a candidate from offering material benefits to voters in consideration for their votes, as applied to petitioner's promise to lower his public salary if elected, was violative of the petitioner's First Amendment free speech rights. The Court stated that "a candidate's promise to confer some ultimate benefit on the voter, *qua* taxpayer, citizen or member of the general public, does not lie beyond the pale of the First Amendment protection."

Page 1269. At the end of Note 2 add:

See Democratic Party of United States v. LaFollette, 450 U.S. 107, 101 S. Ct. 1010, 67 L. Ed. 2d 82 (1981), where the Court was called on to resolve a conflict between the rules of the national Democratic Party and the Wisconsin election laws. The party rules provided that only those who affiliated themselves with the Democratic Party may participate in the process of selecting delegates to the national convention. Wisconsin's election laws allowed voters to participate in the presidential primary without regard to party affiliation (a so-called open primary). Although Wisconsin's delegates were chosen in a separate election, the results of the open primary were binding on the delegates. The national Democratic Party informed the Wisconsin delegation that under its primary rules, they could not be seated at the national convention.

Justice Stewart, writing for the Court, stated: "The issue is whether the State may compel the National Party to seat a delegation chosen in a way that violates the rules of the Party.... [T]his issue was resolved, we believe, in Cousins v. Wigoda, 419 U.S. 477 (1975).... Here, the members of the National Party, speaking through their rules, chose to define their associational rights by limiting those who could participate in the processes leading to the selection of delegates to their national convention. On several occasions this Court has recognized that the inclusion of persons unaffiliated with a political party may seriously distort its collective decisions — thus impairing the Party's essential functions — and that political parties may accordingly protect themselves 'from intrusion by those with adverse political principles.' ... A political party's choice among the various ways of determining the makeup of a State's delegation to the party's national convention is protected by the Constitution. And as is true of all expressions of First Amendment freedoms, the courts may not interfere on the ground that they view a particular expression as unwise or irrational.... [He concluded that] the interests advanced by the State do not justify its substantial intrusion into the associational freedom of members of the National Party."

Justice Powell, joined by Justices Blackmun and Rehnquist, dissented, stating essentially that Wisconsin's election laws did not impose a substantial burden on the associational freedoms of the national party.

Page 1269. Add as a new Note 3:

3. In California Medical Assn. v. Federal Election Commn., 453 U.S. 182, 101 S. Ct. 2712, 69 L. Ed. 2d 567 (1981), the Court rejected both the appellant's First Amendment and Fifth Amendment challenges to a provision of the Federal Election Campaign Act of 1971, 2 U.S.C. 441a(a)(1)(c), which prohibits individuals and unincorporated associations from contributing more than $5,000 per calendar year to any multicandidate political committee. Relying on Buckley v. Valeo, the Court stated that since the First Amendment rights of a contributor are not violated or infringed upon by limitations on the amount that may be contributed to a campaign organization which advocates the views and candidacy of a particular candidate, the rights of a contributor are likewise not impaired by limits on the amount given to a multicandidate political committee which advocates the views and candidacies of a number of candidates. Turning next to the Fifth Amendment equal protection challenge, the Court reasoned that the differing restrictions placed on individuals and unincorporated associations on the one hand, and on corporations and unions on the other, reflect a congressional judgment that those entities have differing structures and purposes and that they therefore may require different forms of regulation.

Page 1269. Add as a new Note 4:

4. In Citizens Against Rent Control/Coalition for Fair Housing v. City of Berkeley, — U.S. — , 102 S. Ct. 434, — L. Ed. 2d — (1981), the Court, per

Chief Justice Burger, struck down a city ordinance which placed a $250 limit on individual contributions made to committees formed to support or oppose local ballot issues. Relying on Buckley v. Valeo, the Court held that the dollar limitation imposed on individuals seeking to band together and advance their views on a ballot measure constituted a restraint on the individuals' right of association. The Court also held that the ordinance imposed a significant restraint on the freedom of expression of groups and of individuals wishing to express their views through committees.

Justice Marshall concurred separately in an attempt to clarify the Court's holding. Marshall stated that the Court failed to "indicate whether or not it attaches any constitutional significance to the fact that the Berkeley ordinance seeks to limit *contributions* as opposed to direct *expenditures*." Justice Marshall went on to find such a distinction constitutionally relevant, citing Buckley v. Valeo for the proposition that the Court "has always drawn a distinction between restrictions on contributions, and direct limitations on the amount an individual can expend for his own speech." The former are entitled to less rigorous scrutiny by the Court than a direct restriction on expenditures.

Justice Blackmun and Justice O'Connor also concurred in the outcome. However, in contrast to Justice Marshall's suggestion that an individual's right to contribute to a political action committee may be entitled to less than full First Amendment protection, they opined that any statute which directly encroaches upon an individual's right of association and expression required the Court's exercise of strict scrutiny, because it triggers full First Amendment protection.

In Bread Political Action Committee v. Federal Election Commn., — U.S. —, 102 S. Ct. 1235, — L. Ed. 2d — (1982), the Court held that only three categories of plaintiffs may challenge the constitutional validity of Federal Election Campaign Act under §310(a). Section 310(a) permits the "FEC," "the national committee of any political party," or "any individual eligible to vote in any election for the office of President" to file suit in district court. Thus, trade associations, political action committees and other groups may not challenge the Act's validity.

Page 1272. At the end of Note 1 add:

Note, Freeing Public Broadcasting from Unconstitutional Restraints, 89 Yale L.J. 719 (1980); Lively, Media Access and a Free Press: Pursuing First Amendment Values Without Imperiling First Amendment Rights, 58 Den. L.J. 17 (1980); BeVier, An Informed Public, An Informing Press: The Search for a Constitutional Principle, 68 Calif. L. Rev. 482 (1980).

Page 1275. At the end of the carryover paragraph add:

Compare CBS, Inc. v. Federal Communications Commn., 453 U.S. 367, 101 S. Ct. 2813, 69 L. Ed. 2d 706 (1981), where the Court considered the FCC's implementation, as well as the constitutionality, of §312(a)(7) of the

Communications Act, as amended in 1972, which authorizes the revocation of broadcast licenses for refusal to allow candidates for federal elective office reasonable amounts of broadcast time and which also gives legally qualified candidates an affirmative, promptly enforceable right of reasonable access to purchase air time from broadcast stations. FCC standards limiting the right of access to the period after a campaign has begun, as determined by the Commission, and requiring broadcasters to evaluate access requests individually, were found not to be arbitrary or capricious. And, the Court concluded, such a right of access does not violate the First Amendment by unduly circumscribing the editorial discretion of broadcasters. Chief Justice Burger's majority opinion relied extensively on administrative interpretation of the statutory provisions, as acquiesced in by Congress. With respect to the First Amendment contention, the Court cited and quoted from CBS, Inc. v. Democratic National Committee, putting emphasis on the regulated nature of the broadcasting industry and the paramount rights of listeners and viewers to receive information, relying on *Red Lion*. While agreeing that "the Court has never approved a *general* right of access to the media," Burger stated that §312(a)(7) "creates [only] a *limited* right to 'reasonable' access that pertains only to legally qualified federal candidates and may be invoked by them only for the purpose of advancing their candidacies once a campaign has commenced." It "represents an effort by Congress to assure that an important resource — the airwaves — will be used in the public interest" and "properly balances the First Amendment rights of federal candidates, the public, and broadcasters."

Justice White, joined by Justices Rehnquist and Stevens, dissented, primarily on the ground that "the Commission seriously misconstrued the statute when it assumed that it had been given authority to insist on its own views as to reasonable access." This resulted in "an administratively created right of access which, in light of the pre-existing statutory policies [as well as "media judgments representing different but nevertheless reasonable reactions to access requests"], is far broader than Congress could have intended to allow." Justice Stevens also wrote a brief separate dissent.

Page 1277. At end of Note 5 add:

See FCC v. WNCN Listeners Guild, 450 U.S. 532, 101 S. Ct. 1266, 67 L. Ed. 2d 521 (1981), where the Court refined its holding in *Red Lion*, stating: "*Red Lion* held that the Commission's 'fairness doctrine' was consistent with the public interest standard of the Communications Act and did not violate the First Amendment, but rather enhanced First Amendment values by promoting 'the presentation of vigorous debate of controversial issues of importance and concern to the public. . . .' Although observing that the interests of the people as a whole were promoted by debate of public issues on the radio, we did not imply that the First Amendment grants individual listeners the right to have the Commission review the abandonment of their favorite entertainment programs. The Commission seeks to further the interests of the listening public as a whole by relying on market forces to promote diversity in radio entertainment formats and to satisfy the entertainment preferences of radio listeners. This policy does not conflict with the First Amendment."

Justice Marshall, joined by Justice Brennan, dissented, stating: "[N]either the 'fairness doctrine' nor the political broadcasting rules have anything to do with the various situations ... in which the Commission has not hesitated to consider program formats in making the 'public interest' determination. The fairness doctrine imposes an obligation on licensees to devote a 'reasonable percentage' of broadcast time to controversial issues of public importance, and it requires that the coverage be fair in that it accurately reflects the opposing views.... The political broadcasting rules regulate broadcasts by candidates for federal and non-federal public office.... The Commission's examination of whether a broadcaster's format includes programming directed at women or at residents of local community, or its requirement that licensees providing programming designed to serve the unique needs of children, simply have nothing to do with either the fairness doctrine or the political broadcasting rules."

Page 1280. At the end of Note 2 add:

For the same reasons advanced in Greer v. Spock, the Court upheld Air Force regulations which required members of the service to obtain approval from their commanders before circulating petitions on Air Force bases. Brown v. Glines, 444 U.S. 348, 100 S. Ct. 594, 63 L. Ed. 2d 516 (1980). Finding that "nothing in the Constitution ... disables a military commander from acting to prevent what he considers to be a clear danger to the loyalty, discipline, or morale of troops on the base under his command," Justice Powell, writing for the majority, stated that the government clearly had a substantial interest that it was seeking to protect and that this interest was "unrelated to the suppression of free expression." Because the regulations did not restrict speech any more than was reasonably necessary to maintain respect for the duty and discipline which are vital to military effectiveness and because they did not unduly interfere with a serviceman's right to communicate directly with members of Congress, they were not an unconstitutional prior restraint in violation of the First Amendment nor in conflict with the prohibition on restrictions of communications from servicemen to members of Congress contained in 10 U.S.C. 1034. Justices Brennan, Stewart, and Stevens dissented.

The Court applied the *Glines* rationale in Secretary of the Navy v. Huff, 444 U.S. 453, 100 S. Ct. 606, 62 L. Ed. 2d 607 (1980). Concluding that the "special characteristics" of military service require that civilian authorities accord military commanders some flexibility in dealing with internal matters affecting discipline and morale, a requirement for prior approval by commanders before military personnel on overseas bases could circulate petitions to members of Congress was upheld, despite §1034. Justices Brennan, Stewart and Stevens again dissented.

Page 1289. Add as new Note 6:

6. Metromedia, Inc. v. City of San Diego, 453 U.S. 490, 101 S. Ct. 2882, 69 L. Ed. 2d 800 (1981), involved the constitutionality of a municipal ordinance imposing substantial prohibitions on the erection of outdoor advertising displays within the city. San Diego's stated purpose was "to eliminate hazards to pedestrians and motorists brought about by distracting sign displays" and "to preserve and improve the appearance of the City." On-site commercial advertising was permitted, but other commercial advertising and most non-commercial advertising was prohibited by the ordinance. Justice White's plurality opinion, joined by Justices Stewart, Marshall, and Powell, concluded that the city's general ban on non-commercial advertising was facially invalid under the First and Fourteenth Amendments, and that the ordinance did not constitute a reasonable "time, place, and manner" restriction. Justice Brennan, joined by Justice Blackmun, concurred separately, construing the ordinance even more broadly than Justice White and finding that the city's virtually total ban on billboards was impermissible absent a sufficiently substantial governmental interest directly furthered thereby and absent a showing that a more narrowly drawn restriction would less effectively promote such an objective. Justice Stevens concurred in part and dissented in part. Chief Justice Burger, Justice Rehnquist, and Justice Stevens filed dissenting opinions.

After noting that the Court "has often faced the problem of applying the broad principles of the First Amendment to unique forms of expression" and that "at times First Amendment values must yield to other societal interests," Justice White addressed himself to what he described as "the law of billboards." He wrote: "Billboards are a well-established medium of communication, used to convey a broad range of different kinds of messages. . . . [But,] because it is designed to stand out and apart from its surroundings [as a "large, immobile, and permanent structure"], the billboard creates a unique set of problems for land-use planning and development." He continued:

"Billboards, then, like other media of communication, combine communicative and noncommunicative aspects. As with other media, the government has legitimate interests in controlling the noncommunicative aspects of the medium, . . . but the First and Fourteenth Amendments foreclose a similar interest in controlling the communicative aspects. Because regulation of the noncommunicative aspects of a medium often impinges to some degree on the communicative aspects, it has been necessary for the courts to reconcile the government's regulatory interests with the individual's right to expression. '[A] court may not escape the task of assessing the First Amendment interest at stake and weighing it against the public interest allegedly served by the regulation.' Linmark Associates, Inc. v. Willingboro, 431 U.S. 85, 91 (1977), quoting Bigelow v. Virginia, 421 U.S. 809, 826 (1975). Performance of this task requires a particularized inquiry into the nature of the conflicting interests at stake here, beginning with a precise appraisal of the character of the ordinance as it affects communication."

After concluding that "[t]o determine if any billboard is prohibited by the ordinance, one must determine how it is constructed, where it is located, and what message it carried," White continued:

"The extension of First Amendment protections to purely commercial speech is a relatively recent development in First Amendment jurisprudence. Prior to 1975, purely commercial advertisements of services or goods for sale were considered to be outside the protection of the First Amendment. Valentine v. Chrestensen, 316 U.S. 52 (1942). That construction of the First Amendment was severely cut back in Bigelow v. Virginia, 421 U.S. 809 (1975). In Virginia Pharmacy Board v. Virginia Consumer Council, 425 U.S. 748 (1976), we plainly held that speech proposing no more than a commercial transaction enjoys a substantial degree of First Amendment protection: A state may not completely suppress the dissemination of truthful information about an entirely lawful activity merely because it is fearful of that information's effect upon its disseminators and its recipients. That decision, however, did not equate commercial and noncommercial speech for First Amendment purposes; indeed, it expressly indicated the contrary. . . .

"Although the protection extended to commercial speech has continued to develop, commercial and noncommercial communications, in the context of the First Amendment, have been treated differently. Bates v. State Bar of Arizona, 433 U.S. 350 (1977), held that advertising by attorneys may not be subjected to blanket suppression and that the specific advertisement at issue there was constitutionally protected. However, we continued to observe the distinction between commercial and noncommercial speech, indicating that the former could be forbidden and regulated in situations where the latter could not be. 433 U.S., at 379-381; 383-384 [and citing and discussing *Ohralik* and *American Mini Theatres*].

"Finally, in Central Hudson .v. Public Service Commn., 447 U.S. 557 (1980), we held that: 'The Constitution . . . accords a lesser protection to commercial speech than to other constitutionally guaranteed expression. The protection available for a particular commercial expression turns on the nature both of the expression and of the governmental interests served by its regulation.' Id., at 562-563 (citation omitted). We then adopted a four-part test for determining the validity of government restrictions on commercial speech as distinguished from more fully protected speech. (1) The First Amendment protects commercial speech only if that speech concerns lawful activity and is not misleading. A restriction on otherwise protected commercial speech is valid only if it (2) seeks to implement a substantial governmental interest, (3) directly advances that interest, and (4) reaches no farther than necessary to accomplish the given objective. Id., at 563-566."

Justice White conceded that the ordinance's "twin goals" of "traffic safety and the appearance of the city" were legitimate, but questioned whether the law as written "directly advance[s]" those objectives. Ultimately, though, he concluded that "insofar as it regulates commercial speech the San Diego ordinance meets the constitutional requirements of *Central Hudson.*" However, the fatal flaw in the ordinance, according to White, was in its "general ban on signs carrying noncommercial advertising." He concluded:

"Although the city may distinguish between the relative value of different categories of commercial speech, the city does not have the same range of choice in the area of noncommercial speech to evaluate the strength of, or distinguish between, various communicative interests. . . . With respect to noncommercial speech, the city may not choose the appropriate subjects for public discourse. . . . Because some noncommercial messages may be conveyed on billboards throughout the commercial and industrial zones, San Diego must similarly allow billboards conveying other noncommercial messages throughout those zones. . . . It is apparent as well that the ordinance distinguishes in several ways between permissible and impermissible signs at a particular location by reference to their content. Whether or not these distinctions are themselves constitutional, they take the regulation out of the domain of time, place, and manner restrictions, [citing the *Consolidated Edison* case].

"There can be no question that a prohibition on the erection of billboards infringes freedom of speech: The exceptions do not create the infringement, rather the general prohibition does. But the exceptions to the general prohibition are of great significance in assessing the strength of the city's interest in prohibiting billboards. We conclude that by allowing commercial establishments to use billboards to advertise the products and services they offer, the city necessarily has conceded that some communicative interests, e.g., on-site commercial advertising, are stronger than its competing interests in esthetics and traffic safety. It has nevertheless banned all noncommercial signs except those specifically excepted. . . .

"Because the San Diego ordinance reaches too far into the realm of protected speech, we conclude that it is unconstitutional on its face."

Justice Brennan concurred separately because he felt that "this case in effect presents the total ban [of billboards] question," and because he regarded "the plurality's bifurcated approach itself [as raising] serious First Amendment problems and [relying] on a distinction between commercial and noncommercial speech unanticipated by . . . prior cases." Cities "may totally ban [billboards only if they] can show that a sufficiently substantial governmental interest is directly furthered by the total ban, and that any more narrowly drawn restriction, i.e., anything less than a total ban, would promote less well the achievement of that goal," Brennan asserted. Here San Diego had "failed to provide adequate justification for its substantial restriction on protected activity," he concluded. Moreover, he wrote, "[t]he plurality's treatment of the commercial-noncommercial distinction is mistaken in its factual analysis and departs from this Court's precedents." The plurality's bifurcated approach, he said, "presents a real danger of curtailing noncommercial speech in the guise of regulating commercial speech," for it allows too much discretion to be exercised by local officials. He further observed:

"It is one thing for a court to classify in specific cases whether commercial or noncommercial speech is involved, but quite another — and for me dispositively so — for a city to do so regularly for the purpose of deciding what messages may be communicated by way of billboards. Cities are equipped to make traditional police power decisions, see Saia v. New York, supra, at 564-565 (Frankfurter, J., dissenting), not decisions based on the content of speech. . . . I have no doubt that those who seek to convey commercial messages will engage in the most imaginative of exercises to place themselves within the safe haven of noncommercial speech, while at the same time conveying their commercial message. Encouraging such behavior can only make the job of city officials — who already are inclined to ban billboards — that much more difficult and potentially intrusive upon legitimate noncommercial expression."

Chief Justice Burger felt the ordinance should be sustained as a reasonable police power measure that had only a limited impact on protected speech, and thus dissented. Local government has the authority, he asserted, "to protect its citizens' legitimate interests in traffic safety and the environment by eliminating distracting and ugly structures from its buildings and roadways, to define which billboards actually pose that danger, and to decide whether, in certain instances, the public's need for information outweighs the dangers perceived." Justice Stevens took the position that, since a city may in his view prohibit outdoor advertising entirely, consistent with the First Amendment, San Diego's less restrictive approach should survive constitutional challenge. Justice Rehnquist stated that he agreed substantially with the Burger and Stevens positions.

Page 1294. At the end of Note 1 add:

See also Consolidated Edison Co. of New York, Inc. v. Public Service Commn., 447 U.S. 530, 100 S. Ct. 2326, 65 L. Ed. 2d 319 (1980), and Central Hudson Gas & Electric Corp. v. Public Service Commn., 447 U.S. 557, 100 S. Ct. 2343, 65 L. Ed. 2d 341 (1980), invalidating the New York Public Service Commission's prohibition of an electric utility's use of bill inserts to promote its position on controversial public policy issues as violative of the First Amendment, and also holding that the commission's ban on all promotional advertising by electric utilities was more extensive than necessary to further the state's substantial interest in energy conservation. Referring to *First National Bank of Boston* as having "rejected the contention that a State may confine corporate speech to specified issues," the Court in *Consolidated Edison* concluded that "the regulation could not stand absent a showing of a compelling state interest." The agency's action did not constitute a valid time, place, and manner regulation or a permissible subject-matter regulation; the former may not be based on the content of expression, as here, and the latter can be justified only if narrowly drawn so as to foster a significant government interest. The Court did not deal with the question whether ratepayers could effectively be required to subsidize such speech, since the record did not indicate that this was in fact so. *Lehman* was distinguished, since the recipients of the bill inserts were not a captive audience in the sense of that and like cases. Justices Marshall and Stevens concurred.

In *Central Hudson*, again speaking through Justice Powell, the Court found the commission's ban violative of the First Amendment. Citing *Virginia State Board of Pharmacy* and related decisions, the Court noted that, while commercial speech is protected from "unwarranted governmental regulation," the "Constitution ... accords a lesser protection to commercial speech than to other constitutionally guaranteed expression," relying on *Bates* and *Ohralik*. Since "[t]he First Amendment's concern for commercial speech is based on the informational function of advertising, ... there can be no constitutional objection to the suppression of commercial messages that do not accurately inform the public about lawful activity ... or commercial speech related to illegal activity...." But here the commission did not claim that "the expression at issue either is inaccurate or relates to unlawful activity." Nor, in the instant circumstances, did the utility's monopoly position alter its First Amendment rights. The two justifications offered for the ban on promotional advertising — energy conservation and rate reduction — were unpersuasive, the Court concluded, for the restriction was more extensive than necessary to further the state's legitimate interests, which could be adequately protected "by more limited regulation of appellant's commercial expression." Justices Brennan and Stevens concurred, while Justice Rehnquist dissented, emphasizing the appellant's status as a state-created monopoly as well as the importance of energy conservation measures, and further arguing that commercial speech should not be accorded the same protection as political speech.

Page 1294. At the end of Note 2 add:

Bolton, Constitutional Limitations on Restrictive Corporate and Union Political Speech, 22 Ariz. L. Rev. 373 (1980).

Page 1307. At the end of Note 2 add:

Cf. Snepp v. United States, 444 U.S. 507, 100 S. Ct. 763, 62 L. Ed. 2d 704 (1980), holding that the need to protect classified information allows the government to require a contractual obligation on the part of a CIA employee to submit writings for prepublication review, and concluding that in such a situation the prior restraint doctrine does not apply in the same manner as in the Pentagon Papers case. Justice Stevens, joined by Justices Brennan and Marshall, dissented.

In Haig v. Agee, 453 U.S. 280, 101 S. Ct. 2766, 69 L. Ed. 2d 640 (1981), infra in this Supplement, addition to Casebook p.1597, the Court rejected a First Amendment challenge to the State Department's revocation of an American citizen's passport, on the grounds that action not speech was involved and that, in any event, the respondent through his activities abroad posed a serious threat to national security, so that the *Near* case exception to the ban on prior restraint, preserved in the Pentagon Papers case, was applicable.

Page 1308. Prior to Sheppard v. Maxwell, add:

CHANDLER v. STATE OF FLORIDA, 449 U.S. 560, 101 S. Ct. 802, 66 L. Ed. 2d 740 (1981). Here the Court again found it necessary to assess the constitutional considerations relating to permitting the limited access of the electronic media into the courtroom and its subsequent effects on a criminal defendant's due process protections. Two Miami Beach policemen were charged with conspiracy to commit burglary, grand larceny, and possession of burglary tools. The defendants sought to have Florida's Experimental Canon 3A(7), which permits the limited access of electronic equipment into the courtroom under specific guidelines, declared unconstitutional on its face and as applied.

The trial court denied the relief requested and permitted electronic media coverage of the trial. The defendants, found guilty on all counts, moved for a new trial, claiming that they had been denied a fair and impartial trial because of the television coverage. The Florida District Court of Appeals affirmed the convictions and the Florida Supreme Court denied review.

After canvassing the historical development of the judicial proscription barring the use of all photographic, radio, and television coverage of courtroom proceedings, the Court proceeded to analyze the plurality decision in *Estes*, concluding that it was "satisfied that *Estes* did not announce a constitutional rule that all photographic or broadcast coverage of criminal trials is inherently a denial of due process. . . ." The Court then turned to the consideration of whether such a *per se* rule was constitutionally required. Concluding that it was not and that at least limited and controlled access of electronic media into courtrooms was not inconsistent with due process, Chief Justice Burger, writing for the Court, stated:

"Any criminal case that generates a great deal of publicity presents some risks that the publicity may compromise the right of the defendant to a fair trial. Trial courts must be especially vigilant to guard against any impairment of the defendant's right to a verdict based solely upon the evidence and the relevant law. . . . [But an] absolute constitutional ban on broadcast coverage of trials cannot be justified simply because there is a danger that, in some cases, prejudicial broadcast accounts of pretrial and trial events may impair the ability of jurors to decide the issue of guilt or innocence uninfluenced by extraneous matter. The risk of juror prejudice in some cases does not justify an absolute ban on news coverage of trials by the printed media; so also the risk of such prejudice does not warrant an absolute constitutional ban on all broadcast coverage. A case attracts a high level of public attention because of its intrinsic interest to the public and the manner of reporting the event. The risk of juror prejudice is present in any publication of a trial, but the appropriate safeguard against such prejudice is the defendant's right to demonstrate that the media's coverage of his case — be it printed or broadcast — compromised the ability of the particular jury that heard the case to adjudicate fairly.

"As we noted earlier, the concurring opinions in *Estes* expressed concern that the very presence of media cameras and recording devices at a trial inescapably gives rise to an adverse psychological impact on the participants in the trial. This kind of general psychological prejudice, allegedly present whenever there is broadcast coverage of a trial, is different from the more particularized problem of prejudicial impact.... If it could be demonstrated that the mere presence of photographic and recording equipment and the knowledge that the event would be broadcast invariably and uniformly affected the conduct of participants so as to impair fundamental fairness, our task would be simple; prohibition of broadcast coverage of trials would be required....

"Not unimportant to the position asserted by Florida and other states is the change in television technology since 1962, when Estes was tried. It is urged, and some empirical data are presented, that many of the negative factors found in *Estes* — cumbersome equipment, cables, distracting lighting, numerous camera technicians — are less substantial factors today than they were at that time.

"It is also significant that safeguards have been built into the experimental programs in state courts, and into the Florida program, to avoid some of the most egregious problems envisioned by the six opinions in the *Estes* case. Florida admonishes its courts to take special pains to protect certain witnesses — for example, children, victims of sex crimes, some informants, and even the very timid witness or party — from the glare of publicity and the tensions of being 'on camera.'

"The Florida guidelines place on trial judges positive obligations to be on guard to protect the fundamental right of the accused to a fair trial. The Florida statute, being one of thè few permitting broadcast coverage of criminal trials over the objection of the accused, raises problems not present in the statutes of other states. Inherent in electronic coverage of a trial is the risk that the very awareness by the accused of the coverage and the contemplated broadcast may adversely affect the conduct of the participants and the fairness of the trial, yet leave no evidence of how the conduct or the trial's fairness was affected. Given this danger, it is significant that Florida requires that objections of the accused to coverage be heard and considered on the record by the trial court. In addition to providing a record for appellate review, a pretrial hearing enables a defendant to advance the basis of his objection to broadcast coverage and allows the trial court to define the steps necessary to minimize or eliminate the risks of prejudice to the accused. Experiments such as the one presented here may well increase the number of appeals by adding a new basis for claims to reverse, but this is a risk Florida has chosen to take after preliminary experimentation. Here, the record does not indicate that appellants requested an evidentiary hearing to show adverse impact or injury. Nor does the record reveal anything more than generalized allegations of prejudice. . . .

"Whatever may be the 'mischievous potentialities [of broadcast coverage] for intruding upon the detached atmosphere which should always surround the judicial process,' Estes v. Texas, 381 U.S., at 587, at present no one has been able to present empirical data sufficient to establish that the mere presence of the broadcast media inherently has an adverse effect on that process. The appellants have offered nothing to demonstrate that their trial was subtly tainted by broadcast coverage — let alone that all broadcast trials would be so tainted.

"Where, as here, we cannot say that a denial of due process automatically results from activity authorized by a state, the admonition of Justice Brandeis, dissenting in New State Ice Co. v. Liebmann, 285 U.S. 262, 311 (1932), is relevant, [quoting from the passage regarding the desirability of allowing "experimentation in things social and economic [a]s a grave responsibility," where Brandeis concluded that "it is one of the happy incidents of the federal system that a single courageous state may, if its citizens choose, serve as a laboratory; and try novel social and economic experiments without risk to the rest of the country"]. This concept of federalism, echoed by the states favoring Florida's experiment, must guide our decision.

"To say that the appellants have not demonstrated that broadcast coverage is inherently a denial of due process is not to say that the appellants were in fact accorded all of the protections of due process in their trial. As noted earlier, a defendant has the right on review to show that the media's coverage of his case — printed or broadcast — compromised the ability of the jury to judge him fairly. Alternatively, a defendant might show that broadcast coverage of his particular case had an adverse impact on the trial participants sufficient to constitute a denial of due process. Neither showing was made in this case.

"To demonstrate prejudice in a specific case a defendant must show something more than juror awareness that the trial is such as to attract the attention of broadcasters. No doubt the very presence of a camera in the courtroom made the jurors aware that the trial was thought to be of sufficient interest to the public to warrant coverage. Jurors, forbidden to watch all broadcasts, would have had no way of knowing that only fleeting seconds of the proceeding would be reproduced. But the appellants have not attempted to show with any specificity that the presence of cameras

155

impaired the ability of the the jurors to decide the case on only the evidence before them or that their trial was affected adversely by the impact on any of the participants of the presence of cameras and the prospect of broadcast. . . . In short, there is no showing that the trial was compromised by television coverage, as was the case in *Estes*.

"It is not necessary either to ignore or to discount the potential danger to the fairness of a trial in a particular case in order to conclude that Florida may permit the electronic media to cover trials in its state courts. Dangers lurk in this, as in most, experiments, but unless we were to conclude that television coverage under all conditions is prohibited by the Constitution, the states must be free to experiment. We are not empowered by the Constitution to oversee or harness state procedural experimentation; only when the state action infringes fundamental guarantees are we authorized to intervene. We must assume state courts will be alert to any factors that impair the fundamental rights of the accused.

"The Florida program is inherently evolutional in nature; the initial project has provided guidance for the new canons which can be changed at will, and application of which is subject to control by the trial judge. The risk of prejudice to particular defendants is ever present and must be examined carefully as cases arise. Nothing of the 'Roman circus' or 'Yankee Stadium' atmosphere, as in *Estes*, prevailed here, however, nor have appellants attempted to show that the unsequestered jury was exposed to 'sensational' coverage, in the sense of *Estes* or of Sheppard v. Maxwell. Absent a showing of prejudice of constitutional dimensions to these defendants, there is no reason for this Court either to endorse or to invalidate Florida's experiment. . . ."

Justice Stewart concurred in the result but concluded that the Court was in effect overruling *Estes*.

Justice White also concurred separately in the judgment, essentially agreeing with Justice Stewart's analysis.

Page 1311. At the end of Note 2 add:

Note, The Free Press — Fair Trial Dilemma: New Dimensions to a Continuing Struggle, 6 Hofstra L. Rev. 1013 (1978).

Page 1333. After Note 4 add:

RICHMOND NEWSPAPERS, INC. v. VIRGINIA, 448 U.S. 555, 100 S. Ct. 2814, 65 L. Ed. 2d 973 (1980). As stated succinctly in Chief Justice Burger's plurality opinion, "[t]he narrow question presented in this case is whether the right of the public and press to attend criminal trials is guaranteed under the United States Constitution." A Virginia trial court had, at the request of the defendant, closed the courtroom to the public, including a reporter for appellant newspaper. The Virginia Supreme Court upheld the closure order and, over objections that the case was moot, the Supreme Court considered the merits. Speaking for himself and Justices White and Stevens, Chief Justice Burger first noted that the decision in *Gannett* was not controlling, for there "the Court was not required to decide whether a right of access to *trials*, as distinguished from hearings on *pre*trial motions, was constitutionally guaranteed." After referring to *Nebraska Press Assn.* and other cases where the Court "has treated questions involving conflicts between publicity and a defendant's right to a fair trial," Burger emphasized that "here for the first time the Court is asked to decide whether the criminal trial itself may be closed to the public upon the unopposed request of a defendant, without any demonstration that closure is required to protect the defendant's superior right to a fair trial, or that some other overriding consideration requires closure." After canvassing the historic background of "the modern criminal trial in Anglo-American justice," Burger stated that "the historical evidence demonstrates conclusively that at the time when our organic laws were adopted, criminal trials both here and in England had long been presumptively open." In modern times, he noted, "[i]nstead of acquiring information about trials by first hand observation or by word of mouth from those who attended, people now acquire it chiefly through the print and electronic media." While agreeing that, "[d]espite the history of criminal trials being presumptively open since long before the Constitution, ... neither the Constitution nor the Bill of Rights contains any provision which by its terms guarantees the public the right to attend criminal trials," the Chief Justice stated that "there remains the question whether, absent an explicit provision, the Constitution [nonetheless] affords protection against exclusion of the public from criminal trials." In answering that question affirmatively he wrote:

"The First Amendment, in conjunction with the Fourteenth, prohibits governments from 'abridging the freedom of speech, or of the press; or the right of the people peaceably to assemble, and to petition the Government for a redress of grievances.' These expressly guaranteed freedoms share a common core purpose of assuring freedom of communication on matters relating to the functioning of government. Plainly it would be difficult to single out any aspect of government of higher concern and importance to the people than the manner in which criminal trials are conducted; as we have shown, recognition of this pervades the centuries-old history of open trials and the opinions of this Court.

"The Bill of Rights was enacted against the backdrop of the long history of trials being presumptively open. Public access to trials was then regarded as an important aspect of the process itself.... In guaranteeing freedoms such as those of speech and press, the First Amendment can [thus] be read as protecting the right of everyone to attend trials so as to give meaning to those explicit guarantees. '[T]he First Amendment goes beyond protection of the press and the self-expression of individuals to prohibit government from limiting the stock of information from which members of the public may draw.' First National Bank of Boston v. Bellotti, 435 U.S. 765, 783 (1978). Free speech carries with it some freedom to listen. 'In a variety of contexts this Court has referred to a First Amendment right to "receive information and ideas." ' Kleindienst v. Mandel, 408 U.S. 753, 762 (1972). What this means in the context of trials is that the First Amendment guarantees of speech and press, standing alone, prohibit government from summarily closing courtroom doors which had long been open to the public at the time that amendment was adopted. . . .

"It is not crucial whether we describe this right to attend criminal trials to hear, see, and communicate observations concerning them as a 'right of access,' cf. *Gannett*, supra, at 397 (Powell, J., concurring); Saxbe v. Washington Post Co., 417 U.S. 843 (1974); Pell v. Procunier, 417 U.S. 817 (1974), or a 'right to gather information,' for we have recognized that 'without some protection for seeking out the news, freedom of the press could be eviscerated.' Branzburg v. Hayes, 408 U.S. 665, 681 (1972). The explicit, guaranteed rights to speak and to publish concerning what takes place at a trial would lose much meaning if access to observe the trial could, as it was here, be foreclosed arbitrarily.

"The right of access to places traditionally open to the public, as criminal trials have long been, may be seen as assured by the amalgam of the First Amendment guarantees of speech and press; and their affinity to the right of assembly is not without relevance. From the outset, the right of assembly was regarded not only as an independent right but also as a catalyst to augment the free exercise of the other First Amendment rights with which it was deliberately linked by the draftsmen. . . . Subject to the traditional time, place, and manner restrictions, see, e.g., Cox v. New Hampshire, 312 U.S. 569 (1941); see also Cox v. Louisiana, 379 U.S. 559, 560-564 (1965), streets, sidewalks, and parks are places traditionally open, where First Amendment rights may be exercised, see Hague v. C.I.O., 307 U.S. 496, 515 (1939) (opinion of Roberts, J.); a trial courtroom also is a public place where the people generally — and representatives of the media — have a right to be present, and where their presence historically has been thought to enhance the integrity and quality of what takes place. . . .

"The State argues that the Constitution nowhere spells out a guarantee for the right of the public to attend trials, and that accordingly no such right is protected. The possibility that such a contention could be made did not escape the notice of the Constitution's draftsmen; they were concerned that some important rights might be thought disparaged because not specifically guaranteed. It was even argued that because of this danger no Bill of Rights should be adopted. . . .

"But arguments such as the State makes have not precluded recognition of important rights not enumerated. Notwithstanding the appropriate caution against reading into the Constitution rights not explicitly defined, the

Court has acknowledged that certain unarticulated rights are implicit in enumerated guarantees. For example, the rights of association and of privacy, the right to be presumed innocent and the right to be judged by a standard of proof beyond a reasonable doubt in a criminal trial, as well as the right to travel, appear nowhere in the Constitution or Bill of Rights. Yet these important but unarticulated rights have nonetheless been found to share constitutional protection in common with explicit guarantees. The concerns expressed by Madison and others have thus been resolved; fundamental rights, even though not expressly guaranteed, have been recognized by the Court as indispensable to the enjoyment of rights explicitly defined.

"We hold that the right to attend criminal trials is implicit in the guarantees of the First Amendment; without the freedom to attend such trials, which people have exercised for centuries, important aspects of freedom of speech and 'of the press could be eviscerated.' *Branzburg*, supra, at 681."

Concluding, Chief Justice Burger stated: "In contrast to the pretrial proceeding dealt with in *Gannett*, . . . there exist in the context of the trial itself various tested alternatives to satisfy the constitutional demands of fairness," citing, e.g., Sheppard v. Maxwell. Since, "[a]bsent an overriding interest articulated in findings, the trial of a criminal case must be open to the public," the decision below was reversed.

Justice White concurred, noting briefly that four justices had dissented in *Gannett* on the basis of the "First Amendment issue . . . here . . . addressed." Justice Stevens also concurred, stating:

"This is a watershed case. Until today the Court has accorded virtually absolute protection to the dissemination of information or ideas, but never before has it squarely held that the acquisition of newsworthy matter is entitled to any constitutional protection whatsoever. An additional word of emphasis is therefore appropriate.

"Twice before, the Court has implied that any governmental restriction on access to information, no matter how severe and no matter how unjustified, would be constitutionally acceptable so long as it did not single out the press for special disabilities not applicable to the public at large, [citing Saxbe v. Washington Post Co. and Houchins v. KQED, Inc.]. Today, however, for the first time, the Court unequivocally holds that an arbitrary interference with access to important information is an abridgment of the freedoms of speech and of the press protected by the First Amendment.

"It is somewhat ironic that the Court should find more reason to recognize a right of access today than it did in *Houchins*. For *Houchins* involved the plight of a segment of society least able to protect itself, an attack on a longstanding policy of concealment, and an absence of any legitimate justification for abridging public access to information about how government operates. In this case we are protecting the interests of the most powerful voices in the community, we are concerned with an almost unique exception to an established tradition of openness in the conduct of criminal trials, and it is likely that the closure order was motivated by the judge's desire to protect the individual defendant from the burden of a fourth criminal trial.

"In any event, ... I agree that the First Amendment protects the public and the press from abridgment of their rights of access to information about the operation of their government, including the Judicial Branch; given the total absence of any record justification for the closure order entered in this case, that order violated the First Amendment."

Justice Brennan, joined by Justice Marshall, wrote a lengthy, separate concurring opinion, discussing a number of decisions dealing with the scope and limitations on the "First Amendment right to gather information," along with the historical background of open trials. Concluding, he wrote:

"As previously noted, resolution of First Amendment public access claims in individual cases must be strongly influenced by the weight of historical practice and by an assessment of the specific structural value of public access in the circumstances. With regard to the case at hand, our ingrained tradition of public trials and the importance of public access to the broader purposes of the trial process, tip the balance strongly toward the rule that trials be open. What countervailing interests might be sufficiently compelling to reverse this presumption of openness need not concern us now, for the statute at stake here authorizes trial closures at the unfettered discretion of the judge and parties."

Justice Stewart also concurred separately, stating:

"Whatever the ultimate answer to that question may be with respect to pretrial suppression hearings in criminal cases, the First and Fourteenth Amendments clearly give the press and the public a right of access to trials themselves, civil as well as criminal. ... [I]t has for centuries been a basic presupposition of the Anglo-American legal system that trials shall be public trials. ... With us, a trial is by very definition a proceeding open to the press and to the public.

"In conspicuous contrast to a military base, Greer v. Spock, 424 U.S. 828; a jail, Adderley v. Florida, 385 U.S. 39; or a prison, Pell v. Procunier, 417 U.S. 817, a trial courtroom is a public place. Even more than city streets, sidewalks, and parks as areas of traditional First Amendment activity, e.g., Shuttleworth v. Birmingham, 394 U.S. 147, a trial courtroom is a place where representatives of the press and of the public are not only free to be, but where their presence serves to assure the integrity of what goes on.

"But this does not mean that the First Amendment right of members of the public and representatives of the press to attend civil and criminal trials is absolute. Just as a legislature may impose reasonable time, place and manner restrictions upon the exercise of First Amendment freedoms, so may a trial judge impose reasonable limitations upon the unrestricted occupation of a courtroom by representatives of the press and members of the public. Cf. Sheppard v. Maxwell, 384 U.S. 333. Much more than a city street, a trial courtroom must be a quiet and orderly place. Compare Kovacs v. Cooper, 336 U.S. 77 with Illinois v. Allen, 397 U.S. 337 and Estes v. Texas, 381 U.S. 532. Moreover, every courtroom has a finite physical capacity, and there may be occasions when not all who wish to attend a trial may do so. And while there exist many alternative ways to satisfy the constitutional demands of a fair trial, those demands may also sometimes justify limitations upon the unrestricted presence of spectators in the courtroom.

"Since in the present case the trial judge appears to have given no recognition to the right of representatives of the press and members of the public to be present at the Virginia murder trial over which he was presiding, the judgment under review must be reversed."

Justice Blackmun, a dissenter in *Gannett*, similarly concurred, stating that it was "gratifying ... to see the Court now looking to and relying upon legal history in determining the fundamental public character of the criminal trial, ... [and] to see the Court wash away at least some of the graffiti that marred the prevailing opinions in *Gannett*." Continuing, he wrote:

"The Court's ultimate ruling in *Gannett*, with such clarification as is provided by the opinions in this case today, apparently is now to the effect that there is no *Sixth* Amendment right on the part of the public — or the press — to an open hearing on a motion to suppress. I, of course, continue to believe that *Gannett* was in error, both in its interpretation of the Sixth Amendment generally, and in its application to the suppression hearing, for I remain convinced that the right to a public trial is to be found where the Constitution explicitly placed it — in the Sixth Amendment.

"The Court, however, has eschewed the Sixth Amendment route. The plurality turns to other possible constitutional sources and invokes a veritable potpourri of them — the speech clause of the First Amendment, the press clause, the assembly clause, the Ninth Amendment, and a cluster of penumbral guarantees recognized in past decisions. This course is troublesome, but it is the route that has been selected and, at least for now, we must live with it. . . . [U]ncertainty marks the nature — and strictness — of the standard of closure the Court adopts, [referring to the varying approaches taken by different justices]. . . .

"Having said all this, and with the Sixth Amendment set to one side in this case, I am driven to conclude, as a secondary position, that the First Amendment must provide some measure of protection for public access to the trial. The opinion in partial dissent in *Gannett* explained that the public has an intense need and a deserved right to know about the administration of justice in general; about the prosecution of local crimes in particular; about the conduct of the judge, the prosecutor, defense counsel, police officers, other public servants, and all the actors in the judicial arena; and about the trial itself. It is clear and obvious to me, on the approach the Court has chosen to take, that, by closing this criminal trial, the trial judge abridged these First Amendment interests of the public."

Justice Rehnquist was the lone dissenter; Justice Powell did not participate. Rehnquist's view, in substance, was that neither "the First or Sixth Amendments, as made applicable to the States by the Fourteenth, require that a State's reasons for denying public access to a trial, where both the prosecuting attorney and the defendant have consented to an order of closure approved by the judge, are subject to any additional constitutional review at our hands." He then proceeded to discuss considerations of federalism which, in his view, argued against the federal judiciary's oversight of state court systems with respect to the matter at issue.

Page 1333. Add as a new Note 5:

The Privacy Protection Act of 1980 (P.L. 96-440) was enacted as a congressional reaction to the *Zurcher* decision and, in particular, reflects the concerns expressed in Justice Stewart's dissent in that case. The Act makes it "unlawful for a government officer or employee, in connection with the investigation or prosecution of a criminal offense, to search for or seize any work product materials possessed by a person reasonably believed to have a purpose to disseminate to a public newspaper, book, broadcast, or other similar form of public communication, in or affecting interstate commerce." The Act goes on to also make it unlawful for a government officer or employee to "search for or seize documentary materials, possessed by a person in connection with a purpose to disseminate to the public a newspaper or other similar form of public communication ... [unless] there is probable cause to believe that the person possessing such materials has committed or is committing the criminal offense to which the materials relate." Assuming the legitimacy of Congress's concerns, is this an appropriate use of the commerce power? The Act leaves enforcement of its provisions to the persons aggrieved in the form of a civil law suit, but makes this civil action subject to a complete defense of an officer's "reasonable good faith."

Page 1340. Add to the footnoted material:

Frakt, Defamation Since Gertz v. Robert Welch Inc.: The Emerging Common Law, 10 Rut.-Cam. L. Rev. 519 (1978); Sowle, Defamation and the Case for a Constitutional Privilege of Fair Report, 54 N.Y.U.L. Rev. 469 (1979).

Page 1364. At the end of the carryover footnoted material add:

Grunes, Obscenity Law and the Justices: Reversing Policy of the Supreme Court, 9 Seton Hall L. Rev. 403 (1978).

Page 1396. At the end of Note 1 add:

Schauer, Speech and "Speech" — Obscenity and "Obscenity": An Exercise in the Interpretation of Constitutional Language, 67 Geo. L. Rev. 899 (1979)

Page 1399. At the end of Note 6 add:

Cf. Cooper v. Mitchell Brothers' Santa Ana Theater, — U.S. — , 102 S. Ct. 172, — L. Ed. 2d — (1981), where the Court held in a per curiam decision that, in a public nuisance abatement action brought against a motion picture theater, "while a state may require proof beyond a reasonable doubt in an obscenity case, that choice is solely a matter of state law. The First and Fourteenth Amendments do not require such a standard." Justice Brennan, joined by Justice Marshall, filed a dissent, essentially adhering to their view that a "state may not constitutionally suppress sexually oriented films. . . ." Justice Stevens dissented separately, stating that the Court should follow its traditional practice of avoiding unnecessary and premature adjudication of constitutional questions.

Page 1402. At the end of Note 2 add:

For resolution of a case involving a zoning ordinance designed to prohibit all forms of live entertainment, see Schad v. Borough of Mount Ephraim, 452 U.S. 61, 101 S. Ct. 2176, 68 L. Ed. 2d 671 (1981). Justice White, writing for the Court, framed the constitutional question: "[Whether] . . . the imposition of criminal penalties under an ordinance prohibiting all live entertainment, including nonobscene nude dancing, violate[s] [the appellants'] rights of free expression guaranteed by the First and Fourteenth Amendments. . . ." White continued: "By excluding live entertainment throughout the Borough, the Mount Ephraim ordinance prohibits a wide range of expression that has long been held to be within the protections of the First and Fourteenth Amendments. Entertainment as well as political and ideological speech, is protected; motion pictures, programs broadcast by radio and television and live entertainment such as musical and dramatic works, fall within the First Amendment guarantees. . . . [N]or may live entertainment be prohibited solely because it displays the nude human figure. 'Nudity alone' does not place otherwise protected material outside the mantle of the First Amendment . . . and nude dancing is not without its First Amendment protection from official regulation. . . . Because the appellants' claims are rooted in the First Amendment, they are entitled to rely on the impact of the ordinance on the expressive activities of others as well as their own. 'Because overbroad laws, like vague ones, deter privileged activities, our cases firmly establish appellants' standing to raise an overbreadth challenge.' Grayned v. City of Rockford, 408 U.S. 104, 114 (1972)."

Further, Justice White wrote: "The power of local governments to zone and control land use is undoubtedly broad and its proper exercise is an essential aspect of achieving a satisfactory quality of life in both urban and rural communities. But the zoning power is not infinite and unchallengable; it 'must be exercised within constitutional limits,' Moore v. City of East Cleveland, 431 U.S. 494, 514 (1977). . . . [W]hen a zoning ordinance infringes upon a protected liberty, it must be narrowly drawn and must further a substantial governmental interest. . . . Because the ordinance challenged in this case significantly limits communicative activity within the Borough, we must scrutinize both the interest advanced by the Borough to justify the limitation . . . and the means chosen to further those interests."

Justice White next distinguished Young v. American Mini Theatres Inc., 427 U.S. 50 (1976), stating: "Although [this] Court there stated that a zoning ordinance is not invalid merely because it regulates activity protected under the First Amendment, it emphasized that the challenged restriction on the location of adult movie theatres imposed a minimal burden on protected speech. . . . The restriction did not affect the number of adult movie theatres that could operate in the city; it merely dispersed them. The Court did not imply that a municipality could ban all adult theatres — much less all live entertainment or all nude dancing — from its commercial districts citywide." Concluding with a discussion of the overbreadth challenge, Justice White stated: "Mount Ephraim contends that it may selectively exclude commercial live entertainment from the broad range of commercial uses permitted in the Borough for reasons normally associated with live entertainment, such as parking, trash, police protection, and medical facilities. . . . [Admittedly,] [i]t may be that some forms of live entertainment would create problems that are not associated with the commercial uses presently permitted in Mount Ephraim. Yet this ordinance is not narrowly drawn to respond to what might be the distinctive problems arising from certain types of live entertainment, and it is not clear that a more selective approach would fail to address those unique problems if any there are. The Borough has not established that its interests could not be met by restrictions that are less intrusive on protected forms of expression."

Justices Blackmun and Stevens concurred separately.

Chief Justice Burger, joined by Justice Rehnquist, dissented, stating: "The residents of this small enclave chose to maintain their town as a placid, 'bedroom' community of a few thousand people. To that end, they passed an admittedly broad regulation prohibiting certain forms of entertainment. Because I believe that a community of people are — within limits — masters of their own environment, I would hold that, as applied, the ordinance is valid. . . . An overconcern about the draftsmanship and overbreadth should not be allowed to obscure the central question before us. It is clear that, in passing the statute challenged here, the citizens of the Borough of Mount Ephraim meant only to preserve the basic character of their community. It is just as clear that, by thrusting its live nude dancing shows on this community, the appellant alters and damages that community over its objections. As applied in this case, therefore, the statute speaks directly and unequivocally. It may be that, as applied in some other case, this statute would violate the First Amendment, but since such a case is not before us, we should not decide it.... [S]ome of the concurring views exhibit an understandable discomfort with the idea of denying this small residential enclave the power to keep this kind of show business from its very doorsteps. The Borough of Mount Ephraim has not attempted to suppress the point of view of anyone or to stifle any category of ideas. To say that there is a First Amendment right to impose every form of expression on every community, including the kind of 'expression' involved here, is sheer nonsense. To enshrine such a notion in the Constitution ignores fundamental values that the Constitution ought to protect. To invoke the First Amendment to protect the activity involved in this case trivializes and demeans that great Amendment."

Page 1427. At the end of Note 3 add:

The criteria developed in Elrod v. Burns were applied in Branti v. Finkel, 445 U.S. 507, 100 S. Ct. 1287, 63 L. Ed. 2d 574 (1980), where the Court held that assistant public defenders who are satisfactorily performing their jobs cannot be discharged solely because of their political affiliation or beliefs. Relying heavily on Perry v. Sindermann, the Court concluded that the practice had the effect of imposing an unconstitutional condition on the exercise of First Amendment rights, in the context of public employment. While "party affiliation may be an acceptable requirement for some types of government employment," the burden was on the state to show that a particular employee's political beliefs would interfere with the discharge of his public duties and that his continued employment was inconsistent with an overriding interest of vital importance involving governmental effectiveness and efficiency. The inquiry should not be into whether the labels "policymaker" or "confidential" fit the public office in question, but rather whether it can be convincingly shown that party affiliation is an appropriate requirement for satisfactory performance of the particular job. Since, as to public defenders, it was manifest that individual clients' needs and not partisan politics took priority, the Court concluded that the state had not only failed to carry its burden but that making office-holding dependent on partisan political considerations would be likely to undermine effective performance in office. Justices Stewart, Powell, and Rehnquist dissented.

Page 1428. At the end of Note 5 add:

Cf. National Labor Relations Board v. Yeshiva University, 444 U.S. 672, 100 S. Ct. 856, 63 L. Ed. 2d 115 (1980), where the Court, though implying no restrictions on academic freedom, in a five-to-four decision held that the University's full-time faculty members are managerial employees, who, as a result, are excluded from the coverage of the National Labor Relations Act.

Chapter Eleven

Religious Liberty Under the First Amendment

Page 1466. Add to the first paragraph of the footnoted material:

Abraham, The Status of the First Amendment's Religious Clauses: Some Reflections on Lines and Limits, 22 J. Church & St. 215 (1980).

Page 1488: Add to the footnoted material:

Merel, The Protection of Individual Choice: A Consistent Understanding of Religion Under the First Amendment, 45 U. Chi. L. Rev. 805 (1978); Pfeffer, Freedom and-or Separation: The Constitutional Dilemma of the First Amendment, 64 Minn. L. Rev. 561 (1980).

Page 1471. At the end of the first full paragraph add:

In Larson v. Valente, — U.S. — , 102 S. Ct. 1673, — L. Ed. 2d — (1982), the appellee Unification Church brought suit in federal court, seeking to have Minnesota's Charitable Contribution Act declared unconstitutional on its face and as applied. The Minnesota act provided that only those religious organizations that receive more than half of their contributions from members or affiliated organizations are exempt from the act's reporting and registration requirements. The district court held that the "overbreadth" doctrine was sufficient to support appellees' standing and further held that the application of the act to religious organizations violated the establishment clause. The court of appeals affirmed. The Supreme Court held that the appellees had standing, finding the appellees' strong demonstration that the church is a religion sufficient to establish standing, thus avoiding the question whether the appellees had standing based upon the "overbreadth" challenge. Addressing the merits, the Court stated: "The clearest command of the Establishment Clause is that one religious denomination cannot be officially preferred over another. . . . This constitutional prohibition of denominational preference is inextricably connected with the continuing vitality of the Free Exercise Clause. . . . The fifty percent rule of [the Minnesota law] clearly grants denominational preferences of the sort consistently and firmly deprecated in our precedents. Consequently, that rule must be invalidated unless it is justified by a compelling governmental interest." After further analysis, Justice Brennan, writing for the Court, concluded that the 50 percent rule was not "closely fitted" to further a "compelling governmental interest." Accordingly, the Court held that appellees cannot be compelled to register and report under the act.

Page 1499. Add to the footnoted material:

Swanson, Accommodating Religion in the Public Schools, 59 Neb. L. Rev. 425 (1980).

Page 1500. At the end of Note 2 add:

Cf. Stone v. Graham, 449 U.S. 39, 101 S. Ct. 904, 66 L. Ed. 2d 199 (1980), where the Court struck down a Kentucky statute which required the posting of the Ten Commandments in school rooms. In a per curiam decision the Court declared that such posting served no secular purpose and therefore violated the establishment clause, applying the test of Lemon v. Kurtzman, Casebook p.1515, and relying on *Schempp* and *Engel*. Justice Rehnquist dissented, stating that "[t]he fact that the asserted secular purpose may overlap with what some may see as a religious objective does not render it unconstitutional." Justice Stewart dissented separately, essentially agreeing with Justice Rehnquist.

Page 1502. At the end of Note 5 add:

In Harris v. McRae, 448 U.S. 297, 100 S. Ct. 2671, 65 L. Ed. 2d 784 (1980), infra in this Supplement, addition to Casebook p.1591, the Court rejected an establishment clause attack on the so-called Hyde Amendment to the Social Security Act's Medicaid program provisions. Appellees argued that the Hyde Amendment, in prohibiting federal financial support for abortions except in certain specified circumstances, "violate[d] the Establishment Clause because it incorporates into law the doctrines of the Roman Catholic Church concerning the sinfulness of abortion and the time at which life commences." Applying the three-factor test of *Lemon* and its progeny, the Court stated that "[t]he Hyde Amendment ... is as much a reflection of 'traditionalist' [attitudes]. toward abortion, as it is an embodiment of the virtues of any particular religion."

Page 1515. At the end of Note 1 add:

Cf. St. Martin Evangelical Lutheran Church v. South Dakota, 451 U.S. 772, 101 S. Ct. 2142, 68 L. Ed. 2d 612 (1981), where the Court held that the petitioner's school, which is not a separate legal entity from the church, can claim an exemption from unemployment compensation taxes for school employees pursuant to the federal unemployment tax act and South Dakota's complementary statutes.

Page 1515. At the end of Note 2 add:

But see Valley Forge Christian College v. Americans United for Separation of Church and State, supra in this Supplement, addition to Casebook p.54, in which the Court denied respondents standing to bring a federal taxpayer suit alleging a violation of the establishment clause. The suit revolved around the Federal Property and Administrative Services Act of 1949, which empowered the Secretary of Education to convey "surplus" government property to public or private entities.

Page 1520. Add to the footnoted material:

Note, General Laws, Neutral Principles, and the Free Exercise Clause, 33 Vand. L. Rev. 149 (1980).

Page 1527. At the end of the carryover paragraph add:

In Widmar v. Vincent, — U.S. — , 102 S. Ct. 269, — L. Ed. 2d — (1981), the Court characterized the University of Missouri's policy of prohibiting the use of University buildings or grounds for religious worship or teaching as a First Amendment issue involving an improper content regulation. Although the Court recognized that the University's interest in complying with the establishment clause may be deemed compelling, it found that an "equal access" policy would not offend the establishment clause as tested by the three-pronged test enunciated in Lemon v. Kurtzman. In dissent, Justice White found the Court's reliance on the First Amendment for resolution of the case ill-founded, pointing out that the religion clauses would, in this context, be "emptied of any independent meaning in circumstances in which religious practice took the form of speech."

Page 1532. At the end of Note 5 add:

Cf. Justice White's concurring opinion (joined by Justice Rehnquist) in McKeesport Area School District v. Pennsylvania Department of Education, 446 U.S. 970, 100 S. Ct. 2953, 64 L. Ed. 2d 831 (1980), discussing the pertinent cases at length.

In Committee for Public Education and Religious Liberty v. Regan, 444 U.S. 646, 100 S. Ct. 840, 63 L. Ed. 2d 94 (1980), a majority of the Court upheld a New York statute providing for payment to nonpublic schools of the costs incurred by them in complying with certain state-mandated testing, reporting, and recordkeeping requirements. Justice White's majority opinion distinguished the Levitt case on the grounds that the new statutory scheme "does not reimburse nonpublic schools for the preparation, administration, or grading of teacher-prepared tests." Unlike the earlier version invalidated in *Levitt*, it "provides a means by which payment of state funds are audited, thus ensuring that only the actual costs incurred in providing the covered secular services are reimbursed out of state funds." Relying in considerable part on Wolman v. Walter, the Court concluded that the New York reimbursement scheme satisfied the three-pronged test delineated in Lemon v. Kurtzman and similar establishment clause cases. The law's purpose was clearly secular, it contained ample safeguards against excessive or misdirected reimbursement, and it nonetheless avoided any undue entanglement between government and religion. Meek v. Pittenger, relied on by dissenting Justices Blackmun, Brennan, and Marshall, was read narrowly and viewed as distinguishable by the majority. The dissenters regarded the scheme as having an impermissible primary effect of advancing religion while at the same time fostering excessive government entanglement with sectarian affairs. *Wolman* had been misconstrued by the majority, they suggested, and the plan, despite the obvious differences, suffered from the same fatal defects as the one invalidated in *Levitt*. Justice Stevens also dissented, expressing concern about "largely ad hoc decisions about what payments may or may not be constitutionally made [by government] to nonpublic [and sectarian] schools" and urging "that the entire enterprise of trying to justify various types of subsidies to [such] schools be abandoned," and instead that all of them be invalidated as violative of the establishment clause.

Page 1542. Add to the footnoted material:

Clark, Comments on Some Policies Underlying the Constitutional Law of Religious Freedom, 64 Minn. L. Rev. 453 (1980).

Page 1543. At the end of the first paragraph of Note 2 add:

For a recent application of free exercise principles, see Thomas v. Review Board of Indiana Employment Security Division, 450 U.S. 707, 101 S. Ct. 1425, 67 L. Ed. 2d 624 (1981), where Chief Justice Burger, writing for the Court, applied the reasoning adopted earlier in Sherbert v. Verner to award unemployment compensation benefits to the petitioner.

Justice Rehnquist, dissenting alone, expressed a concern over the Court's expansive reading of the religion clauses, stating: "The Court correctly acknowledges that there is a 'tension' between the Free Exercise and Establishment Clauses of the First Amendment of the United States Constitution. Although the relationship of the two clauses has been the subject of much commentary, the 'tension' is of fairly recent vintage, unknown at the time of the framing and adoption of the First Amendment. The causes of the tension, it seems to me, are three-fold. First, the growth of the social welfare legislation during the latter half of the 20th century has greatly magnified the potential for conflict between the two clauses, since such legislation touches the individual at so many points in his life. Second, the decision by this Court that the First Amendment was 'incorporated' into the Fourteenth Amendment and thereby made applicable against the States . . . [is another cause]. The third, and perhaps most important, cause of the tension is [this Court's] overly expansive interpretation of both clauses.

"None of these developments could have been foreseen by those who framed and adopted the First Amendment. It was adopted well before the growth of much social welfare legislation and at a time when the Federal Government was in a real sense considered a government of limited delegated powers. Indeed, the principal argument against adopting the Constitution *without* a 'Bill of Rights' was not that such an enactment would be *undesirable*, but that it was unnecessary because the limited nature of the Federal Government applied only to the Federal Government, not the government of the states, [citing Barron v. Baltimore]. The Framers could hardly anticipate *Barron* being superseded by the 'selective incorporation' doctrine adopted by the Court, a decision which greatly expanded the number of statutes which would be subject to challenge under the First Amendment.

"In summary, my difficulty with today's decision is that it reads the Free Exercise Clause too broadly and it fails to squarely acknowledge that such a reading conflicts with many of our Establishment Clause cases. As such, the decision simply exacerbates the 'tension' between the two clauses. If the Court were to construe the Free Exercise Clause as it did in *Braunfeld* and the Establishment Clause as Justice Stewart did in *Schempp*, the circumstances in which there would be a conflict between the two clauses would be far and few between. Although I heartily agree with the Court's tacit abandonment of much of our rhetoric about the Establishment Clause, I regret that the Court cannot see its way clear to restore what was surely intended to have been a greater degree of flexibility to the Federal and State governments in legislating consistently with the Free Exercise Clause."

Page 1547. At the end of Note 1 add:

Note, Toward a Constitutional Definition of Religion, 91 Harv. L. Rev. 1056 (1978).

Page 1551. At the end of Note 1 add:

Whitehead & Conlan, The Establishment of the Religion of Secular Humanism and its First Amendment Implications, 10 Texas Tech. L. Rev. (1979).

Page 1559. At the end of Note 1 add:

Dealing with some questions left open by *Yoder*, the Court in United States v. Lee, – U.S. – , 102 S. Ct. 1051, – L. Ed. 2d – (1982), considered the situation of an Amish farmer who employed several other Amish to work on his farm and who refused to withhold and pay Social Security taxes on his employees' work, claiming that the payment of taxes and receipt of benefits would violate the tenets of his religious faith. After being assessed for unpaid taxes he made a payment and then instituted suit in federal district court seeking a refund, arguing that the imposition of the taxes violated his First Amendment right to free exercise of his religion. The lower court agreed with his contentions, and the government took a direct appeal from the district court under 28 U.S.C. 1252.

The Court began its examination of the case by stating that the statutory exemption from the Social Security taxes (relied on in part by the district court) applied only to self-employed individuals and not to employers or employees. Turning to the constitutional issue, the Court cited Wisconsin v. Yoder for the proposition that a state may justify some limitations on free exercise by showing that they are essential to an overriding governmental objective. Because the Social Security System serves the public interest by providing a comprehensive system of insurance with a variety of other benefits, the government's interest in assuring mandatory and continuous participation in and contribution to was declared by the Court to be "very high." The Court next cited Braunfeld v. Brown, stating that although religious beliefs can be accommodated there comes a point when an accommodation would "radically restrict the operating latitude of the legislature." In a summary statement by Chief Justice Burger, who announced the opinion of the Court, *Yoder* was distinguished. The Chief Justice wrote: "[I]t would be difficult to accommodate the comprehensive Social Security System with myriad exemptions flowing from a wide variety of religious beliefs. The obligation to pay the Social Security tax initially is not fundamentally different from the obligation to pay income taxes; the difference — in theory at least — is that the Social Security tax revenues are segregated for use only in furtherance of a statutory program. There is no principled way, however, for the purposes of this case, to distinguish between general taxes and those imposed under the Social Security Act. . . . Because the broad public interest in maintaining a sound tax system is of such a high order, religious belief in conflict with the payment of taxes affords no basis for resisting the tax. . . . Congress drew a line in . . . exempting self-employed Amish but not all Amish working for an Amish employer. The tax imposed on employees to support the Social Security System must be uniformly applicable to all, except as Congress provides explicitly otherwise."

Justice Stevens concurred separately, stating his agreement with the Court's analysis that there is "virtually no room for a 'constitutionally-required exemption' on religious grounds from a valid tax law that is entirely neutral in its application."

Chapter Twelve

Other Fundamental Rights

Page 1589. At the end of Note 2 add:

Perry, The Abortion Funding Cases: A Comment on the Supreme Court's Role in American Government, 66 Geo. L. Rev. 1191 (1978).

Page 1591. After Note 3 add:

HARRIS v. McRAE
448 U.S. 297, 100 S. Ct. 2671, 65 L. Ed. 2d 784 (1980)

[Presented for decision was the constitutionality of the so-called Hyde Amendment to Title XIX of the Social Security Act, which provides funds for the Medicaid program of federal financial assistance to states providing medical treatment for needy persons. In pertinent part the Hyde Amendment stated that none of the federal funds appropriated under the act "shall be used to perform abortions except where the life of the mother would be endangered if the fetus were carried to term ... or ... for such medical procedures necessary for victims of rape or incest when such rape or incest has been promptly reported to a law enforcement agency or public health service." P.L. 96-123, 93 Stat. 926. After a lengthy trial the district court invalidated the provision as violative of the equal protection component of the Fifth Amendment's due process clause and the free exercise clause of the First Amendment. A five-member majority reversed the decision below and upheld the challenged provision's constitutionality.

Mr. Justice STEWART delivered the opinion of the Court....

We address first the appellees' argument that the Hyde Amendment, by restricting the availability of certain medically necessary abortions under Medicaid, impinges on the "liberty" protected by the Due Process Clause as recognized in Roe v. Wade, 410 U.S. 113, and its progeny.

In the *Wade* case, this Court held unconstitutional a Texas statute making it a crime to procure or attempt an abortion except on medical advice for the purpose of saving the mother's life. The constitutional underpinning of *Wade* was a recognition that the "liberty" protected by the Due Process

Clause of the Fourteenth Amendment includes not only the freedoms explicitly mentioned in the Bill of Rights, but also a freedom of personal choice in certain matters of marriage and family life. This implicit constitutional liberty, the Court in *Wade* held, includes the freedom of a woman to decide whether to terminate a pregnancy.

But the Court in *Wade* also recognized that a State has legitimate interests during a pregnancy in both ensuring the health of the mother and protecting potential human life. These state interests ... pose a conflict with a woman's untrammeled freedom of choice. In resolving this conflict, the Court held that before the end of the first trimester of pregnancy, neither state interest is sufficiently substantial to justify any intrusion on the woman's freedom of choice. In the second trimester, the state interest in maternal health was found to be sufficiently substantial to justify regulation reasonably related to that concern. And, at viability, usually in the third trimester, the state interest in protecting the potential life of the fetus was found to justify a criminal prohibition against abortions, except where necessary for the preservation of the life or health of the mother. Thus, inasmuch as the Texas criminal statute allowed abortions only where necessary to save the life of the mother and without regard to the stage of the pregnancy, the Court held in *Wade* that the statute violated the Due Process Clause of the Fourteenth Amendment.

In Maher v. Roe, 432 U.S. 464, the Court was presented with the question whether the scope of personal constitutional freedom recognized in Roe v. Wade included an entitlement to Medicaid payments for abortions that are not medically necessary. At issue in *Maher* was a Connecticut welfare regulation under which Medicaid recipients received payments for medical services incident to childbirth, but not for medical services incident to nontherapeutic abortions. The District Court held that the regulation violated the Equal Protection Clause of the Fourteenth Amendment because the unequal subsidization of childbirth and abortion impinged on the "fundamental right to abortion" recognized in *Wade* and its progeny.

It was the view of this Court that "the District Court misconceived the nature and scope of the fundamental right recognized in *Roe*." 432 U.S., at 471. The doctrine of Roe v. Wade, the Court held in *Maher*, "protects the woman from unduly burdensome interference with her freedom to decide whether to terminate her pregnancy," id., at 473-474, such as the severe criminal sanctions at issue in Roe v. Wade, supra, or the absolute requirement of spousal consent for an abortion challenged in Planned Parenthood of Central Missouri v. Danforth, 428 U.S. 52.

But the constitutional freedom recognized in *Wade* and its progeny, the *Maher* Court explained, did not prevent Connecticut from making "a value judgment favoring childbirth over abortion, and ... implement[ing] that judgment by the allocation of public funds." Id., at 474. ...

The Court in *Maher* noted that its description of the doctrine recognized in *Wade* and its progeny signaled "no retreat" from those decisions. In explaining why the constitutional principle recognized in *Wade* and later cases — protecting a woman's freedom of choice — did not translate into a constitutional obligation of Connecticut to subsidize abortions, the Court cited the "basic difference between direct state interference with a protected activity and state encouragement of an alternative activity consonant with legislative policy. Constitutional concerns are greatest when the State attempts to impose its will by force of law; the State's power to encourage actions deemed to be in the public interest is necessarily far broader." Id., at 475-476. Thus, even though the Connecticut regulation favored childbirth over abortion by means of subsidization of one and not the other, the Court in *Maher* concluded that the regulation did not impinge on the constitutional freedom recognized in *Wade* because it imposed no governmental restriction on access to abortions.

The Hyde Amendment, like the Connecticut welfare regulation at issue in *Maher*, places no governmental obstacle in the path of a woman who chooses to terminate her pregnancy, but rather, by means of unequal subsidization of abortion and other medical services, encourages alternative activity deemed in the public interest. The present case does differ factually from *Maher* insofar as that case involved a failure to fund nontherapeutic abortions, whereas the Hyde Amendment withholds funding of certain medically necessary abortions. Accordingly, the appellees argue that because the Hyde Amendment affects a significant interest not present or asserted in *Maher* — the interest of a woman in protecting her health during pregnancy — and because that interest lies at the core of the personal constitutional freedom recognized in *Wade*, the present case is constitutionally different from *Maher*. It is the appellees' view that to the extent that the Hyde Amendment withholds funding for certain medically necessary abortions, it clearly impinges on the constitutional principle recognized in *Wade*.

It is evident that a woman's interest in protecting her health was an important theme in *Wade*. In concluding that the freedom of a woman to decide whether to terminate her pregnancy falls within the personal liberty protected by the Due Process Clause, the Court in *Wade* emphasized the fact that the woman's decision carries with it significant personal health implications — both physical and psychological. 410 U.S., at 153. In fact, although the Court in *Wade* recognized that the state interest in protecting potential life becomes sufficiently compelling in the period after fetal viability to justify an absolute criminal prohibition of nontherapeutic abortions, the Court held that even after fetal viability a State may not prohibit abortions "necessary to preserve the life or health of the mother." Id., at 164. Because even the compelling interest of the State in protecting potential life after fetal viability was held to be insufficient to outweigh a woman's decision to protect her life or health, it could be argued that the freedom of a woman to decide whether to terminate her pregnancy for health reasons does in fact lie at the core of the constitutional liberty identified in *Wade*.

But, regardless of whether the freedom of a woman to choose to terminate her pregnancy for health reasons lies at the core or the periphery of the due process liberty recognized in *Wade*, it simply does not follow that a woman's freedom of choice carries with it a constitutional entitlement to the financial resources to avail herself of the full range of protected choices. The reason why was explained in *Maher*: although government may not place obstacles in the path of a woman's exercise of her freedom of choice, it need not remove those not of its own creation. Indigency falls in the latter category. The financial constraints that restrict an indigent woman's ability to enjoy the full range of constitutionally protected freedom of choice are the product not of governmental restrictions on access to abortions, but rather of her indigency. Although Congress has opted to subsidize medically necessary services generally, but not certain medically necessary abortions, the fact remains that the Hyde Amendment leaves an indigent woman with at least the same range of choice in deciding whether to obtain a medically necessary abortion as she would have had if Congress had chosen to subsidize no health care costs at all. We are thus not persuaded that the Hyde Amendment impinges on the constitutionally protected freedom of choice recognized in *Wade*.

Although the liberty protected by the Due Process Clause affords protection against unwarranted government interference with freedom of choice in the context of certain personal decisions, it does not confer an entitlement to such funds as may be necessary to realize all the advantages of that freedom. To hold otherwise would mark a drastic change in our understanding of the Constitution. It cannot be that because government may not prohibit the use of contraceptives, Griswold v. Connecticut, 381 U.S. 479, or prevent parents from sending their child to a private school, Pierce v. Society of Sisters, 268 U.S. 510, government, therefore, has an affirmative constitutional obligation to ensure that all persons have the financial resources to obtain contraceptives or send their children to private schools. To translate the limitation on governmental power implicit in the Due Process Clause into an affirmative funding obligation would require Congress to subsidize the medically necessary abortion of an indigent woman even if Congress had not enacted a Medicaid program to subsidize other medically necessary services. Nothing in the Due Process Clause supports such an extraordinary result. Whether freedom of choice that is constitutionally protected warrants federal subsidization is a question for Congress to answer, not a matter of constitutional entitlement. Accordingly, we conclude that the Hyde Amendment does not impinge on the due process liberty recognized in *Wade*.

[The Court's discussion of appellees' argument that "the Hyde Amendment contravenes rights severed by the Religious Clauses of the First Amendment" is omitted. A summary of the reasons underlying the Court's rejection of the establishment clause argument is included supra in this Supplement, addition to Casebook p.1502. The Court did not address the free exercise clause question, concluding that "appellees lack standing to raise a free exercise challenge to the Hyde Amendment."

Continuing, Justice Stewart wrote:]

It remains to be determined whether the Hyde Amendment violates the equal protection component of the Fifth Amendment. This challenge is premised on the fact that, although federal reimbursement is available under Medicaid for medically necessary services generally, the Hyde Amendment does not permit federal reimbursement of all medically necessary abortions. The District Court held, and the appellees argue here, that this selective subsidization violates the constitutional guarantee of equal protection.

The guarantee of equal protection under the Fifth Amendment is not a source of substantive rights or liberties, but rather a right to be free from invidious discrimination in statutory classifications and other governmental activity. It is well-settled that where a statutory classification does not itself impinge on a right or liberty protected by the Constitution, the validity of classification must be sustained unless "the classification rests on grounds wholly irrelevant to the achievement of [any legitimate governmental] objective." McGowan v. Maryland, supra, 366 U.S., at 425. This presumption of constitutional validity, however, disappears if a statutory classification is predicated on criteria that are, in a constitutional sense, "suspect," the principal example of which is a classification based on race, e.g., Brown v. Board of Education, 347 U.S. 483.

For the reasons stated above, we have already concluded that the Hyde Amendment violates no constitutionally protected substantive rights. We now conclude as well that it is not predicated on a constitutionally suspect classification. In reaching this conclusion, we again draw guidance from the Court's decision in Maher v. Roe. As to whether the Connecticut welfare regulation providing funds for childbirth but not for nontherapeutic abortions discriminated against a suspect class, the Court in *Maher* observed: "An indigent woman desiring an abortion does not come within the limited category of disadvantaged classes so recognized by our cases. Nor does the fact that the impact of the regulation falls upon those who cannot pay lead to a different conclusion. In a sense, every denial of welfare to an indigent creates a wealth classification as compared to nonindigents who are able to pay for the desired goods or services. But this Court has never held that financial need alone identifies a suspect class for purposes of equal protection analysis." 432 U.S., at 471, citing San Antonio School Dist. v. Rodriguez, 411 U.S. 1, 29; Dandridge v. Williams, 397 U.S. 471. Thus, the Court in *Maher* found no basis for concluding that the Connecticut regulation was predicated on a suspect classification.

It is our view that the present case is indistinguishable from *Maher* in this respect. Here, as in *Maher*, the principal impact of the Hyde Amendment falls on the indigent. But the fact does not itself render the funding restriction constitutionally invalid, for this Court has held repeatedly that poverty, standing alone, is not a suspect classification. See, e.g., James v. Valtierra,

402 U.S. 137. That *Maher* involved the refusal to fund nontherapeutic abortions, whereas the present case involves the refusal to fund medically necessary abortions, has no bearing on the factors that render a classification "suspect" within the meaning of the constitutional guarantee of equal protection.

The remaining question then is whether the Hyde Amendment is rationally related to a legitimate governmental objective. It is the Government's position that the Hyde Amendment bears a rational relationship to its legitimate interest in protecting the potential life of the fetus. We agree.

In *Wade*, the Court recognized that the State has "an important and legitimate interest in protecting the potentiality of human life." 410 U.S., at 162. That interest was found to exist throughout a pregnancy, "grow[ing] in substantiality as the woman approaches term." Id., at 162-163. See also Beal v. Doe, 432 U.S. 438, 445-446. Moreover, in *Maher*, the Court held that Connecticut's decision to fund the costs associated with childbirth but not those associated with nontherapeutic abortions was a rational means of advancing the legitimate state interest in protecting potential life by encouraging childbirth, 432 U.S., at 478-479. See also Poelker v. Doe, 432 U.S. 519, 520-521.

It follows that the Hyde Amendment, by encouraging childbirth except in the most urgent circumstances, is rationally related to the legitimate governmental objective of protecting potential life. By subsidizing the medical expenses of indigent women who carry their pregnancies to term while not subsidizing the comparable expenses of women who undergo abortions (except those whose lives are threatened), Congress has established incentives that make childbirth a more attractive alternative than abortion for persons eligible for Medicaid. These incentives bear a direct relationship to the legitimate congressional interest in protecting potential life. Nor is it irrational that Congress has authorized federal reimbursement for medically necessary services generally, but not for certain medically necessary abortions. Abortion is inherently different from other medical procedures, because no other procedure involves the purposeful termination of a potential life. ...

Where, as here, the Congress has neither invaded a substantive constitutional right or freedom, nor enacted legislation that purposefully operates to the detriment of a suspect class, the only requirement of equal protection is that congressional action be rationally related to a legitimate governmental interest. The Hyde Amendment satisfies that standard. It is not the mission of this Court or any other to decide whether the balance of competing interests reflected in the Hyde Amendment is wise social policy. ... Rather, "when an issue involves policy choices as sensitive as those implicated [here] ..., the appropriate forum for their resolution in a democracy is the legislature." Maher v. Roe, supra, at 479.

For the reasons stated in this opinion, we hold that a State that participates in the Medicaid program is not obligated under Title XIX to continue to fund those medically necessary abortions for which federal reimbursement is unavailable under the Hyde Amendment. We further hold that the funding restrictions of the Hyde Amendment violate neither the Fifth Amendment nor the Establishment Clause of the First Amendment. . . .

[Justice White, while joining in the Court's opinion and judgment, wrote a concurring opinion, relying largely on Maher v. Roe.]

Mr. Justice BRENNAN, with whom Mr. Justice MARSHALL and Mr. Justice BLACKMUN join, dissenting. . . .

[After voicing his "continuing disagreement with the Court's mischaracterization of the nature of the fundamental right recognized in Roe v. Wade . . . , and its misconception of the manner in which that right is infringed by federal and state legislation withdrawing all funding for medically necessary abortions," he wrote:]

Roe v. Wade held that the constitutional right to personal privacy encompasses a woman's decision whether or not to terminate her pregnancy. *Roe* and its progeny established that the pregnant woman has a right to be free from state interference with her choice to have an abortion — a right which, at least prior to the end of the first trimester, absolutely prohibits any governmental regulation of that highly personal decision. The proposition for which these cases stand thus is not that the State is under an affirmative obligation to ensure access to abortions for all who may desire them; it is that the State must refrain from wielding its enormous power and influence in a manner that might burden the pregnant woman's freedom to choose whether to have an abortion. The Hyde Amendment's denial of public funds for medically necessary abortions plainly intrudes upon this constitutionally protected decision, for both by design and in effect it serves to coerce indigent pregnant women to bear children that they would otherwise elect not to have.

When viewed in the context of the Medicaid program to which it is appended, it is obvious that the Hyde Amendment is nothing less than an attempt by Congress to circumvent the dictates of the Constitution and achieve indirectly what Roe v. Wade said it could not do directly. Under Title XIX of the Social Security Act, the Federal Government reimburses participating States for virtually all medically necessary services it provides to the categorically needy. The sole limitation of any significance is the Hyde Amendment's prohibition against the use of any federal funds to pay for the costs of abortions (except where the life of the mother would be endangered if the fetus were carried to term). As my Brother Stevens persuasively demonstrates, exclusion of medically necessary abortions from Medicaid coverage cannot be justified as a cost-saving device. Rather, the Hyde Amendment is a transparent attempt by the Legislative Branch to impose the political majority's judgment of the morally acceptable and socially desirable preference on a sensitive and intimate decision that the

Constitution entrusts to the individual. Worse yet, the Hyde Amendment does not foist that majoritarian viewpoint with equal measure upon everyone in our Nation, rich and poor alike; rather, it imposes that viewpoint only upon that segment of our society which, because of its position of political powerlessness, is least able to defend its privacy rights from the encroachments of state-mandated morality. The instant legislation thus calls for more exacting judicial review than in most other cases.... Though it may not be this Court's mission "to decide whether the balance of competing interests reflected in the Hyde Amendment is wise social policy," it most assuredly is our responsibility to vindicate the pregnant woman's constitutional right to decide whether to bear children free from governmental intrusion.

Moreover, it is clear that the Hyde Amendment not only was designed to inhibit, but does in fact inhibit the woman's freedom to choose abortion over childbirth.... In every pregnancy, one of ... two courses of treatment is medically necessary, and the poverty-stricken woman depends on the Medicaid Act to pay for the expenses associated with that procedure. But under the Hyde Amendment, the Government will fund only those procedures incidental to childbirth. By thus injecting coercive financial incentives favoring childbirth into a decision that is constitutionally guaranteed to be free from governmental intrusion, the Hyde Amendment deprives the indigent woman of her freedom to choose abortion over maternity, thereby impinging on the due process liberty right recognized in Roe v. Wade....

The fundamental flaw in the Court's due process analysis, then, is its failure to acknowledge that the discriminatory distribution of the benefits of governmental largesse can discourage the exercise of fundamental liberties just as effectively as can an outright denial of those rights through criminal and regulatory sanctions. Implicit in the Court's reasoning is the notion that as long as the government is not obligated to provide its citizens with certain benefits or privileges, it may condition the grant of such benefits on the recipient's relinquishment of his constitutional rights.

It would belabor the obvious to expound at any great length on the illegitimacy of a state policy that interferes with the exercise of fundamental rights through the selective bestowal of governmental favors. It suffices to note that we have heretofore never hesitated to invalidate any scheme of granting or withholding financial benefits that incidentally or intentionally burdens one manner of exercising a constitutionally protected choice. To take but one example of many, Sherbert v. Verner, 374 U.S. 398 (1963), involved a South Carolina unemployment insurance statute that required recipients to accept suitable employment when offered, even if the grounds for refusal stemmed from religious convictions. Even though the recipients possessed no entitlement to compensation, the Court held that the State could not cancel the benefits of a Seventh Day Adventist who had refused a job requiring her to work on Saturdays....

The Medicaid program cannot be distinguished from these other statutory schemes that unconstitutionally burdened fundamental rights. Here, as in *Sherbert*, the government withholds financial benefits in a manner that discourages the exercise of a due process liberty: The indigent woman who chooses to assert her constitutional right to have an abortion can do so only on pain of sacrificing health care benefits to which she would otherwise be entitled. . . .

Mr. Justice MARSHALL, dissenting.

. . . Under the Hyde Amendment, federal funding is denied for abortions that are medically necessary and that are necessary to avert severe and permanent damage to the health of the mother. The Court's opinion studiously avoids recognizing the undeniable fact that for women eligible for Medicaid — poor women — denial of a Medicaid-funded abortion is equivalent to denial of legal abortion altogether. By definition, these women do not have the money to pay for an abortion themselves. If abortion is medically necessary and a funded abortion is unavailable, they must resort to back-alley butchers, attempt to induce an abortion themselves by crude and dangerous methods, or suffer the serious medical consequences of attempting to carry the fetus to term. Because legal abortion is not a realistic option for such women, the predictable result of the Hyde Amendment will be a significant increase in the number of poor women who will die or suffer significant health damage because of an inability to procure necessary medical services.

The legislation before us is the product of an effort to deny to the poor the constitutional right recognized in Roe v. Wade, 410 U.S. 113 (1973), even though the cost may be serious and long-lasting health damage. As my Brother Stevens has demonstrated, . . . the premise underlying the Hyde Amendment was repudiated in Roe v. Wade, where the Court made clear that the state interest in protecting fetal life cannot justify jeopardizing the life or health of the mother. The denial of Medicaid benefits to individuals who meet all the statutory criteria for eligibility, solely because the treatment that is medically necessary involves the exercise of the fundamental right to choose abortion, is a form of discrimination repugnant to the equal protection of the laws guaranteed by the Constitution. The Court's decision today marks a retreat from Roe v. Wade and represents a cruel blow to the most powerless members of our society. . . .

The Court resolves the equal protection issue in this case through a relentlessly formalistic catechism. Adhering to its "two-tiered" approach to equal protection, the Court first decides that so-called strict scrutiny is not required because the Hyde Amendment does not violate the Due Process Clause and is not predicated on a constitutionally suspect classification. . . .

I continue to believe that the rigid "two-tiered" approach is inappropriate and that the Constitution requires a more exacting standard of review than mere rationality in cases such as this one. Further, in my judgment the Hyde Amendment cannot pass constitutional muster even under the rational-basis standard of review. . . .

The Court treats this case as though it were controlled by *Maher*. To the contrary, this case is the mirror image of *Maher*. The result in *Maher* turned on the fact that the legislation there under consideration discouraged only nontherapeutic, or medically unnecessary, abortions. In the Court's view, denial of Medicaid funding for nontherapeutic abortions was not a denial of equal protection because Medicaid funds were available only for medically necessary procedures. Thus the plaintiffs were seeking benefits which were not available to others similarly situated. I continue to believe that *Maher* was wrongly decided. But it is apparent that while the plaintiffs in *Maher* were seeking a benefit not available to others similarly situated, respondents are protesting their exclusion from a benefit that is available to all others similarly situated. This, it need hardly be said, is a crucial difference for equal protection purposes. . . .

The consequences of today's opinion — consequences to which the Court seems oblivious — are not difficult to predict. Pregnant women denied the funding necessary to procure abortions will be restricted to two alternatives. First, they can carry the fetus to term — even though that route may result in severe injury or death to the mother, the fetus, or both. If that course appears intolerable, they can resort to self-induced abortions or attempt to obtain illegal abortions — not because bearing a child would be inconvenient, but because it is necessary in order to protect their health. The result will not be to protect what the Court describes as "the legitimate governmental objective of protecting potential life," but to ensure the destruction of both fetal and maternal life. . . .

Ultimately, the result reached today may be traced to the Court's unwillingness to apply the constraints of the Constitution to decisions involving the expenditure of governmental funds. In today's decision, as in Maher v. Roe, the Court suggests that a withholding of funding imposes no real obstacle to a woman deciding whether to exercise her constitutionally protected procreative choice, even though the government is prepared to fund all other medically necessary expenses, including the expenses of childbirth. The Court perceives this result as simply a distinction between a "limitation on governmental power" and "an affirmative funding obligation." For a poor person attempting to exercise her "right" to freedom of choice, the difference is imperceptible. As my Brother Brennan has shown . . . the differential distribution of incentives — which the Court concedes is present here — can have precisely the same effect as an outright prohibition. It is no more sufficient an answer here than it was in Roe v. Wade to say "the appropriate forum" for the resolution of sensitive policy choices is the legislature.

In this case, the Federal Government has taken upon itself the burden of financing practically all medically necessary expenditures. One category of medically necessary expenditure has been singled out for exclusion, and the sole basis for the exclusion is a premise repudiated for purposes of constitutional law in Roe v. Wade. The consequence is a devastating impact on the lives and health of poor women. I do not believe that a Constitution committed to the equal protection of the laws can tolerate this result....

Mr. Justice BLACKMUN [the author of the Court's opinion in *Roe*] dissenting....

[What] I said in dissent in Beal v. Doe, 432 U.S. 438, 462 (1977), and its two companion cases, Maher v. Roe, 432 U.S. 464 (1977), and Poelker v. Doe, 432 U.S. 519 (1977), continues for me to be equally pertinent and equally applicable in these Hyde Amendment cases. There is "condescension" in the Court's holding "that she may go elsewhere for her abortion"; this is "disingenuous and alarming"; the Government "punitively impresses upon a needy minority its own concepts of the socially desirable, the publicly acceptable, and the morally sound"; the "financial argument, of course, is specious"; there truly is "another world 'out there,' the existence of which the Court, I suspect, either chooses to ignore or fears to recognize"; the "cancer of poverty will continue to grow"; and "the lot of the poorest among us," once again, and still, is not to be bettered.

Mr. Justice STEVENS, dissenting.
... When the sovereign provides a special benefit or a special protection for a class of persons, it must define the membership in the class by neutral criteria; it may not make special exceptions for reasons that are constitutionally insufficient. ...

[After distinguishing *Maher*, like Justice Marshall, as involving "[a] fundamentally different question" where the "neutral criterion of medical need" was not satisfied, Stevens continued:]

This case involves a special exclusion of women who, by definition, are confronted with a choice between two serious harms: serious health damage to themselves on the one hand and abortion on the other. The competing interests are the interest in maternal health and the interest in protecting potential human life. It is now part of our law that the pregnant woman's decision as to which of these conflicting interests shall prevail is entitled to constitutional protection.

In Roe v. Wade, 410 U.S. 113, and Doe v. Bolton, 410 U.S. 179, the court recognized that the States have a legitimate and protectible interest in potential human life. But the Court explicitly held that prior to fetal viability that interest may not justify any governmental burden on the woman's choice to have an abortion nor even any regulation of abortion except in furtherance of the State's interest in the woman's health. In effect, the Court held that a woman's freedom to elect to have an abortion prior to viability has absolute constitutional protection, subject only to valid health regulations. . . . We have a duty to respect that holding. The Court simply shirks that duty in this case.

If a woman has a constitutional right to place a higher value on avoiding either serious harm to her own health or perhaps an abnormal childbirth than on protecting potential life, the exercise of that right cannot provide the basis for the denial of a benefit to which she would otherwise be entitled. The Court's sterile equal protection analysis evades this critical though simple point. The Court focuses exclusively on the "legitimate interest in protecting the potential life of the fetus." It concludes that since the Hyde amendments further that interest, the exclusion they create is rational and therefore constitutional. But it is misleading to speak of the Government's legitimate interest in the fetus without reference to the context in which that interest was held to be legitimate. For Roe v. Wade squarely held that the States may not protect that interest when a conflict with the interest in a pregnant woman's health exists. It is thus perfectly clear that neither the Federal Government nor the States may exclude a woman from medical benefits to which she would otherwise be entitled solely to further an interest in potential life when a physician, "in appropriate medical judgment," certifies that an abortion is necessary "for the preservation of the life or health of the mother." Roe v. Wade, supra, 410 U.S., at 165. The Court totally fails to explain why this reasoning is not dispositive here.

It cannot be denied that the harm inflicted upon women in the excluded class is grievous. . . . Because a denial of benefits for medically necessary abortions inevitably causes serious harm to the excluded women, it is tantamount to severe punishment. In my judgment, that denial cannot be justified unless Government may, in effect, punish women who want abortions. But as the Court unequivocally held in Roe v. Wade, this the Government may not do. . . .

Having decided to alleviate some of the hardships of poverty by providing necessary medical care, the Government must use neutral criteria in distributing benefits. It may not deny benefits to a financially and medically needy person simply because he is a Republican, a Catholic, or an Oriental — or because he has spoken against a program the Government has a legitimate interest in furthering. In sum, it may not create exceptions for the sole purpose of furthering a governmental interest that is constitutionally subordinate to the individual interest that the entire program was designed to protect. The Hyde amendments not only exclude financially and medically needy persons from the pool of benefits for a constitutionally insufficient reason; they also require the expenditure of millions and millions of dollars in order to thwart the exercise of a constitutional right, thereby effectively inflicting serious and long lasting harm on impoverished women who want and need abortions for valid medical reasons. In my judgment, these amendments constitute an unjustifiable, and indeed blatant violation of the sovereign's duty to govern impartially.

Page 1592. At the end of Note 5 add:

See H.L. v. Matheson, 450 U.S. 398, 101 S. Ct. 1164, 67 L. Ed. 2d 388 (1981), where the Court upheld a Utah statute requiring a physician to "notify, if possible, the parents or guardian of a minor upon whom an abortion is to be performed." Chief Justice Burger, writing for the Court, stated that although the requirement of notice to parents may inhibit some minors from seeking abortions, this in itself is not a valid basis for invalidating the statute. "The Constitution does not compel a state to fine-tune its statutes so as to encourage or facilitate abortions. To the contrary State action 'encouraging childbirth except in the most urgent circumstances' is 'rationally related to the legitimate governmental objective or protecting potential life. . . .' " Burger concluded that "the statute plainly serves important state interests, is narrowly drawn to protect only those interests, and does not violate any guarantees of the Constitution."

Justice Powell and Justice Stewart concurred in the opinion, essentially finding that the Utah statute does not unconstitutionally burden the appellant's right to an abortion. Justice Stevens also concurred separately, basing his opinion on the state's strong interest in establishing a procedure which will "enhance the probability that a pregnant young woman exercise as wisely as possible her right to make the abortion decision." Justice Marshall, joined by Justices Brennan and Blackmun, dissented, finding the statute unconstitutional because it placed an undue burden on the "minor's fundamental right to choose, with her physician, whether to terminate her pregnancy," while not serving any legitimate state interest.

Page 1593. At the end of Note 7 add:

See also the Privacy Protection Act of 1980 (P.L. 96-440), supra in this Supplement, addition to Casebook p.1333.

Page 1595. At the end of the carryover paragraph add:

Cf. Jones v. Helms, 452 U.S. 412, 101 S. Ct. 2434, 69 L. Ed. 2d 118 (1981), where the Court rejected a challenge to Georgia's system of classification, which differentiates between a parent who abandons a dependent child and remains in Georgia and a parent who abandons such a child and leaves the state, despite the appellee's right to travel claim. The Court, per Justice Stevens, stated: "The right to travel has been described as a privilege of national citizenship, and as an aspect of liberty that is protected by the Due Process Clause of the Fifth and Fourteenth Amendments. Whatever its source, a State may neither tax nor penalize a citizen for exercising his right to leave one state and enter another. . . . Despite the fundamental nature of this right, [however,] there nonetheless are situations in which a state may prevent a citizen from leaving. Most obvious is the case in which a person has been convicted of a crime within a State. . . . In this case, [the] appellee's guilty plea [to the charge that he voluntarily abandoned his dependent child] was an acknowledgement that he had committed a misdemeanor before he initially left Georgia for Alabama. Upon conviction of that misdemeanor, he was subject to imprisonment for a period of up to a year. Therefore, ... appellee's own misconduct has *qualified* his right to travel interstate before he sought to exercise that right." (Emphasis added.)

Stevens next distinguished Crandall v. Nevada and Edwards v. California, stating that in these cases, as well as in more recent cases such as Dunn v. Blumstein and Sosna v. Iowa, "the statute at issue imposed a burden on the exercise of the right to travel by citizens whose right to travel had not been qualified in any way. In contrast, in this case, appellee's criminal conduct within the state of Georgia necessarily qualified his right thereafter freely to travel interstate.... The question presented by this case is not whether Georgia can justify disparate treatment of residents and nonresidents, or new and old residents. Rather, the question is whether the state may enhance the misdemeanor of child abandonment to a felony if the resident offender leaves the state after committing the offense.... The Georgia Supreme Court has held that ... [the statute's] enhancement provision serves the 'legislative purpose of causing parents to support their children since the General Assembly could have concluded that the parental support obligation is more difficult to enforce if the parent charged with child abandonment leaves the state.'.... [The] appellee has not provided us with any basis for questioning the validity of the legislative judgment that this purpose is served by making abandonment within the State followed by departure a more serious offense than mere abandonment within the State. We therefore are unwilling to accept the suggestion that this enhancement is an impermissible infringement of appellee's constitutional right to travel...."

Page 1597. After the carryover paragraph add:

HAIG v. AGEE, 453 U.S. 280, 101 S. Ct. 2766, 69 L. Ed. 2d 640 (1981). Respondent is an American citizen currently residing in West Germany. Formerly an employee of the Central Intelligence Agency, for the past several years he had been engaged in the writing of books and giving of speeches for the self-announced purpose of "expos[ing] CIA officers and agents and ... tak[ing] the measures necessary to drive them out of the countries where they are operating." In December of 1979 the Secretary of State notified the respondent that his American passport had been revoked, because his "activities abroad are causing or are likely to cause serious damage to the national security or the foreign policy of the United States." Respondent promptly filed suit, alleging that the regulation relied on by the Secretary was not authorized by the Passport Act of 1926 (22 U.S.C. 211a), as well as challenging the constitutionality of the revocation on procedural due process and First Amendment grounds. In addition, he maintained that the government's action violates his constitutionally guaranteed right to travel. The district court granted summary judgment for Agee, holding that the regulation exceeded the Secretary's statutory authority. A divided court of appeals affirmed. Speaking through Chief Justice Burger, the Court reversed, rejecting all of the respondent's arguments.

Relying largely on Zemel v. Rusk, the Court held that "consistent administrative construction" of the Passport Act supported the Secretary of State's implied authority to revoke passports. Amplifying, Burger stated:

"*Zemel* recognized that congressional acquiescence may sometimes be found from nothing more than silence in the face of an administrative policy. . . . Here, however, the inference of congressional approval 'is supported by more than mere congressional inaction.' *Zemel*, 381 U.S., at 11-12. Twelve years after the promulgation of the regulations at issue and 22 years after promulgation of the similar 1956 regulation, Congress enacted the statute making it unlawful to travel abroad without a passport even in peacetime. 8 U.S.C. §1185(b) (1976 ed., Supp. II). Simultaneously, Congress amended the Passport Act of 1926 to provide that '[u]nless authorized by law,' in the absence of war, armed hostilities, or imminent danger to travelers, a passport may not be geographically restricted. Section 1185(b) of Title 8 must be read *in pari materia* with the Passport Act. . . .

"The 1978 amendments are weighty evidence of congressional approval of the Secretary's interpretation, particularly that in the 1966 regulations. Despite the longstanding and officially promulgated view that the Executive had the power to withhold passports for reasons of national security and foreign policy, Congress in 1978, 'though it once again enacted legislation relating to passports, left completely untouched the broad rule-making authority granted in the earlier Act.' *Zemel*, 381 U.S., at 12. . . .

"A passport is, in a sense, a letter of introduction in which the issuing sovereign vouches for the bearer and requests other sovereigns to aid the bearer. 3 G. Hackworth, Digest of International Law §268, at p.499 (1942). . . . With the enactment of travel control legislation making a passport generally a requirement for travel abroad, a passport took on certain added characteristics. Most important for present purposes, the only means by which an American can lawfully leave the country or return to it — absent a Presidentially granted exception — is with a passport. See 8 U.S.C. §1185(b) (1976 ed., Supp. II). As a travel control document, a passport is both proof of identity and proof of allegiance to the United States. Even under a travel control statute, however, a passport remains in a sense a document by which the Government vouches for the bearer and for his conduct."

Chief Justice Burger's discussion of the "history of passport controls," showing "since the earliest days of the Republic . . . congressional recognition of Executive authority to withhold passports on the basis of substantial reasons of national security and foreign policy," is omitted. He noted that "[b]y enactment of the first travel control statute in 1918, Congress made clear its expectation that the Executive would curtail or prevent international travel by American citizens if it was contrary to the national security" and then addressed Agee's contention that "the only way the Executive can establish implicit congressional approval is by proof of longstanding and consistent *enforcement* of the claimed power: that is, by showing that many passports were revoked on national security and foreign policy grounds," stating:

"The history is clear that there have been few situations involving substantial likelihood of serious damage to the national security or foreign policy of the United States as a result of a passport holder's activities abroad, and that in the cases which have arisen, the Secretary has consistently exercised his power to withhold passports. . . . The Secretary has construed and applied his regulations consistently, and it would be anomalous to fault the Government because there were so few occasions to exercise the announced policy and practice. Although a pattern of actual enforcement is one indicator of Executive policy, it suffices that the Executive has 'openly asserted' the power at issue. *Zemel*, 381 U.S., at 9; see id., at 10.

"[Kent v. Dulles] is not to the contrary. There, it was shown that the claimed governmental policy had not been enforced consistently. The Court stressed that 'as respects Communists these are scattered rulings and not consistently of one pattern.' 357 U.S., at 128. In other words, the Executive had allowed passports to some Communists, but sought to deny one to Kent. The Court had serious doubts as to whether there was in reality any definite policy in which Congress could have acquiesced. Here, by contrast, there is no basis for a claim that the Executive has failed to enforce the policy against others engaged in conduct likely to cause serious damage to our national security or foreign policy. It would turn *Kent* on its head to say that simply because we have had only a few situations involving conduct such as that in this record, the Executive lacks the authority to deal with the problem when it is encountered.

"Agee also contends that the statements of Executive policy are entitled to diminished weight because many of them concern the powers of the Executive in wartime. However, the statute provides no support for this argument. History eloquently attests that grave problems of national security and foreign policy are by no means limited to times of formally declared war.

"Relying on the statement of the Court in *Kent* that 'illegal conduct' and problems of allegiance were 'so far as relevant here, . . . the only [grounds] which it could fairly be argued were adopted by Congress in light of prior administrative practice,' 357 U.S., at 127-128, Agee argues that this enumeration was exclusive and is controlling here. This is not correct.

"The *Kent* Court had no occasion to consider whether the Executive had the power to revoke the passport of an individual whose *conduct* is damaging the national security and foreign policy of the United States. *Kent* involved denials of passports solely on the basis of political beliefs entitled to First Amendment protection. See Aptheker v. Secretary of State, 378 U.S. 500 (1964). Although finding it unnecessary to reach the merits of that constitutional problem, the *Kent* Court emphasized the fact that it dealt 'with *beliefs*, with *associations*, with *ideological* matters.' 357 U.S., at 130 (emphasis supplied). . . .

"The protection accorded beliefs standing alone is very different from the protection accorded conduct. Thus, in *Aptheker* . . ., the Court held that a statute which, like the policy at issue in *Kent*, denied passports to Communists solely on the basis of political beliefs unconstitutionally 'establishes an irrebuttable presumption that individuals who are members of the specified organizations will, if given passports, engage in activities inimical to the security of the United States.' 378 U.S., at 511. The Court recognized that the legitimacy of the objective of safeguarding our national security is 'obvious and unarguable.' Id., at 509. The Court explained that the statute at issue was not the least restrictive alternative available: 'The prohibition against travel is supported only by a tenuous relationship between the bare fact of organizational membership and the activity Congress sought to proscribe.' Id., at 514.

"Beliefs and speech are only part of Agee's 'campaign to fight the United States CIA.' In that sense, this case contrasts markedly with the facts in *Kent* and *Aptheker*. No presumptions, rebuttable or otherwise, are involved, for Agee's conduct in foreign countries presents a serious danger to American officials abroad and serious danger to the national security.

"We hold that the policy announced in the challenged regulations is 'sufficiently substantial and consistent' to compel the conclusion that Congress has approved it. See *Zemel*, 381 U.S., at 12.

"Agee also attacks the Secretary's action on three constitutional grounds: first, that the revocation of his passport impermissibly burdens his freedom to travel; second, that the action was intended to penalize his exercise of free speech and deter his criticism of government policies and practices; and third, that failure to accord him a prerevocation hearing violated his Fifth Amendment right to procedural due process.

"In light of the express language of the passport regulations, which permits their application only in cases involving likelihood of 'serious damage' to national security or foreign policy, these claims are without merit.

"Revocation of a passport undeniably curtails travel, but the freedom to travel abroad with a 'letter of introduction' in the form of a passport issued by the sovereign is subordinate to national security and foreign policy considerations; as such, it is subject to reasonable governmental regulation. The Court has made it plain that the *freedom* to travel outside the United States must be distinguished from the *right* to travel within the United States. This was underscored in Califano v. Aznavorian, 439 U.S. 170, 176 (1978):

Aznavorian urges that the freedom of international travel is basically equivalent to the constitutional right to interstate travel, recognized by this Court for over 100 years. Edwards v. California, 314 U.S. 160; Twining v. New Jersey, 211 U.S. 78, 97; Williams v. Fears, 179 U.S. 270, 274; Crandall v. Nevada, 6 Wall. 35, 43-44; Passenger Cases, 7 How. 283, 492 (Taney, C.J., dissenting). But this

Court has often pointed out the crucial difference between the freedom to travel internationally and the right of interstate travel.

"The constitutional right of interstate travel is virtually unqualified, United States v. Guest, 383 U.S. 745, 757-758 (1966); Griffin v. Breckenridge, 403 U.S. 88, 105-106 (1971). By contrast the 'right' of international travel has been considered to be no more than an aspect of the 'liberty' protected by the Due Process Clause of the Fifth Amendment. As such this 'right,' the Court has held, can be regulated within the bounds of due process." (Citations omitted.) Califano v. Torres, 435 U.S. 1, 4, n.6.

"It is 'obvious and unarguable' that no governmental interest is more compelling than the security of the Nation. Aptheker v. Secretary of State, 378 U.S., at 509; accord Cole v. Young, 351 U.S. 536, 546 (1956); see *Zemel*, 381 U.S., at 13-17. Protection of the foreign policy of the United States is a governmental interest of great importance, since foreign policy and national security considerations cannot neatly be compartmentalized.

"Measures to protect the secrecy of our Government's foreign intelligence operations plainly serve these interests. Thus, in Snepp v. United States, 444 U.S. 507, 509, n.3 (1980), we held that '[t]he Government has a compelling interest in protecting both the secrecy of information so important to our national security and the appearance of confidentiality so essential to the effective operation of our foreign intelligence service.' See also id., at 511-513. The Court in United States v. Curtiss-Wright Export Corp., supra, properly emphasized: '[The President] has his confidential sources of information. He has his agents in the form of diplomatic, consular and other officials. Secrecy in respect of information may be highly necessary, and the premature disclosure of it productive of harmful results.' 299 U.S., at 320. Accord, Chicago & Southern Air Lines, Inc. v. Waterman Steamship Corp., 333 U.S., at 111; The Federalist No. 64, pp. 392-393 (Mentor ed. 1961).

"Not only has Agee jeopardized the security of the United States, but he has endangered the interests of countries other than the United States — thereby creating serious problems for American foreign relations and foreign policy. Restricting Agee's foreign travel, although perhaps not certain to prevent all of Agee's harmful activities, is the only avenue open to the Government to limit these activities.

"Assuming *arguendo* that First Amendment protections reach beyond our national boundaries, Agee's First Amendment claim has no foundation. The revocation of Agee's passport rests in part on the content of his speech: specifically, his repeated disclosures of intelligence operations and names of intelligence personnel. Long ago, however, this Court recognized that 'No one would question but that a government might prevent actual obstruction to its recruiting service or the publication of the sailing dates of transports or the number and location of troops.' Near v. Minnesota, 283 U.S. 697, 716 (1931), citing Chafee, Freedom of Speech 10 (1920). Agee's disclosures, among other things, have the declared purpose of obstructing intelligence operations and the recruiting of intelligence personnel. They are clearly not protected by the Constitution. The mere fact that Agee is also engaged in criticism of the Government does not render his conduct beyond the reach of the law.

"To the extent the revocation of his passport operates to inhibit Agee, 'it is an inhibition of *action*,' rather than of speech. *Zemel*, 381 U.S., at 16-17 (emphasis supplied). Agee is as free to criticize the United States Government as he was when he held a passport — always subject, of course, to express limits on certain rights by virtue of his contract with the Government. . . .

"On this record, the Government is not required to hold a prerevocation hearing. In Cole v. Young, supra, we held that federal employees who hold 'sensitive' positions 'where they could bring about any discernible effects on the Nation's security' may be suspended without a presuspension hearing. 351 U.S., at 546-547. For the same reasons, when there is a subantial likelihood of 'serious damage' to national security or foreign policy as a result of a passport holder's activities in foreign countries, the Government may take action to ensure that the holder may not exploit the sponsorship of his travels by the United States. '[W]hile the Constitution protects against invasions of individual rights, it is not a suicide pact.' Kennedy v. Mendoza-Martinez, 372 U.S. 144, 160 (1963). The Constitution's due process guarantees call for no more than what has been accorded here: a statement of reasons and an opportunity for a prompt postrevocation hearing."

Justice Blackmun concurred, suggesting that perhaps the Court "is cutting back somewhat upon the opinions in [*Kent* and *Zemel*] *sub silentio*."

Justice Brennan, joined by Justice Marshall, dissented, asserting that the Court's reliance on prior decisions was "fundamentally misplaced" and "that the Court instead has departed from the express holdings of those decisions." In pertinent part he wrote:

"This is not a complicated case. The Court has twice articulated the proper mode of analysis for determining whether Congress has delegated to the Executive Branch the authority to deny a passport under the Passport Act of 1926. Zemel v. Rusk, 381 U.S. 1 (1965); Kent v. Dulles, 357 U.S. 116 (1958). The analysis is hardly confusing, and I expect that had the Court faithfully applied it, today's judgment would affirm the decision below. . . .

"As in *Kent* and *Zemel*, there is no dispute here that the Passport Act of 1926 does not *expressly* authorize the Secretary to revoke Agee's passport. . . . Therefore, the sole remaining inquiry is whether there exists 'with regard to the sort of passport [revocation] involved [here], an administrative *practice* sufficiently substantial and consistent to warrant the conclusion that Congress had implicitly approved it. Zemel v. Rusk, supra, at 12 (emphasis added). The Court today, citing to this same page in *Zemel*, applies a test markedly different from that of *Zemel* and *Kent* and in fact expressly disavowed by the latter. . . .

"Not only does the Court ignore the *Kent-Zemel* requirement that Executive discretion be supported by a consistent administrative practice, but it also relies on the very Executive construction and policy deemed irrelevant in *Kent*. . . . The Court's reliance on material expressly abjured in *Kent* becomes understandable only when one appreciates the paucity of recorded administrative practice — the only evidence upon which *Kent* and *Zemel* permit reliance — with respect to passport denials or revocations based on foreign policy or national security considerations relating to an individual. The Court itself identifies only three occasions over the past 33 years when the Secretary has revoked passports for such reasons. . . . And only one of these cases involved a revocation pursuant to the regulations challenged in this case. Yet, in 1979 alone, there were 7,835,000 Americans travelling abroad. . . . The presumption is that Congress must expressly delegate authority to the Secretary to deny or revoke passports for foreign policy or national security reasons before he may exercise such authority. To overcome the presumption against an implied delegation, the Government must show 'an administrative practice sufficiently substantial and consistent.' *Zemel v. Rusk, supra,* at 12. Only in this way can the Court satisfy itself that Congress has implicitly approved such exercise of authority by the Secretary.

"I suspect that this case is a prime example of the adage that 'bad facts make bad law.' Philip Agee is hardly a model representative of our Nation. And the Executive Branch has attempted to use one of the only means at its disposal, revocation of a passport, to stop respondent's damaging statements. But just as the Constitution protects both popular and unpopular speech, it likewise protects both popular and unpopular travelers. And it is important to remember that this decision applies not only to Philip Agee, whose activities could be perceived as harming the national security, but also to other citizens who may merely disagree with Government foreign policy and express their views.

"The Constitution allocates the lawmaking function to Congress, and I fear that today's decision has handed over too much of that function to the Executive. In permitting the Secretary to stop this unpopular traveler and critic of the CIA, the Court professes to rely on, but in fact departs from, the two precedents in the passport regulation area, *Zemel* and *Kent.* Of course it is always easier to fit oneself within the safe haven of *stare decisis* than boldly to overrule precedents of several decades' standing. Because I find myself unable to reconcile those cases with the decision in this case, however, and because I disagree with the Court's *sub silentio* overruling of those cases, I dissent."

Page 1598. At the end of the fourth paragraph add:

The Court held that indigent parents do not have the right to appointed counsel in *all* parental terminations proceedings. Lassiter v. Department of Social Services of Durham County, supra in this Supplement, addition to Casebook p.785.

Addendum

Page 14. At the end of Note 9 add:

See United States v. Johnson, — U.S. — , 102 S. Ct. — , — L. Ed. 2d —
(1982), where the Court upheld a retroactive application of one of its recent
decisions construing the Fourth Amendment to a conviction not yet final at
the time the Court's decision was rendered. Except where a case would be
controlled by retroactivity precedents, the retroactive application of all new-
ly declared constitutional rules of criminal procedure to convictions not final
when the rule is established is "consonant with [the] Court's original understanding in Linkletter v. Walker," Casebook p.14, the Court concluded.

Page 43. At the end of the footnote add:

Alfred L. Snapp & Son v. Puerto Rico, — U.S. — , 102 S. Ct. — , — L. Ed.
2d — (1982), involved the question whether the Commonwealth of Puerto
Rico had standing to bring suit in its capacity as *parens patriae* against
Virginia apple growers who allegedly discriminated against citizens of Puerto Rico in favor of temporary foreign workers, in violation of several
federal statutes. Reviewing the considerations relevant to determining standing in such circumstances, the Court concluded that Puerto Rico did have
parens patriae standing here. It had a "quasi-sovereign" interest in the general well-being of its citizens, which includes not only physical and economic
aspects but also a substantial interest in securing its residents from the
harmful effects of discrimination. Puerto Rico also had standing in its sovereign capacity to seek to ensure that its residents obtained the intended
benefits of the federal employment service scheme established by the applicable statutes. Puerto Rico was seeking to assert a cognizable injury to an
identifiable group of individual residents, but also to protect a substantial
segment of its population from the indirect effects of the alleged violations of
federal law. A state (or, in this case, commonwealth) also has a quasi-
sovereign interest in attempting to ensure that it is not excluded from its
rightful status within the federal system. Thus, Puerto Rico was more than
a nominal party and, since it had significant interests apart from those of
particular private parties, could sue as *parens patriae* in a federal court consistent with Article III and prior precedents, e.g., Georgia v. Pennsylvania

R. Co., 324 U.S. 439 (1945), and Maryland v. Louisiana, 451 U.S. 725 (1981), infra in this Supplement, addition to Casebook p.103.

Page 103. At the end of Note 2 add:

See California v. Grace Brethren Church, — U.S. —, 102 S. Ct. —, — L. Ed. 2d — (1982), where the Court exercised its jurisdiction under 28 U.S.C. 1252 to hear an appeal from a California district court's decision holding California's unemployment compensation tax scheme (which is federally approved under the Federal Unemployment Tax Act) as violative of the First Amendment religion clauses.

Page 104. At the end of the carryover paragraph add:

See California v. Texas, — U.S. —, 102 S. Ct. —, — L. Ed. 2d — (1982), for a per curiam decision which granted the State of California leave to file a complaint against Texas under the Court's original jurisdiction, 28 U.S.C. 1251. Although the Court had previously denied California leave to file, it concluded that California's bill of complaint now states a "controversy" within the meaning of the Article III provision. The Court also acknowledged that it was proper for it to exercise its original jurisdiction in this case despite its self-imposed prudential and equitable limitations on the exercise of original jurisdiction. Previously, the Court had felt that statutory interpleader might obviate the need to exercise original jurisdiction. However, the decision in Cory v. White, infra in this Supplement, addition to Casebook p.129, determined that such a statutory interpleader action could not be brought; hence, the precondition for the exercise of original jurisdiction had been met. The Court concluded by saying that California and Texas had asserted inconsistent claims and were "undeniably adversaries." Justices Powell, Marshall, Rehnquist, and Stevens dissented, noting the speculative nature of the claims resulting in such prematurity that there was not, in their judgment, "a case or controversy in the constitutional sense."

Page 127. At the end of the first full paragraph add:

For a challenge to the Bankruptcy Reform Act of 1978, and in particular Congress's power to create non-Article III courts with the ability to adjudicate non-bankruptcy cases, see Northern Pipeline Construction Co. v. Marathon Pipe Line Co., — U.S. —, 102 S. Ct. —, — L. Ed. 2d — (1982). The Act allowed for the appointment of bankruptcy court judges for 14-year terms and for their salaries to be subject to adjustment. The Act also granted bankruptcy courts jurisdiction over all civil proceedings arising under Title 11 (bankruptcy) of the United States Code.

Justice Brennan, representing a plurality, stated that "the judicial power of the United States must be exercised by judges who have the attributes of life tenure and protection against salary diminution" specified in Article III.

"[Our] Constitution unambiguously enunciates a fundamental principle — that the 'judicial power' of the United States must be reposed in an independent judiciary. It is undisputed that the bankruptcy judges ... do not enjoy protection constitutionally afforded to Article III judges." After Brennan identified three historically recognized legislatively created courts not prohibited by Article III to be "territorial courts," "courts martial," and legislative courts to adjudicate cases involving "public rights," he stated that the bankruptcy courts created by the Act did not fall within the narrow definitions of those limited exceptions. He concluded: "Article III bars Congress from establishing legislative courts to exercise jurisdiction over all matters related to [cases] arising under bankruptcy laws. [The] broad grant of jurisdiction to the bankruptcy courts is unconstitutional ... and the Act has impermissibly removed most, if not all, of 'the essential attributes of the judicial power' from Article III district courts, and vested those attributes in a non-Article III adjunct."

The Court further held that its decision "shall apply prospectively only, in order to avoid the injustice and hardship a retroactive application would surely visit upon those litigants who relied on the Act's vesting of jurisdiction in the bankruptcy courts."

Justices Rehnquist and O'Connor concurred in the judgment, but felt that the issues could have been greatly narrowed.

Chief Justice Burger and Justices White and Powell dissented, reading Article III literally to mean "Congress [is] free to establish such lower courts as it saw fit, [and] any court that it did establish would be an 'inferior' court exercising 'judicial power of the United States' "; therefore, the creation of the bankruptcy courts and appointment of bankruptcy court judges was not unconstitutional under the mandates of the Act.

Page 129. At the end of Note 2 add:

See Cory v. White, — U.S. —, 102 S. Ct. —, — L. Ed. 2d — (1982), where the Court held that the Eleventh Amendment barred the administrator of the late Howard Hughes' estate from using statutory interpleader to resolve a dispute between California and Texas regarding Hughes' domicile at the time of death. The Court preferred to follow Worcester County Trust Co. v. Riley, 302 U.S. 292 (1937), instead of the dissent's reliance on Edelman v. Jordan, Casebook p.129, and stated that the Eleventh Amendment controlled in actions seeking injunctive relief against states as well as in suits seeking monetary damages from state treasuries.

Page 136. At the end of the carryover paragraph add:

For an application of the Younger doctrine to state supreme court attorney disciplinary proceedings, see Middlesex County Ethics Comm. v. Garden State Bar Assn., — U.S. —, 102 S. Ct. —, — L. Ed. 2d — (1982). Finding that New Jersey has an extremely important interest in maintaining and assuring the professional conduct of the attorneys it licenses, and that the New Jersey Supreme Court considers its disciplinary proceedings as "judicial in nature," the Court held the "proceedings [were] of a character to warrant federal court deference." Moreover, federal courts should abstain from interfering with ongoing disciplinary proceedings once the pertinent inquiry is satisfied, i.e., "whether the state proceedings afford an adequate opportunity to raise constitutional issues," citing Huffman v. Pursue, Casebook p.135. In his brief concurring opinion, Justice Brennan cautioned, "I continue to adhere to my view, however, that [*Younger*] is in general inapplicable to civil proceedings."

Page 137. At the end of Note 7 add:

See also Lehman v. Lycoming County Children's Services, — U.S. — , 102 S. Ct. — , — L. Ed. 2d — (1982), holding that Section 2254 does not provide a jurisdictional basis for federal courts to consider collateral challenges to state-court judgments involuntarily terminating parental rights, since the children in question were not in the "custody" of the state in the way in which that term has consistently been used in determining the availability of federal habeas corpus. In addition, the Court stated, considerations of federalism and the exceptional need for finality in child-custody disputes argue strongly against allowing such an action to be brought. Justices Blackmun, Brennan, and Marshall dissented.

Page 137. At the end of the carryover paragraph in the footnote add:

See California v. Grace Brethren Church, — U.S. — , 102 S. Ct. — , — L. Ed. 2d — (1982), where the Court held that 28 U.S.C. 1341 deprived a California district court of jurisdiction to issue declaratory and injunctive relief against collection of any state tax where a "plain, speedy, and efficient remedy" may be had in the state courts.

Page 226. At the end of Note 2 add:

Compare Federal Energy Regulatory Commn. v. Mississippi, — U.S. — , 102 S. Ct. 2126, — L. Ed. 2d — (1982), where the State of Mississippi sought a declaratory judgment that certain provisions of the Public Utilities Regulatory Act of 1978 (PURPA) were both outside Congress's power under the commerce clause and an entrenchment on state sovereignty in violation of the Tenth Amendment. Relying on Carter v. Carter Coal Co., 298 U.S. 239 (1936), Casebook p.181, Mississippi asserted that nothing in the commerce clause authorized or justified the federal government's taking over the regulation or control of an intrastate public utility. Citing National League of Cities v. Usery, Casebook p.218, Mississippi also claimed that the provisions of PURPA constituted a direct intrusion into integral and traditional functions of the state protected by the Tenth Amendment from federal regulation.

In rejecting Mississippi's contentions and upholding PURPA's constitutionality, the Court distinguished *National League of Cities* and relied instead on *Hodel* as stating the "applicable standard." Federal regulation of intrastate power transmission is proper, the Court stated, because of the interstate nature of the generation and supply of electrical power. The Court further noted that it was difficult to conceive of a more basic element of interstate commerce than electrical energy, a product used in virtually every home and commercial facility, and concluded that even if Mississippi was correct in its criticisms of PURPA, congressional findings compel the conclusion that "the means chosen by Congress are reasonably related and adapted to the end permitted by the Constitution." In contrast to the situation in *National League of Cities*, the federal government is attempting through PURPA to use state regulatory machinery to advance federal goals. The regulations involved do not compel or control the exercise of Mississippi's sovereign powers; rather they establish requirements for continued state activity in an otherwise "pre-emptible area." The Court concluded that if Congress could require a state administrative body to consider proposed regulations as a condition to its continued involvement in such a field, as it can, then there is nothing unconstitutional about Congress's requiring certain procedural minima as that body goes about its tasks, relying on Testa v. Katt, Casebook p.533, and Fry v. United States, 421 U.S. 542 (1975). Moreover, the Court stated, "it has always been the law that state legislative and judicial decisionmakers must give preclusive effect to federal enactments concerning nongovernmental activity, no matter what the strength of the competing local interests," citing, e.g., Martin v. Hunter's Lessee, Casebook p.15.

Page 325. At the end of Note 10 add:

Cf. Nixon v. Fitzgerald, — U.S. —, 102 S. Ct. —, — L. Ed. 2d — (1982), where the Court directly confronted the issue of the scope of the immunity from suit possessed by the President of the United States. The President had been named as a party-defendant in a civil damages action brought by a former Department of the Air Force management analyst who claimed he was vindictively dismissed for "purely personal reasons" by the President, for the analyst's participation in disclosing extremely significant defense contract cost overruns on the C-5A project. A severely divided Court held that "the petitioner, as a former President of the United States, is entitled to absolute immunity from damages liability predicated on his official acts." Justice Powell, writing for the majority, explained that certiorari was granted to decide this important issue, which the Court had not heretofore been called upon to resolve. He stated that the Court had consistently recognized government officials as being entitled to some form of immunity from suits for civil damages. He said: "In the absence of immunity, executive officials would hesitate to exercise their discretion ... even when the public interest required bold and unhesitating action." He continued, stating that the Court's decisions concerning immunity of governent officials from civil damages liability have been guided by the "Constitution, federal statutes, and history." Powell viewed Butz v. Economou, Casebook p.325, as recognizing that federal officials generally have the same qualified immunity possessed by state officials but that a blanket recognition of absolute immunity would be anomalous; however, a functional approach requires "an absolute immunity for certain officials — notably judges and prosecutors — who have especially sensitive duties." This applies to Presidents as well.

Justice Powell stated: "We consider this immunity a functionally mandated incident of the President's unique office, noted in the constitutional tradition of the separation of powers and supported by our history.... The President occupies a unique position in the constitutional scheme." The Article II grant of authority establishes the President as the "chief constitutional officer of the Executive Branch, entrusted with supervisory and policy responsibilities of utmost discretion and sensitivity ... [in] the conduct of foreign affairs — a realm [in] which the Court has recognized that it would be intolerable that courts, without relevant information, should review and perhaps nullify actions of the Executive taken on information properly held secret." He said that the concern is compelling for an officeholder to be able to deal fearlessly and impartially when making sensitive and far-reaching decisions incident to the duties of his office. In defining the scope of an official's absolute privilege, the Court has recognized that the sphere of protected action must be related closely to the immunity's justifying purposes. Citing *Butz* and Barr v. Mateo, Casebook p.324, he said, "[f]requently, our decisions have held that an official's absolute immunity should extend only to acts in performance of particular functions of his office. In view of the special nature of the President's constitutional office and functions, we think it appropriate to recognize absolute presidential immunity from damages liability for acts within the 'outer perimeter' of his official responsibility." In stating that the alleged wrongful acts lay well within the "outer perimeter" of the President's authority, Justice Powell concluded that "[t]he existence of alternative remedies and deterrents establishes that absolute immunity will not place the President 'above the law.' For the President, as for judges and prosecutors, absolute immunity merely precludes a particular private remedy for alleged misconduct in order to advance compelling public ends."

Chief Justice Burger wrote a concurring opinion, while Justices White, Brennan, Marshall, and Blackmun dissented, stating that the majority was now applying "the dissenting view in *Butz* to the office of the President," so that a chief executive "acting within the outer boundaries of what Presidents normally do may, without liability, deliberately cause serious injury to any number of citizens even though he knows his conduct violates a statute or tramples on the constitutional rights of those who are injured." Such a conclusion does not necessarily flow from our constitutional scheme, the dissenters asserted, and the office of the President may operate effectively without having a license to inflict deliberate injury on others by conduct known to be unlawful. Absolute immunity should be attached only to certain activities of the President, not to the office as such, they stated, relying, e.g., on Marbury v. Madison as well as Scheuer v. Rhodes, Casebook p.534. In contrast to the speech or debate clause, guaranteeing absolute immunity to certain actions by members of Congress, the Constitution contains no express provision relating to presidential immunity. Citing the *Nixon* and *Bivens* cases, the dissenters concluded that, consistent with the separation of powers concept as well as sound public policy, "[t]he scope of immunity is determined by function, not office." Dismissal of employees is not, they said, a function that would be "substantially impaired" because of a possible damages action. Justice Blackmun also wrote a dissent.

Compare Harlow v. Fitzgerald, – U.S. – , 102 S. Ct. – , – L. Ed. 2d – (1982), where the Court held that presidential aides and executive branch officials are generally entitled to only a qualified or good-faith immunity from civil litigation, one which permits defeat of insubstantial claims without resort to trial. To establish entitlement to absolute immunity from personal liability, "the one seeking the privilege has the burden of showing that public policy requires an exemption of that scope," the Court stated. A presidential aide first must show that the responsibilities of his office embrace a function so sensitive as to require a total shield from liability. He must then be able to demonstrate that he was discharging the protected function while performing the act for which liability is asserted. The Court concluded that government officials performing discretionary functions are henceforth generally shielded from liability for civil damages, insofar as their conduct does not violate "clearly established" statutory or constitutional rights of which a reasonable person would be cognizant, but that the immunity, unlike the President's, is not absolute.

Page 387. At the end of Note 1 add:

For an application of the commerce clause protection of interstate commerce in the context of business takeovers, mergers, or acquisitions, see Edgar v. MITE Corp., – U.S. – , 102 S. Ct. – , – L. Ed. 2d – (1982). The Court held the Illinois Business Takeover Act to be unconstitutional as excessively burdening interstate commerce in light of the local interests the Act purports to further. Illinois' asserted interests in protecting resident security holders and regulating the internal affairs of companies incorporated under Illinois law are insufficient to outweigh the burdens imposed by the Act on interstate commerce.

Page 455. At the end of Note 2 add:

In Rice v. Norman Williams Co., — U.S. — , 102 S. Ct. — , — L. Ed. 2d — (1982), the Court rejected a series of constitutional challenges to a California alcoholic beverage law requiring that those importing liquor into the state be "designated" as an authorized inspector of the brand in question. The Court held that the California designation statute was not invalid on 'its face as being preempted by the Sherman Act. Nor was it preempted by the Federal Alcohol Administration Act. There was no denial of due process since respondents lacked a constitutionally protected liberty or property interest in obtaining a distiller's permission to deal in its products. Nor, finally, was equal protection denied, as the law was rationally related to the legitimate purpose of restraining intrabrand competition to foster interbrand competition.

Page 456. At the end of Note 3 add:

For cases distinguishing *Mobil* and *Exxon* and elaborating on the "unitary-business principle," see Asarco Inc. v. Idaho State Tax Commn., — U.S. — , 102 S. Ct. — , — L. Ed. 2d — (1982), and F.W. Woolworth Co. v. Taxation and Revenue Department of New Mexico, — U.S. — , 102 S. Ct. — , — L. Ed. 2d — (1982), both of which address the central issue of a state's ability to include within a non-domiciliary corporation's apportionable income a portion of the intangible income — such as dividends, interest, or capital gains from sale of stock — that the parent corporation derives from its subsidiaries which themselves have no other connection with the taxing state.

Quoting from *Mobil* that "the linchpin of apportionability [for] state income taxation of an interstate enterprise is the 'unitary-business principle,' " the Court in *Asarco*, speaking through Justice Powell, stated, "[a]s a general principle, a state may not tax values earned outside its borders ... ; however, due process limitations on an attempted tax would be satisfied if there is a 'minimal connection' between the interstate activities and the taxing state, and a rational relationship between the income attributed to the state and the intrastate values of the enterprise ... ; in other words, has the state given anything for which it can ask return." When income is earned from activities which are part of a "unitary business" conducted in several states, then the requirement that the income sought to be taxed bear a relationship to the benefits and privileges conferred by the several states has been met. The Court concluded that Idaho's attempt to tax intangible income of Asarco not properly related to that state was a violation of due process.

At the same time, the Court also invalidated New Mexico's effort to tax a portion of F.W. Woolworth Co.'s dividend income received from its foreign subsidiaries, none of which conducted business in New Mexico, as a violation of due process. The Court again stressed the required necessity of a nexus between the benefits and values of the taxing state and the income to be taxed. The Court stated, "under the principles articulated in *Mobil* and *Exxon,* and today reiterated in *Asarco,* F.W. Woolworth Co. and its subsidiaries are not fundamentally integrated so as to constitute a 'unitary business,' nor does New Mexico's [attempted] tax bear the necessary relationship to opportunities, benefits, or protections conferred or afforded by the state." Mere potential to operate a company as part of a "unitary business" is not in itself dispositive that a single enterprise exists.

Justices O'Connor, Blackmun, and Rehnquist dissented in both cases.

Page 465. At the end of Note 4 add:

For an application of the preemption doctrine in the context of home mortgages, see Fidelity Federal Savings & Loan Assn. v. Cuesta, — U.S. — , 102 S. Ct. — , — L. Ed.2d — (1982), where the Court dealt with a challenge to the enforcement of a "due-on-sale" provision of a mortgage contract by a federal savings and loan association. In 1976, the Federal Home Loan Bank Board authorized federal savings and loan associations to "continue to have to include ... in a loan instrument" a "due-on-sale clause," i.e., a contractual provision permitting the lender to declare an entire loan balance due and payable if the property securing the loan was sold or otherwise transferred without the association's prior written consent. The preamble to the "due-on-sale" regulation contained an expressed intent that "due-on-sale practices" of federal savings and loan associations shall be governed "exclusively by federal law, and that federal associations" shall not be bound or subject to any conflicting state law imposing different requirements. The Court addressed the assertion that a state law which limited a lender's ability to exercise "due-on-sale" rights to transfers of property which impair a lender's security was controlling rather than a regulation of a federal agency.

Justice Blackmun, speaking for the majority, began by stating that the "preemption doctrine" has its roots in the supremacy clause of Article VI of the Constitution, and that preemption may be either express or implied; however, it "is compelled whether Congress' command is explicitly stated in the statute's language or implicitly contained in its structure or purpose." Citing Florida Lime and Avocado Growers, Inc. v. Paul, Casebook p.456, Blackmun said: "[W]hen state law stands as an obstacle to the accomplishment and execution of the full purposes and objectives of Congress, ... state law is nullified to the extent that it actually conflicts with federal law. [Moreover,] [t]hese principles are not inapplicable here simply because real property law is a matter of special concern to the states; [indeed,] [f]ederal regulations have no less preemptive effect than federal statutes." Blackmun concluded "that the Board's due-on-sale regulation was meant to preempt conflicting state limitations on the due-on-sale practices of federal savings and loans."

Justices Rehnquist and Stevens dissented.

Page 470. At the end of Note 1 add:

See Blum v. Bacon, — U.S. — , 102 S. Ct — , — L. Ed. 2d — (1982), for a case invalidating on supremacy clause grounds New York's exclusion of AFDC recipients from its emergency assistance program, which is federally funded under the Social Security Act.

Page 534. At the end of the third paragraph of Note 3 add:

Concerning the question of whether the exhaustion of state administrative remedies is a prerequisite to an action under 42 U.S.C. 1983, see Patsy v. Board of Regents of the State of Florida, — U.S. — , 102 S. Ct. — , — L. Ed. 2d — (1982). Consistent with its general no-exhaustion rule, the Court decided that, based on the legislative histories of §1983 and §1997e (part of the Civil Rights of Institutionalized Persons Act, enacted in 1980), exhaustion of state administrative remedies should not be required as a prerequisite to bringing an action pursuant to §1983.

Page 537. At the end of second paragraph add:

In the area of employment discrimination, the Court in Kremer v. Chemical Construction Corp., — U.S. — , 102 S. Ct. 1883, — L. Ed. 2d — (1982), held that a petitioner whose claim had been dismissed as meritless by an appropriate state agency, and was upheld both administratively and judicially, was precluded from litigating the same claim in federal court. A state court judgment which was not constitutionally infirm must receive full faith and credit from federal courts, the Court concluded, as "there is no 'affirmative showing' of a 'clear and manifest' legislative purpose in Title VII to deny res judicata or collateral estoppel effect to a state court judgment."

Page 628. At the end of Note 4 add:

See also Plyler v. Doe, — U.S. — , 102 S. Ct. — , — L. Ed. 2d — (1982), infra in this Supplement, addition to Casebook p.1053, invalidating as a denial of equal protection a Texas law discriminating against illegal aliens with respect to access to public education.

Page 642. At the end of the first paragraph of Note 2 add:

Cf. Florida Dept. of State v. Treasure Salvors, Inc., — U.S. — , 102 S. Ct. — , — L. Ed. 2d — (1982), holding that the Eleventh Amendment did not bar proceedings against Florida officials seeking the recovery of valuable artifacts obtained from the wreck of a sunken Spanish galleon located off the Florida coast. Suits against state officials for acting beyond the scope of statutory authority or unconstitutionally are allowed consistent with the Eleventh Amendment, under Ex parte Young, Casebook p.642. And since there was no attempt to compel Florida to expend state funds to compensate the claimants for any injury, the principles of Edelman v. Jordan, Casebook p.129, were complied with. Here, the Court concluded, state officers "acted without legitimate authority in withholding the property at issue." Four justices dissented on the Eleventh Amendment question.

Page 694. At the end of Note 5 add:

See Rendell-Baker v. Kohn, – U.S. – , 102 S. Ct. – , – L. Ed. 2d – (1982), for a case presenting a "state action" question in the education context involving a private school operated for maladjusted students, most of whom were referred by city school committees. The city would pay for each pupil it referred, and funds were disbursed to the school from the state. Although the school is state-regulated in order to participate in tuition funding, the school remains independent in the administration of personnel policies. Petitioners were former employees who were discharged and subsequently initiated actions under 42 U.S.C. 1983, claiming that state action was involved. Referring to Blum v. Yaretsky, infra in this Supplement, addition to Casebook p.694, a decision handed down on the same day, the Court found no "state action" in the school's discharge of the petitioner employees, adding that "the school's receipt of public funds does not make the discharge decisions acts of the state."

Justices Marshall and Brennan dissented.

Compare Blum v. Yaretsky, – U.S. – , 102 S. Ct. – , – L. Ed. 2d – (1982), which was referred to by *Rendell-Baker* several times, for an application of "state action" inquiry in the nursing home context. Medicaid recipients who are eligible have access to both "skilled nursing facilities" and "health related facilities," both of which are privately owned and reimbursed directly by the state for the reasonable cost of health care services. A utilization review committee, required by federal regulations, can transfer patients from one type of facility to the other or discharge patients. The respondents claimed, upon one such transfer, of being shifted to a lower level of care without receiving adequate notice of the pending action, and sought to prove "state action" incident to the discharge and transfer decisions. The Court decided that no "state action" had been proved and that respondents' Fourteenth Amendment rights were thus not implicated. The Court stressed that "[t]he mere fact that a business is subject to state regulation does not by itself convert its action into that of the state for purposes of the Fourteenth Amendment." The Court's precedents, in particular Flagg Bros., Inc. v. Brooks, Casebook p.693, Moose Lodge No. 107 v. Irvis, Casebook p.686, and Jackson v. Metropolitan Edison Co., Casebook p.692, indicate that a state normally can be held responsible for private decisions only when it has exercised coercive power "or has provided such significant encouragement that the choice must in law be deemed to be that of the state." In finding insufficient governmental involvement in the decisions to dischargc or transfer, the Court concluded that, "even though the state subsidizes the costs of the facilities, pays the expenses of the patients, and licenses the facilities, the actions of the nursing home are not thereby converted into 'state action.'"

Justices Brennan and Marshall dissented.

Page 740. After O'Connor v. Donaldson add:

YOUNGBERG v. ROMEO, — U.S. —, 102 S. Ct. —, — L. Ed. 2d — (1982). Respondent, a profoundly retarded patient who had been involuntarily committed to a Pennsylvania state mental institution, sought damages from petitioner institution officials for injuries allegedly suffered while confined, in an action brought by his mother under 42 U.S.C. 1983. She claimed that respondent possessed constitutional rights to safe conditions of confinement, freedom from bodily restraint, and training and treatment (or "habilitation"), and that his rights in these respects had been denied, resulting in violation of the Eighth and Fourteenth Amendments. In the ensuing jury trial, the federal district court instructed the jurors that the Eighth Amendment provided the proper standard of possible liability, and the jury returned a verdict for petitioners upon which judgment was entered. On appeal the Court of Appeals for the Third Circuit reversed and remanded for a new trial, holding that the Fourteenth, rather than the Eighth, Amendment was the correct constitutional predicate for the asserted rights. With Justice Powell writing the opinion, a unanimous Court concluded that "the jury was erroneously instructed on the assumption that the proper standard of liability was that of the Eighth Amendment," and accordingly remanded for further proceedings. In assessing the constitutional contentions Justice Powell wrote:

"We consider here for the first time the substantive rights of involuntarily-committed mentally retarded persons under the Fourteenth Amendment to the Constitution. In this case, respondent has been committed under the laws of Pennsylvania, and he does not challenge the commitment. Rather, he argues that he has a constitutionally protected liberty interest in safety, freedom of movement, and training within the institution; and that petitioners infringed these rights by failing to provide constitutionally required conditions of confinement.

"The mere fact that Romeo has been committed under proper procedures does not deprive him of all substantive liberty interests under the Fourteenth Amendment. . . . Indeed, the state concedes that respondent has a right to adequate food, shelter, clothing, and medical care. We must decide whether liberty interests also exist in safety, freedom of movement, and training. If such interests do exist, we must further decide whether they have been infringed in this case."

Justice Powell then stated that "[r]espondent's first two claims involve liberty interests recognized by prior decisions of this Court, interests that involuntary commitment proceedings do not extinguish," referring to the rights to safe conditions and to freedom from bodily restraint, citing, e.g., Ingraham v. Wright, Casebook p.786, and Greenholtz v. Nebraska Penal Inmates, Casebook p.791. But, Powell continued, the "remaining claim is more troubling," involving a constitutional right to "minimally adequate habilitation" or, stated differently, to "training and development of needed skills," as "a substantive due process claim that is said to be grounded in the liberty component of the Due Process Clause of the Fourteenth Amendment." With regard to this claim, the Court said:

"In addressing the asserted right to training, we start from established principles. As a general matter, a State is under no constitutional duty to provide substantive services for those within its border. See Harris v. McRae, 448 U.S. 297, 318 (1980) (publicly funded abortions); Maher v. Roe, 432 U.S. 464, 469 (1977) (medical treatment). When a person is institutionalized — and wholly dependent on the State — it is conceded by petitioner that a duty to provide certain services and care does exist, although even then a State necessarily has considerable discretion in determining the nature and scope of its responsibilities. . . .

"Respondent, in light of the severe character of his retardation, concedes that no amount of training will make possible his release. And he does not argue that if he were still at home, the State would have an obligation to provide training at its expense. The record reveals that respondent's primary needs are bodily safety and a minimum of physical restraint, and respondent clearly claims training related to these needs. As we have recognized that there is a constitutionally protected liberty interest in safety and freedom from restraint, training may be necessary to avoid unconstitutional infringement of those rights. . . . If, as seems the case, respondent seeks only training related to safety and freedom from restraints [essentially "self-care programs . . . needed to reduce his aggressive behavior"], this case does not present the difficult question whether a mentally retarded person, involuntarily committed to a state institution, has some general constitutional right to training *per se,* even when no type or amount of training would lead to freedom.

"Chief Judge Seitz [of the Third Circuit], in language apparently adopted by respondent, observed: 'I believe that the plaintiff has a constitutional right to minimally adequate care and treatment. The existence of a constitutional right to care and treatment is no longer a novel legal proposition.' Chief Judge Seitz did not identify or otherwise define — beyond the right to reasonable safety and freedom from physical restraint — the 'minimally adequate care and treatment' that appropriately may be required for this respondent. In the circumstances presented by this case, and on the basis of the record developed to date, we agree with his view and conclude that respondent's liberty interests require the State to provide minimally adequate or reasonable training to ensure safety and freedom from undue restraint. In view of the kinds of treatment sought by respondent and the evidence of record, we need go no further in this case."

Continuing, Justice Powell further stated:

"We have established that Romeo retains liberty interests in safety and freedom from bodily restraint. Yet these interests are not absolute; indeed to some extent they are in conflict. In operating an institution such as Pennhurst, there are occasions in which it is necessary for the State to restrain the movement of residents — for example, to protect them as well as others from violence. Similar restraints may also be appropriate in a training program. And an institution cannot protect its residents from all danger of violence if it is to permit them to have any freedom of movement. The question then is not simply whether a liberty interest has been infringed but whether the extent or nature of the restraint or lack of absolute safety is such as to violate due process, ... [analogizing to the approach taken in deciding procedural due-process challenges to civil commitment proceedings," citing Parham v. J.R., 442 U.S. 584 (1979), Casebook p.792]. Accordingly, whether respondent's constitutional rights have been violated must be determined by balancing his liberty interests against the relevant state interests. If there is to be any uniformity in protecting these interests, this balancing cannot be left to the unguided discretion of a judge or jury. We therefore turn to consider the proper standard for determining whether a State adequately has protected the rights of the involuntarily-committed mentally retarded.

"We think the standard articulated by Chief Judge Seitz affords the necessary guidance and reflects the proper balance between the legitimate interests of the State and the rights of the involuntarily committed to reasonable conditions of safety and freedom from unreasonable restraints. He would have held that 'the Constitution only requires that the courts make certain that professional judgment in fact was exercised. It is not appropriate for the courts to specify which of several professionally acceptable choices should have been made.' 644 F.2d, at 178. Persons who have been involuntarily committed are entitled to more considerate treatment and conditions of confinement than criminals whose conditions of confinement are designed to punish. Cf. Estelle v. Gamble, 429 U.S. 97, 104 (1976). At the same time, this standard is lower than the 'compelling' or 'substantial' necessity tests the [majority of the] Court of Appeals would require a state to meet to justify use of restraints or conditions of less than absolute safety. We think this requirement would place an undue burden on the administration of institutions such as Pennhurst and also would restrict unnecessarily the exercise of professional judgment as to the needs of residents.

"Moreover, we agree that respondent is entitled to minimally adequate training. In this case, the minimally adequate training required by the Constitution is such training as may be reasonable in light of respondent's liberty interests in safety and freedom from unreasonable restraints. In determining what is 'reasonable' — in this and in any case presenting a claim for training by a state — we emphasize that courts must show deference to the judgment exercised by a qualified professional. By so limiting judicial review of challenges to conditions in state institutions, interference by the federal judiciary with the internal operations of these institutions should be minimized. Moreover, there certainly is no reason to think judges or juries are better qualified than appropriate professionals in making such decisions. . . . For these reasons, the decision, if made by a professional, is presumptively valid; liability may be imposed only when the decision by the professional is such a substantial departure from accepted professional judgment, practice or standards as to demonstrate that the person responsible actually did not base the decision on such a judgment. In an action for damages against a professional in his individual capacity, however, the professional will not be liable if he was unable to satisfy his normal professional standards because of budgetary constraints; in such a situation, good-faith immunity would bar liability. . . ."

Concluding, Justice Powell wrote:

"In deciding this case, we have weighed those post-commitment interests cognizable as liberty interests under the Due Process Clause of the Fourteenth Amendment against legitimate state interests and in light of the constraints under which most state institutions necessarily operate. We repeat that the state concedes a duty to provide adequate food, shelter, clothing and medical care. These are the essentials of the care that the state must provide. The state also has the unquestioned duty to provide reasonable safety for all residents and personnel within the institution. And it may not restrain residents except when and to the extent professional judgment deems this necessary to assure such safety or to provide needed training. In this case, therefore, the state is under a duty to provide respondent with such training as an appropriate professional would consider reasonable to ensure his safety and to facilitate his ability to function free from bodily restraints. It may well be unreasonable not to provide training when training could significantly reduce the need for restraints or the likelihood of violence.

"Respondent thus enjoys constitutionally protected interests in conditions of reasonable care and safety, reasonably non-restrictive confinement conditions, and such training as may be required by these interests. Such conditions of confinement would comport fully with the purpose of respondent's commitment. Cf. Jackson v. Indiana, 406 U.S. 715, 738 (1972). . . . In determining whether the state has met its obligations in these respects, decisions made by the appropriate professional are entitled to a presumption of correctness. Such a presumption is necessary to enable institutions of this type — often, unfortunately, overcrowded and understaffed — to continue to function. A single professional may have to make decisions with respect to a number of residents with widely varying needs and problems in the course of a normal day. The administrators, and particularly professional personnel, should not be required to make each decision in the shadow of an action for damages."

Justice Blackmun, joined by Justices Brennan and O'Connor, wrote a concurring opinion that sought "to make clear why [the Court's] opinion properly leaves unresolved two difficult and important issues." One is whether a state could accept a mental patient for "care and treatment" and then, consistent with due process, "refuse to provide him with any 'treatment,' as that term is defined by state law," referring to Jackson v. Indiana. The other "question left open today," Blackmun continued, "is whether respondent has an independent constitutional claim . . . to that 'habilitation' or training necessary to *preserve* those basic self-care skills he possessed when he first entered Pennhurst," also as an aspect of Fourteenth Amendment due process, in order to "prevent losses of additional liberty as a result of his confinement." Blackmun agreed that it was premature to resolve these issues "on this less-than-fully-developed record."

Chief Justice Burger concurred only in the judgment. He wrote separately that he "would hold flatly that respondent has no constitutional right to training, or 'habilitation,' *per se*," asserting that under the circumstances "the State's provision of food, shelter, medical care, and living conditions as safe as the inherent nature of the institutional environment reasonably allows, serve to justify the State's custody of respondent." Liability could be imposed on petitioners, in Burger's view, only for "unreasonable infringement of a mentally-retarded person's interests in safety and freedom from restraint."

Page 740. At the end of the carryover paragraph add:

See Mills v. Rogers, — U.S. — , 102 S. Ct. — , — L. Ed. 2d — (1982), decided the same day as Youngberg v. Romeo, supra in this Supplement, addition to Casebook p.740. Justice Powell delivered the opinion of a unanimous Court, identifying the principal issue as whether involuntarily committed mental patients have a constitutional right to refuse treatment with antipsychotic drugs, a question encompassing both substantive and procedural aspects. The litigants in this Massachusetts case agreed that the Constitution recognizes a "liberty interest" in avoiding the unwarranted administration of antipsychotic drugs; thus the substantive issue involved the defining of the constitutionally protected interest as well as the identification of the circumstances under which competing state interests might outweigh it. The procedural issue was delineated as concerning the constitutionally required procedures for determining that an individual's "liberty interest" actually is outweighed in a particular instance. Justice Powell stated that the substantive and procedural issues were intertwined with questions of state law, which could not be avoided for purposes of determining actual rights and obligations since the constitutionally provided substantive rights were only a minimum. Further, he said, "where a state creates liberty interests broader than those protected directly by the Federal Constitution, the procedures mandated to protect the federal substantive interests might fail to determine the actual procedural rights and obligations of persons within the state." Maintaining that the full scope of a patient's due process rights may depend on the substantive "liberty interest" created by state as well as federal law, the Court reiterated that a state may confer procedural protections of liberty interests that extend beyond those minimally required by the Constitution of the United States; if so, the minimal federal requirements would not be controlling nor in need of delineation in order to determine the legal rights and duties of persons within that state.

Justice Powell then referred to "a case recently decided by the Supreme Judicial Court of Massachusetts," dealing with the right to refuse antipsychotic drug therapy, which held that a person does not forfeit his protected liberty interest by virtue of becoming incompetent, but rather remains entitled to have his substituted judgment exercised on his behalf. Concluding that it was the Court's settled policy to avoid unnecessary decisions of constitutional issues, and that the intervening Massachusetts case may have changed Massachusetts law, the Court vacated the judgment and remanded the case for further proceedings.

Page 754. Add as a new Note 3:

3. In Greene v. Lindsey, — U.S. — , 102 S. Ct. 1874, — L. Ed. 2d — (1982), the Court held that the posting of a "writ of forcible entry and detainer" on a tenant's apartment door in a public housing project was insufficient notice to comply with procedural due process requirements. Relying on Mullane v. Central Hanover Bank & Trust, 339 U.S. 306 (1950), Casebook, p.752, the Court concluded that the due process clause of the Fourteenth Amendment prescribes a constitutional minimum of adequate notice, stating: "An elementary and fundamental requirement of due process in any proceeding which is to be accorded finality is notice reasonably calculated, under all circumstances, to apprise interested parties of the pendency of the action and afford them an opportunity to present their objections." The dissenters preferred the system chosen by the Kentucky legislature of posting a summons on the door of a residence as opposed to the preference of the majority for notice by means of the U.S. mail.

Page 759. Add as a new Note 5:

5. Cf. Insurance Corporation of Ireland, Ltd. v. Compagnie des Bauxites de Guinee, — U.S. — , 102 S. Ct. 2099, — L. Ed. 2d — (1982), where the lower federal courts "legally presumed" that petitioner had consented to in personam jurisdiction as a result of repeated non-compliance with court-ordered production of documents. In affirming, the Court carefully distinguished subject matter jurisdiction, a non-waivable Article III and statutory requirement, from personal jurisdiction, which flows not from Article III

but from the due process clause. The personal jurisdiction requirement recognizes and protects an individual liberty interest, the Court indicated.

Here personal jurisdiction results from petitioner's "waiver" by not timely objecting to personal jurisdiction, and from sanctions authorized by discovery rules contained in Rule 37 of the Federal Rules of Civil Procedure. Such a sanction was both "just" and specifically related to the particular "claim" that was at issue in the discovery order. Due process is violated by a rule attributing legal consequences to a failure to produce evidence only if the defendant's conduct fails to suggest a presumption that such failure was essentially an admission that the defense was without merit.

Page 761. At the end of the first paragraph of Note 2 add:

For a case dealing with the distinction between the requirement of "state action" to establish a Fourteenth Amendment violation and the requirement of action "under color of state law" to establish a right to recover under 42 U.S.C. 1983, in the context of a prejudgment attachment procedure of the debtor's property, see Lugar v. Edmondson Oil Co., Inc., – U.S. – , 102 S. Ct. – , – L. Ed. 2d – (1982). Citing Sniadach v. Family Finance Corp., Casebook p.761, the Court held the petitioner was deprived of his property through state action and since Virginia's prejudgment attachment statute has been challenged as to its constitutionality, petitioner had a valid §1983 claim. Chief Justice Burger and Justices Powell, Rehnquist, and O'Connor dissented.

Page 792. At the end of Note 5 add:

In Lehman v. Lycoming County Children's Services, – U.S. – , 102 S. Ct. – , – L. Ed. 2d – (1982), the Court distinguished *Santosky* in holding federal habeas corpus actions under 28 U.S.C. §2254 unavailable in regard to child-custody disputes.

Page 840. At the end of Note 3 add:

Compare Loretto v. Teleprompter Manhattan CATV Corp., – U.S. – , 102 S. Ct. – , – L. Ed. 2d – (1982), which involved consideration of whether a "taking" of property without compensation resulted from a New York statute requiring a landlord to permit a cable television company to install its cable facilities on an apartment building in New York City. Holding that there was a taking for Fifth and Fourteenth Amendment purposes, the Court focused on the fact that permanent occupation of physical property occurred incident to the installation of cable facilities on a building. Thus, without regard to whether the activity achieves an important public benefit or has only a minimal economic impact on the property owner, a taking to the extent of the physical occupation results. Distinguishing the *Penn Central* case as involving a situation where "substantial regulation of an owner's use of his own property [was] deemed necessary to promote the public interest," the Court noted that it has "[a]t the same time ... long considered a physical intrusion by government to be a property restriction of an unusually serious character for purpose of the Taking Clause. . . . [W]hen the physical intrusion reaches the extreme form of a permanent physical occupation," the Court concluded, "a taking has occurred." In contrast to the dissenters' view, the majority asserted that "application of the physical occupation rule [in this context will not have] dire consequences for the government's power to adjust landlord-tenant relationships." Justices Blackmun, Brennan, and White dissented, characterizing the majority's approach as formalistic and unduly rigid. Since the economic effect of the New York requirement was *de minimis*, the dissent maintained, application of the traditional balancing test should produce the conclusion that no taking occurred.

Page 871. At the end of the carryover paragraph add:

For a discussion of Article IV's interstate privileges and immunities clause as the source of a constitutionally protected "right to travel," as a ground for invalidating Alaska's dissimilar treatment of its residents based on duration of residency in lieu of an equal protection analysis, see Justice O'Connor's concurring opinion in Zobel v. Williams, — U.S. —, 102 S. Ct. —, — L. Ed. 2d — (1982). Disagreeing with the majority's evaluation of Alaska's expressed purpose to reward its citizens for past contributions as being illegitimate, she stated: "[A] full reading of Shapiro v. Thompson [Casebook p.1085] reveals the Court has rejected this objective only when its implementation would abridge an interest in interstate travel or migration. A desire to compensate citizens for their prior contributions is neither inherently invidious nor irrational." In declaring "Alaska's purpose wholly illegitimate, the Court establishes an uncertain jurisprudence," O'Connor asserted. Discussing the right to travel, she assessed the potential constitutional infringement of schemes such as Alaska's to be the necessarily less favorable treatment of new residents of a state as compared to longer-term residents. She continued: "Stripped of its essentials, the plan denies non-Alaskans settling in the state the same privileges afforded longer-term residents." She stressed that the privileges and immunities clause of Article IV addresses just this type of discrimination, i.e., Alaska's forcing "nonresidents settling in the state to accept a status inferior to that of old-timers. [R]esidents who arrived in Alaska after that date [Alaska's statehood in 1959] have a less valuable citizenship right. . . . [C]itizens who arrive in the state tomorrow will receive an even smaller claim on Alaska's resources." Referring to Baldwin v. Fish & Game Commn. of Montana, Casebook p.1095, she stated the proper standard of review is for the Court to ascertain whether the state is treating residents and nonresidents "without unnecessary distinctions" when the resident seeks to engage in "an essential activity or exercise a basic right." If the nonresident engages in conduct not deemed "fundamental" because it does not "bea[r] upon the vitality of the Nation as a single entity," the privileges and immunities clause extends no protection. Defining the right to travel infringed upon in this case as "fundamental," Justice O'Connor concluded that "[i]t is difficult to imagine a right more essential to the Nation as a whole than the right to establish residency in a new state."

Page 948. At the end of Note 1 add:

For extended consideration as well as application of *Rodrigeuz* in the context of a Texas law denying access to public schools to illegal aliens, see Plyler v. Doe, — U.S. — , 102 S. Ct. — , — L. Ed. 2d — (1982), infra in this Supplement, addition to Casebook p.1053.

Page 988. Add as a new Note 3:

3. In Rodriguez v. Popular Democratic Party, — U.S. — , 102 S. Ct. 2194, — L. Ed. 2d — (1982), a unanimous Court upheld a Puerto Rico statute which vests in a political party the initial authority to appoint an interim replacement — until the next general election — for one of its members who vacates the position of district senator or representative. Noting that the Constitution does not expressly require a prescribed method for filling vacancies in a state or commonwealth legislature, the Court emphasized that the methods chosen by the people of Puerto Rico (just as with any state) and their representatives to structure the Commonwealth's electoral system are entitled to "substantial deference."

Chief Justice Berger stressed that the voting rights of Puerto Rican citizens are constitutionally protected to the same extent as those of all other United States citizens. However, quoting from Minor v. Happersett, 88 U.S (21 Wall.) 162 (1875), Casebook, p.987, he reiterated the Court's position that "the Constitution does not confer the right of suffrage upon anyone." Relying on San Antonio School District v. Rodriguez, Casebook p.930, the Court reemphasized that "the right to vote, *per se*, is not a constitutionally guaranteed right." The Court concluded that Puerto Rico's party appointment system served several "compelling interests": first, the system protected the "electoral mandate" of the previous election, and, second, it ensured the stability and continuity of the "legislative balance" until the next general election. Reliance was placed on Valenti v. Rockefeller, 399 U.S. 405 (1969), where the Court sustained the authority of the Governor of New York to fill a vacancy in the United States Senate by appointment pending the next regularly scheduled congressional election, and concluded that although most members of the legislature hold office by virtue of popular election, some members, at any given time, may hold office through interim appointment.

Is Chief Justice Burger's quote from Minor v. Happersett, overturned in any event by the Nineteenth Amendment, a correct statement of currently held views on the source of the right to vote in federal elections? See, e.g., Art. I., §2, and the Seventeenth Amendment, as well as Oregon v. Mitchell, Casebook p.1125. And, with respect to Burger's reference to *Rodriguez*, compare the Court's statement in that case (411 U.S. at 34, n.74).

Page 1011. At the end of first paragraph of Note 5 add:

In Rogers v. Lodge, — U.S. — , 102 S. Ct. — , — L. Ed. 2d — (1982), the Court invalidated a Georgia county's at-large system for electing members of its board of commissioners, on the ground that it violated Fourteenth and Fifteenth Amendment rights by diluting the voting power of black citizens. Blacks had always made up a substantial majority of the county's population but comprised a minority of the registered voters. Bloc voting along racial lines had been present and past discrimination restricted the present opportunity of blacks to participate effectively in the local political process. Perhaps most significantly, no black had ever been elected to the county board. The lower federal courts required proof of discriminatory intent "as a requisite to a finding of unconstitutional vote dilution," but concluded that, although the at-large electoral system was "neutral in origin," the policy was being maintained for discriminatory purposes. These findings of intentional discrimination were not clearly erroneous, the Court concluded, and thus they should not be disturbed. Nor did the lower courts act incorrectly in ordering the utilization of single-member districts for the election of board members. The majority reviewed Washington v. Davis, Casebook p.981, and the *Arlington Heights* case (Casebook p.985), and in particular their application in the election context, discussing and distinguishing Mobile v. Bolden in this regard. Whitcomb v. Chavis was similarly distinguished, while White v. Regester was relied upon. Justices Powell, Rehnquist, and Stevens dissented, noting that there were no direct barriers to voting or evident dilution of the weight of votes, that cases such as this did not differ significantly from gerrymandering situations, and, finally, that "the standard used to identify unlawful racial discrimination in this area should be defined in terms that are judicially manageable and reviewable." Reliable "objective" factors should be used in assessing whether discriminatory intent is present, they stated.

Page 1037. After the second paragraph of Note 1 add:

Compare Clements v. Fashing, — U.S. — , 102 S. Ct. — , — L. Ed. 2d — (1982), involving provisions of the Texas Constitution making current office-holders ineligible for service in the legislature and providing for "automatic resignation" from positions if they became candidates in any other state or federal election. A 5-4 majority held these "ballot access" provisions valid against an equal protection challenge. The majority ruled that Texas' asserted interests were sufficient to warrant a *"de minimis"* interference with the appellees' "First Amendment interest in candidacy." Relying on Bullock v. Carter, Casebook p.1035, the Court held that candidacy is not a "fundamental right," and "the existence of barriers to a candidate's access to the ballot does not itself compel close scrutiny." Texas needs only to show a rational relationship between the classifications created by its provisions and the legitimate interests it seeks to protect, and had done so here, the majority concluded.

Justices Brennan, Marshall, White, and Blackmun dissented.

Page 1054. At the end of Note 6 add:

PLYLER v. DOE
—————————————————————————————
— U.S. —, 102 S. Ct. —, — L. Ed. 2d — (1982)

[At issue in two companion cases was the constitutionality, under the Fourteenth Amendment's equal protection clause, of a 1975 Texas statute that withheld from local school districts any state funding for the education of children not "legally admitted" into the United States. School districts either denied enrollment entirely to illegal-alien children or sought to charge them tuition for attending the public schools. The lower federal courts which considered the cases rejected the school officials' contentions that this was a legitimate financial measure designed to maintain the fiscal integrity of the school systems, that exclusion of "undocumented" school-age children from the public educational system improved the quality of education provided, and that the measure reduced the number of illegal aliens coming into the State of Texas. One of the district courts applied a strict scrutiny test, while the other determined that the restriction was unconstitutional regardless of the equal protection standard that was applied. The Court noted probable jurisdiction and consolidated the cases for briefing and argument.]

Justice BRENNAN delivered the opinion of the Court....

The Fourteenth Amendment provides that "No State shall ... deprive any person of life, liberty, or property, without due process of law; nor deny to *any person within its jurisdiction* the equal protection of the laws." Appellants argue at the outset that undocumented aliens, because of their immigration status, are not "persons within the jurisdiction" of the State of Texas, and that they therefore have no right to the equal protection of Texas law. We reject this argument. Whatever his status under the immigration laws, an alien is surely a "person" in any ordinary sense of that term. Aliens, even aliens whose presence in this country is unlawful, have long been recognized as "persons" guaranteed due process of law by the Fifth and Fourteenth Amendments.... Yick Wo v. Hopkins, 118 U.S. 356,

369 (1886). Indeed, we have clearly held that the Fifth Amendment protects aliens whose presence in this country is unlawful from invidious discrimination by the Federal Government. Mathews v. Diaz, 426 U.S. 67, 77 (1976).

Appellants seek to distinguish our prior cases, emphasizing that the Equal Protection Clause directs a State to afford its protection to persons *within its jurisdiction* while the Due Process Clauses of the Fifth and Fourteenth Amendments contain no such assertedly limiting phrase. In appellants' view, persons who have entered the United States illegally are not "within the jurisdiction" of a State even if they are present within a State's boundaries and subject to its laws. Neither our cases nor the logic of the Fourteenth Amendment supports that constricting construction of the phrase "within its jurisdiction," [citing United States v. Wong Kim Ark, 169 U.S. 649 (1898), Casebook p.603]. We have never suggested that the class of persons who might avail themselves of the equal protection guarantee is less than coextensive with that entitled to due process. To the contrary, we have recognized that both provisions were fashioned to protect an identical class of persons, and to reach every exercise of State authority. . . .

In concluding that "all persons within the territory of the United States," including aliens unlawfully present, may invoke the Fifth and Sixth Amendment to challenge actions of the Federal Government, we reasoned from the understanding that the Fourteenth Amendment was designed to afford its protection to all within the boundaries of a State. . . . Our cases applying the Equal Protection Clause reflect the same territorial theme. . . .

There is simply no support for appellants' suggestion that "due process" is somehow of greater stature than "equal protection" and therefore available to a larger class of persons. To the contrary, each aspect of the Fourteenth Amendment reflects an elementary limitation on state power. To permit a State to employ the phrase "within its jurisdiction" in order to identify subclasses of persons whom it would define as beyond its jurisdiction, thereby relieving itself of the obligation to assure that its laws are designed and applied equally to those persons, would undermine the principal purpose for which the Equal Protection Clause was incorporated in the Fourteenth Amendment. The Equal Protection Clause was intended to work nothing less than the abolition of all caste- and invidious class-based legislation. That objective is fundamentally at odds with the power the State asserts here to classify persons subject to its law as nonetheless excepted from its protection. . . .

Use of the phrase "within its jurisdiction" [as the congressional debates indicate] does not detract from, but rather confirms, the understanding that the protection of the Fourteenth Amendment extends to anyone, citizen or stranger, who *is* subject to the laws of a State, and reaches into every corner of a States territory. That a person's initial entry into a State, or into the United States, was unlawful, and that he may for that reason be expelled, cannot negate the simple fact of his presence within the State's territorial perimeter. Given such presence, he is subject to the full range of obligations imposed by the State's civil and criminal laws. And until he leaves the jurisdiction — either voluntarily, or involuntarily in accordance with the Constitution and laws of the United States — he is entitled to the equal protection of the laws that a State may choose to establish.

Our conclusion that the illegal aliens who are plaintiffs in these cases may claim the benefit of the Fourteenth Amendment's guarantee of equal protection only begins the inquiry. The more difficult question is whether the Equal Protection Clause has been violated by the refusal of the State of Texas to reimburse local school boards for the education of children who cannot demonstrate that their presence within the United States is lawful, or by the imposition by those school boards of the burden of tuition on those children. It is to this question that we now turn. . . .

[While "[i]n applying the Equal Protection Clause to most forms of state action [the Court] seek[s] only the assurance that the classification at issue bears some fair relationship to a legitimate public purpose"], we would not be faithful to our obligations under the Fourteenth Amendment if we applied so deferential a standard to every classification. The Equal Protection Clause was intended as a restriction on state legislative action inconsistent with elemental constitutional premises. Thus we have treated as presumptively invidious those classifications that disadvantage a "suspect class,"[14] or that impinge upon the exercise of a "fundamental right."[15] With respect to such classifications, it is appropriate to enforce the mandate of equal protec-

14. Several formulations might explain our treatment of certain classifications as "suspect." Some classifications are more likely than others to reflect deep-seated prejudice rather than legislative rationality in pursuit of some legitimate objective. Legislation predicated on such prejudice is easily recognized as incompatible with the constitutional understanding that each person is to be judged individually and is entitled to equal justice under the law. Classifications treated as suspect tend to be irrelevant to any proper legislative goal. See McLaughlin v. Florida, 379 U.S. 184, 192 (1964): Hirabayashi v. United States, 320 U.S. 81, 100 (1943). Finally, certain groups, indeed largely the same groups, have historically been "relegated to such a position of political powerlessness as to command extraordinary protection from the majoritarian political process." San Antonio School District v. Rodriguez, 411 U.S. 1, 28 (1973); Graham v. Richardson, 403 U.S. 365, 372 (1971); see United States v. Carolene Products Co., 304 U.S. 144, 152-153, n.4 (1938). The experience of our Nation has shown that prejudice may manifest itself in the treatment of some groups. Our response to that experience is reflected in the Equal Protection Clause of the Fourteenth Amendment. Legislation imposing special disabilities upon groups disfavored by virtue of circumstances beyond their control suggests the kind of "class or caste" treatment that the Fourteenth Amendment was designed to abolish.

15. In determining whether a class-based denial of a particular right is deserving of strict scrutiny under the Equal Protection Clause, we look to the Constitution to see if the right infringed has its source, explicitly or implicitly, therein. But we have also recognized the fundamentality of participation in state "elections on an equal basis with other citizens in the jurisdiction," Dunn v. Blumstein, supra, at 336, even though "the right to vote *per se*, is not a constitutionally protected right." *San Antonio School District*, 411 U.S., at 35, n.78. With respect to suffrage, we have explained the need for strict scrutiny as arising from the significance of the franchise as the guardian of all other rights. See Harper v. Virginia Bd. of Elections, 383 U.S.

tion by requiring the State to demonstrate that its classification has been precisely tailored to serve a compelling governmental interest. In addition, we have recognized that certain forms of legislative classification, while not facially invidious, nonetheless give rise to recurring constitutional difficulties; in these limited circumstances we have sought the assurance that the classification reflects a reasoned judgment consistent with the ideal of equal protection by inquiring whether it may fairly be viewed as furthering a substantial interest of the State.[16] We turn to a consideration of the standard appropriate for the evaluation of [the Texas statute].

Sheer incapability or lax enforcement of the laws barring entry into this country, coupled with the failure to establish an effective bar to the employment of undocumented aliens, has resulted in the creation of a substantial "shadow population" of illegal migrants — numbering in the millions — within our borders. This situation raises the specter of a permanent caste of undocumented resident aliens, encouraged by some to remain here as a source of cheap labor, but nevertheless denied the benefits that our society makes available to citizens and lawful residents. The existence of such an underclass presents most difficult problems for a Nation that prides itself on adherence to principles of equality under law.

The children who are plaintiffs in these cases are special members of this underclass. Persuasive arguments support the view that a State may withhold its benificence from those whose very presence within the United States is the product of their own unlawful conduct. These arguments do not apply with the same force to classifications imposing disabilities on the minor *children* of such illegal entrants. At the least, those who elect to enter our territory by stealth and in violation of our law should be prepared to bear the consequences, including, but not limited to, deportation. But the children of those illegal entrants are not comparably situated. Their "parents have the ability to conform their conduct to societal norms," and presumably the ability to remove themselves from the State's jurisdiction; but the children who are plaintiffs in these cases "can affect neither their parents' conduct nor their own status." Trimble v. Gordon, 430 U.S. 762, 770 (1977). Even if the State found it expedient to control the conduct of adults by acting against their children, legislation directing the onus of a parent's

---

663, 667 (1966); Reynolds v. Sims, 377 U.S. 533, 562 (1964): Yick Wo v. Hopkins, 118 U.S. 356, 370 (1886).

16. See Craig v. Boren, 429 U.S. 190 (1976); Lalli v. Lalli, 439 U.S. 259 (1978). This technique of "intermediate" scrutiny permits us to evaluate the rationality of the legislative judgment with reference to well-settled constitutional principles. "In expounding the Constitution, the Court's role is to discern 'principles sufficiently absolute to give them roots throughout the community and continuity over significant periods of time, and to lift them above the level of the pragmatic political judgments of a particular time and place.'" University of California Regents v. Bakke, 438 U.S. 265, 299 (1978) (Opinion of Powell, J.), quoting A. Cox, The Role of the Supreme Court in American Government 114 (1976). Only when concerns sufficiently absolute and enduring can be clearly ascertained from the Constitution and our cases do we employ this standard to aid us in determining the rationality of the legislative choice.

misconduct against his children does not comport with fundamental conceptions of justice. . . .

Of course, undocumented status is not irrelevant to any proper legislative goal. Nor is undocumented status an absolutely immutable characteristic since it is the product of conscious, indeed unlawful, action. But §21.031 [of the Texas Education Code] is directed against children, and imposes its discriminatory burden on the basis of a legal characteristic over which children can have little control. It is thus difficult to conceive of a rational justification for penalizing these children for their presence within the United States. Yet that appears to be precisely the effect of §21.031.

Public education is not a "right" granted to individuals by the Constitution. *San Antonio School District,* supra, at 35. But neither is it merely some governmental "benefit" indistinguishable from other forms of social welfare legislation. Both the importance of education in maintaining our basic institutions, and the lasting impact of its deprivation on the life of the child, mark the distinction. The "American people have always regarded education and the acquisition of knowledge as matters of supreme importance." Meyer v. Nebraska, 262 U.S. 390, 400 (1923). We have recognized "the public school as a most vital civic institution for the preservation of a democratic system of government," Abington School District v. Schempp, 374 U.S. 203, 230 (1963) (Brennan, J., concurring), and as the primary vehicle for transmitting "the values on which our society rests." Ambach v. Norwick, 441 U.S. 68, 76 (1979). As noted early in our history, "some degree of education is necessary to prepare citizens to participate effectively and intelligently in our open political system if we are to preserve freedom and independence." Wisconsin v. Yoder, 406 U.S. 205, 221 (1972). And these historic "perceptions of the public schools as inculcating fundamental values necessary to the maintenance of a democratic political system have been confirmed by the observations of social scientists." Ambach v. Norwich, supra, at 77. In addition, education provides the basic tools by which individuals might lead economically productive lives to the benefit of us all. In sum, education has a fundamental role in maintaining the fabric of our society. We cannot ignore the significant social costs borne by our Nation when select groups are denied the means to absorb the values and skills upon which our social order rests.

In addition to the pivotal role of education in sustaining our political and cultural heritage, denial of education to some isolated group of children poses an affront to one of the goals of the Equal Protection Clause: the abolition of governmental barriers presenting unreasonable obstacles to advancement on the basis of individual merit. Paradoxically, by depriving the children of any disfavored group of an education, we foreclose the means by which that group might raise the level of esteem in which it is held by the majority. But more directly, "education prepares individuals to be self-reliant and self-sufficient participants in society." Wisconsin v. Yoder, supra, at 221. Illiteracy is an enduring disability. The inability to read and write will handicap the individual deprived of a basic education each and every day of his life. The inestimable toll of that deprivation on the social, economic, intellectual and psychological well-being of the individual, and the obstacle it poses to individual achievement, makes it most difficult to reconcile the cost or the principle of a status-based denial of basic education with the framework of equality embodied in the Equal Protection Clause, [quoting at length from Brown v. Board of Education, Casebook p.899].

These well-settled principles allow us to determine the proper level of deference to be afforded §21.031. Undocumented aliens cannot be treated as a suspect class because their presence in this country in violation of federal law is not a "constitutional irrelevancy." Nor is education a fundamental right; a State need not justify by compelling necessity every variation in the manner in which education is provided to its population. ... But more is involved in this case than the abstract question whether §21.031 discriminates against a suspect class, or whether education is a fundamental right. Section 21.031 imposes a lifetime hardship on a discrete class of children not accountable for their disabling status. The stigma of illiteracy will mark them for the rest of their lives. By denying these children a basic education, we deny them the ability to live within the structure of our civic institutions, and foreclose any realistic possibility that they will contribute in even the smallest way to the progress of our Nation. In determining the rationality of §21.031, we may appropriately take into account its costs to the Nation and to the innocent children who are its victims. In light of these countervailing costs, the discrimination contained in §21.031 can hardly be considered rational unless it furthers some substantial goal of the State.

It is the State's principal argument, and apparently the view of the dissenting Justices, that the undocumented status of these children *vel non* establishes a sufficient rational basis for denying them benefits that a State might choose to afford other residents. The State notes that while other aliens are admitted "on an equality of legal privileges with all citizens under non-discriminatory laws," Takahashi v. Fish & Game Commn., 334 U.S. 410, 420 (1948), the asserted right of these children to an education can claim no implicit congressional imprimatur. Indeed, on the State's view, Congress' apparent disapproval of the presence of these children within the United States, and the evasion of the federal regulatory program that is the mark of undocumented status, provides authority for its decision to impose upon them special disabilities. Faced with an equal protection challenge respecting the treatment of aliens, we agree that the courts must be attentive to congressional policy; the exercise of congressional power might well affect the State's prerogatives to afford differential treatment to a particular class of aliens. But we are unable to find in the congressional immigration scheme any statement of policy that might weigh significantly in arriving at an equal protection balance concerning the State's authority to deprive these children of an education, [especially since "States enjoy no power with respect to the classification of aliens" in view of the Constitution's commitment of plenary power under Art. I to Congress.]

To be sure, like all persons who have entered the United States unlawfully, these children are subject to deportation. 8 U.S.C. §§1251-1252. But there is no assurance that a child subject to deportation will ever be deported. An illegal entrant might be granted federal permission to continue to reside in this country, or even to become a citizen. See, e.g., 8 U.S.C. §§1252, 1253(h), 1254. In light of the discretionary federal power to grant relief from deportation, a State cannot realistically determine that any particular undocumented child will in fact be deported until after deportation proceedings have been completed. It would of course be most difficult for the State to justify a denial of education to a child enjoying an inchoate federal permission to remain.

We are reluctant to impute to Congress the intention to withhold from these children, for so long as they are present in this country through no fault of their own, access to a basic education. In other contexts, undocumented status, coupled with some articulable federal policy, might enhance State authority with respect to the treatment of undocumented aliens. But in the area of special constitutional sensitivity presented by this case, and in the absence of any contrary indication fairly discernible in the present legislative record, we perceive no national policy that supports the State in denying these children an elementary education. . . . We therefore turn to the state objectives that are said to support §21.031.

Appellants argue that the classification at issue furthers an interest in the "preservation of the state's limited resources for the education of its lawful residents." . . . Of course, a concern for the preservation of resources standing alone can hardly justify the classification used in allocating those resources. Graham v. Richardson, supra, 403 U.S., at 374-375. The State must do more than justify its classification with a concise expression of an intention to discriminate. Examining Board v. Flores de Otero, 426 U.S. 572, 605 (1976). Apart from the asserted state prerogative to act against undocumented children solely on the basis of their undocumented status — an asserted prerogative that carries only minimal force in the circumstances of this case — we discern three colorable state interests that might support §21.031.

First, appellants appear to suggest that the State may seek to protect the State from an influx of illegal immigrants. While a State might have an interest in mitigating the potentially harsh economic effects of sudden shifts in population, §21.031 hardly offers an effective method of dealing with an urgent demographic or economic problem. There is no evidence in the record suggesting that illegal entrants impose any significant burden on the State's economy. To the contrary, the available evidence suggests that illegal aliens underutilize public services, while contributing their labor to the local economy and tax money to the State fisc. . . . The dominant incentive for illegal entry into the State of Texas is the availability of employment;

few if any illegal immigrants come to this country, or presumably to the State of Texas, in order to avail themselves of a free education. Thus, even making the doubtful assumption that the net impact of illegal aliens on the economy of the State is negative, we think it clear that [excluding or charging tuition to undocumented children is ineffectual in stemming the tide of illegal immigration], at least when compared with the alternative of prohibiting the employment of illegal aliens. ...

Second, while it is apparent that a state may "not ... reduce expenditures for education by barring [some arbitrarily chosen class of] children from its schools," Shapiro v. Thompson, 394 U.S. 618, 633 (1969), appellants suggest that undocumented children are appropriately singled out for exclusion because of the special burdens they impose on the State's ability to provide high quality public education. But the record in no way supports the claim that exclusion of undocumented children is likely to improve the overall quality of education in the State. ... [And], even if improvement in the quality of education were a likely result of barring some *number* of children from the schools of the State, the State must support its selection of *this* group as the appropriate target for exclusion. In terms of educational cost and need, however, undocumented children are "basically indistinguishable" from legally resident alien children. ...

Finally, appellants suggest that undocumented children are appropriately singled out because their unlawful presence within the United States renders them less likely than other children to remain within the boundaries of the State, and to put their education to productive social or political use within the State. Even assuming that such an interest is legitimate, it is an interest that is most difficult to quantify. The State has no assurance that any child, citizen or not, will employ the education provided by the State within the confines of the State's borders. If any event, the record is clear that many of the undocumented children disabled by this classification will remain in this country indefinitely and that some will become lawful residents or citizens of the United States. It is difficult to understand precisely what the State hopes to achieve by promoting the creation and perpetuation of a subclass of illiterates within our boundaries, surely adding to the problems and costs of unemployment, welfare, and crime. It is thus clear that whatever savings might be achieved by denying these children an education, they are wholly insubstantial in light of the costs involved to these children, the State, and the Nation.

If the State is to deny a discrete group of innocent children the free public education that it offers to other children residing within its borders, that denial must be justified by a showing that it furthers some substantial state interest. No such showing was made here. Accordingly, the judgment of the Court of Appeals in each of these cases is affirmed.

[Justices Marshall, Blackmun, and Powell wrote separate concurring opinions. Marshall simply reiterated his view, developed at length in his

Rodriguez dissent, that education is a fundamental right subject to strict scrutiny in the context of an equal protection clause challenge. Blackmun's opinion discussed the "fundamental rights' aspect of the Court's equal protection analysis" at length, indicating his continued adherence to the *Rodriguez* formulation as "the appropriate model for resolving most equal protection disputes." He elaborated:]

With all this said, however, I believe the Court's experience has demonstrated that the *Rodriquez* formulation does not settle every issue of "fundamental rights" arising under the Equal Protection Clause. Only a pedant would insist that there are *no* meaningful distinctions among the multitude of social and political interests regulated by the States, and *Rodriguez* does not stand for quite so absolute a proposition. To the contrary, *Rodriguez* implicitly acknowledged that certain interests, though not constitutionally guaranteed, must be accorded a special place in equal protection analysis. Thus, the Court's decisions long have accorded strict scrutiny to classifications bearing on the right to vote in state elections. . . . In other words, the right to vote is accorded extraordinary treatment because it is, in equal protection terms, an extraordinary right: a citizen cannot hope to achieve any meaningful degree of individual political equality if granted an inferior right of participation in the political process. Those denied the vote are relegated, by state fiat, in a most basic way to second-class status.

It is arguable, of course, that the Court never should have applied fundamental rights doctrine in the fashion outlined above. Justice Harlan, for one, maintained that strict equal protection scrutiny was appropriate only when racial or analogous classifications were at issue. . . . But it is too late to debate that point, and I believe that accepting the principle of the voting cases — the idea that state classifications bearing on certain interests pose the risk of allocating rights in a fashion inherently contrary to any notion of "equality" — dictates the outcome here. . . .

In my view, when the State provides an education to some and denies it to others, it immediately and inevitably creates class distinctions of a type fundamentally inconsistent with those purposes, mentioned above, of the Equal Protection Clause. Children denied an education are placed at a permanent and insurmountable competitive disadvantage, for an uneducated child is denied even the opportunity to achieve. And when those children are members of an identifiable group, that group — through the State's action — will have been converted into a discrete underclass. Other benefits provided by the State, such as housing and public assistance, are of course important; to an individual in immediate need, they may be more desirable than the right to be educated. But classifications involving the complete denial of education are in a sense unique, for they strike at the heart of equal protection values by involving the State in the creation of permanent class distinctions. . . . In a sense, then denial of an education is the analogue of denial of the right to vote: the former relegates the individual to second-class social status; the latter places him at a permanent political disadvantage.

This conclusion is fully consistent with *Rodriguez*. The Court there reserved judgment on the constitutionality of a state system that "occasioned an absolute denial of educational opportunities to any of its children," noting that "no charge fairly could be made that the system [at issue in *Rodriguez*] fails to provide each child with an opportunity to acquire ... basic minimal skills." 411 U.S., at 37. And it cautioned that in a case "involv[ing] the most persistent and difficult questions of educational policy, ... [the] Court's lack of specialized knowledge and experience counsels against premature interference with the informed judgments made at the state and local levels." Id., at 42. Thus *Rodriguez* held, and the Court now reaffirms, that "a State need not justify by compelling necessity every variation in the manner in which education is provided to its population." Similarly, it is undeniable that education is not a "fundamental right" in the sense that it is constitutionally guaranteed. Here, however, the State has undertaken to provide an education to most of the children residing within its borders. And, in contrast to the situation in *Rodriguez*, it does not take an advanced degree to predict the effects of a complete denial of education upon those children targeted by the State's classification. In such circumstances, the voting decisions suggest that the State must offer something more than a rational basis for its classification.

[Justice Blackmun concluded by noting the irony of considering the necessity of education in a case involving individuals whose presence in the country was unlawful, but pointed to the "preeminent role of the Federal Government in regulating immigration" as well as the fact that "a significant number of illegal aliens will remain in this country permanently" and it cannot be determined which will stay and which will be deported at the time they are denied a public education. "Given the extraordinary nature of the interest involved, this makes the classification here fatally imprecise," he stated.

Justice Powell alluded to the "intractability of the problem" of illegal aliens in the United States, and said that he agreed with the Court that "their children should not be left on the streets uneducated." He continued by stating that "[a]lthough the analogy is not perfect, our holding today does find support in decisions of this Court with respect to the status of illegitimates," citing and quoting from Weber v. Aetna Casualty & Surety Co., 406 U.S. 164 (1972), Casebook p.1058. Here children of illegal aliens are denied "the opportunity to attend the free public schools that the State makes available to all residents ... because of a status resulting from the violation by parents or guardians of our immigration laws and the fact that they remain in our country unlawfully." Continuing, he wrote:]

Our review in a case such as this is properly heightened.[2] ... Cf. Craig v.

2. I emphasize the Court's conclusion that strict scrutiny is not appropriately applied to this

Boren, 429 U.S. 190 (1976) [Casebook p.1078]. The classification at issue deprives a group of children of the opportunity for education afforded all other children simply because they have been assigned a legal status due to a violation of law by their parents. These children thus have been singled out for a lifelong penalty and stigma. A legislative classification that threatens the creation of an underclass of future citizens and residents cannot be reconciled with one of the fundamental purposes of the Fourteenth Amendment. In these unique circumstances, the Court properly may require that the State's interests be substantial and that the means bear a "fair and substantial relation" to these interests.[3] See Lalli v. Lalli, 439 U.S. 259, 265 ("classifications based on illegitimacy ... are invalid under the Fourteenth Amendment if they are not substantially related to permissible state interests"); Id. at 271 ("[a]s the State's interests are substantial, we now consider the means adopted").

In my view, the State's denial of education to these children bears no substantial relation to any substantial state interest. [Since] an uncertain but significant percentage of illegal alien children will remain in Texas as residents and many eventually will become citizens, ... the State's purported interests ...are poorly served by the educational exclusions. Indeed, the interests relied upon the State would seem to be insubstantial in view of the consequences to the State itself of wholly uneducated persons living indefinitely within its borders. By contrast, access to the public schools is made available to the children of lawful residents without regard to the temporary nature of their residency in the particular Texas school district. . . .

In reaching this conclusion, I am not unmindful of what must be the exasperation of responsible citizens and government authorities in Texas and other states similarly situated. Their responsibility, if any, for the influx of aliens is slight compared to that imposed by the Constitution on the federal government. So long as the ease of entry remains inviting, and the power to deport is exercised infrequently by the federal government, the additional expense of admitting these children to public schools might fairly be shared by the federal and state governments. But it hardly can be argued rationally that anyone benefits from the creation within our borders of a subclass of illiterate persons many of whom will remain in the State, adding to the

---

classification. This exacting standard of review has been reserved for instances in which a "fundamental" constitutional right or a "suspect" classification is present. Neither is present in this case, as the Court holds.

3. The Chief Justice argues in his dissenting opinion that this heightened standard of review is inconsistent with the Court's decision in San Antonio School District v. Rodriguez, 411 U.S. 1(1973). But in *Rodriguez* no group of children was singled out by the State and then penalized because of their parent's status. Rather, funding for education varied across the State because of the tradition of local control. Nor, in that case, was any group of children totally deprived of all education as in this case. If the resident children of illegal aliens were denied welfare assistance, made available by government to all other children who qualify, this also — in my opinion — would be an impermissible penalizing of children because of their parents' status.

problems and costs of both State and National Governments attendant upon unemployment, welfare and crime.

Chief Justice BURGER, with whom Justice WHITE, Justice REHNQUIST, and Justice O'CONNOR join, dissenting.

Were it our business to set the Nation's social policy, I would agree without hesitation that it is senseless for an enlightened society to deprive any children — including illegal aliens — of an elementary education. I fully agree that it would be folly — and wrong — to tolerate creation of a segment of society made up of illiterate persons, many having a limited or no command of our language. However, the Constitution does not constitute us as "Platonic Guardians" nor does it vest in this Court the authority to strike down laws because they do not meet our standards of desirable social policy, "wisdom," or "common sense." . . . We trespass on the assigned function of the political branches under our structure of limited and separated powers when we assume a policymaking role as the Court does today.

The Court makes no attempt to disguise that it is acting to make up for Congress' lack of "effective leadership" in dealing with the serious national problems caused by the influx of uncountable millions of illegal aliens across our borders. . . . The failure of enforcement of the immigration laws over more than a decade and the inherent difficulty and expense of sealing our vast borders have combined to create a grave socio-economic dilemma. It is a dilemma that has not yet even been fully assessed, let alone addressed. However, it is not the function of the judiciary to provide "effective leadership" simply because the political branches of government fail to do so.

The Court's holding today manifests the justly criticized judicial tendency to attempt speedy and wholesome formulation of "remedies" for the failures — or simply the laggard pace — of the political processes of our system of government. The Court employs, and in my view abuses, the Fourteenth Amendment in an effort to become an omnipotent and omniscient problem solver. That the motives for doing so are noble and compassionate does not alter the fact that the Court distorts our constitutional function to make amends for the defaults of others.

In a sense, the Court's opinion rests on such a unique confluence of theories and rationales that it will likely stand for little beyond the results in these particular cases. Yet the extent to which the Court departs from principal constitutional adjudication is nonetheless disturbing.

I have no quarrel with the conclusion that the Equal Protection Clause of the Fourteenth Amendment *applies* to aliens who, after their illegal entry into this country, are indeed physically "within the jurisdiction" of a State. However, as the Court concedes, this "only begins the inquiry." . . . The Equal Protection Clause does not mandate identical treatment of different categories of persons. . . .

The dispositive issue in these cases, simply put, is whether, for purposes of allocating its finite resources, a State has a legitimate reason to differentiate between persons who are lawfully within the State and those who are unlawfully there. The distinction the State of Texas has drawn — based not only upon its own legitimate interests but on classifications established by the federal government in its immigration laws and policies — is not unconstitutional.

The Court acknowledges that, except in those cases when state classifications disadvantage a "suspect class" or impinge upon a "fundamental right," the Equal Protection Clause permits a State "substantial latitude" in distinguishing between different groups of persons. . . . Moreover, the Court expressly — and correctly — rejects any suggestion that illegal aliens are a suspect class, . . . or that education is a fundamental right. . . . Yet by patching together bits and pieces of what might be termed quasi-suspect-class and quasi-fundamental-rights analysis, the Court spins out a theory custom-tailored to the facts of these cases.

In the end, we are told little more than that the level of scrutiny employed to strike down the Texas law applies only when illegal alien children are deprived of a public education. . . . If ever a court was guilty of an unabashedly result-oriented approach, this case is a prime example.

The Court first suggests that these illegal alien children, although not a suspect class, are entitled to special solicitude under the Equal Protection Clause because they lack "control" over or "responsibility" for their unlawful entry into this country. . . . Similarly, the Court appears to take the position that §21.031 is presumptively "irrational" because it has the effect of imposing "penalties" on "innocent" chidren. . . . However, the Equal Protection Clause does not preclude legislators from classifying among persons on the basis of factors and characteristics over which individuals may be said to lack "control." Indeed, in some circumstances persons generally, and children in particular, may have little control over or responsibility for such things as their ill-health, need for public assistance, or place of residence. Yet a state legislature is not barred from considering, for example, relevant differences between the mentally-healthy and the mentally-ill, or between the residents of different countries, simply because these may be factors unrelated to individual choice or to any "wrongdoing." The Equal Protection Clause protects against arbitrary and irrational classifications, and against invidious discrimination stemming from prejudice and hostility; it is not an all-encompassing "equalizer" designed to eradicate every distinction for which persons are not "responsible."

The Court does not presume to suggest that appellees' purported lack of culpability for their illegal status prevents them from being deported or otherwise "penalized" under federal law. Yet would deportation be any less a "penalty" than denial of privileges provided to legal residents? Illegality of presence in the United States does not — and need not — depend on some amorphous concept of "guilt" or "innocence" concerning an alien's entry.

Similarly, a State's use of federal immigration status as a basis for legislative classification is not necessarily rendered suspect for its failure to take such factors into account.

The Court's analogy to cases involving discrimination against illegitimate children ... is grossly misleading. The State has not thrust any disabilities upon appellees due to their "status of birth." Cf. Weber v. Aetna Casualty & Surety Co., 406 U.S. 164, 176 (1972). Rather, appellees' status is predicated upon the circumstances of their concededly illegal presence in this country, and is a direct result of Congress' obviously valid exercise of its "broad constitutional powers" in the field of immigration and naturalization. U.S. Const., Art. I, §8, cl. 4: see Takahashi v. Fish & Game Commission, 334 U.S. 410, 419 (1948). This Court has recognized that in allocating governmental benefits to a given class of aliens, one "may take into account the character of the relationship between the alien and this country." Mathews v. Diaz, 426 U.S. 67, 80 (1976). When that "relationship" is a federally-prohibited one, there can, of course, be no presumption that a State has a constitutional duty to include illegal aliens among the recipients of its govermental benefits.

The second strand of the Court's analysis rests on the premise that, although public education is not a constitutionally-guaranteed right, "neither is it merely some governmental 'benefit' indistinguishable from other forms of social welfare legislation." ... Whatever meaning or relevance this opaque observation might have in some other context, it simply has no bearing on the issues at hand. Indeed, it is never made clear what the Court's opinion means on this score.

The importance of education is beyond dispute. Yet we have held repeatedly that the importance of a governmental services does not elevate it to the status of a "fundamental right" for purposes of equal protection analysis. San Antonio School District v. Rodriguez, 411 U.S. 1. 30-31 (1973); Lindsey v. Normet, 405 U.S. 56, 73-74 (1972). In *San Antonio School District*, supra, Justice Powell, speaking for the Court, expressly rejected the proposition that state laws dealing with public education are subject to special scrutiny under the Equal Protection Clause. Moreover, the Court points to no meaningful way to distinguish between education and other governmental benefits in this context. Is the Court suggesting that education is more "fundamental" than food, shelter, or medical care?

The Equal Protection Clause guarantees similar treatment of similarly situated persons, but it does not mandate a constitutional hierarchy of governmental services. [Rather,] the central question in these cases, as in every equal protection case not involving truly fundamental rights, "explicitly or implicitly guaranteed by the Constitution," *San Antonio School District*, supra, at 33-34, is whether there is some legitimate basis for a legislative distinction between different classes of persons. The fact that the distinction is drawn in legislation affecting access to public education — as opposed to legislation allocating other important governmental benefits, such as public assistance, health care, or housing — cannot make a difference in the level of scrutiny applied.

Once it is conceded — as the Court does — that illegal aliens are not a suspect class, and that education is not a fundamental right, our inquiry should focus on and be limited to whether the legislative classification at issue bears a rational relationship to a legitimate state purpose. Vance v. Bradley, 440 U.S. 93, 97 (1979): Dandridge v. Williams, 397 U.S. 471, 485-487 (1970)....

The State contends primarily that §21.031 serves to prevent undue depletion of its limited revenues available for education, and to preserve the fiscal integrity of the State's school financing system against an ever-increasing flood of illegal aliens — aliens over whose entry or continued presence it has no control. Of course such fiscal concerns alone could not justify discrimination against a suspect class or an arbitrary and irrational denial of benefits to a particular group of persons. Yet I assume no member of this Court would argue that prudent conservation of finite state revenues is *per se* an illegitimate goal. Indeed, the numerous classifications this Court has sustained in social welfare legislation were invariably related to the limited amount of revenues available to spend on any given program or set of programs. See, e.g., Jefferson v. Hackney, 406 U.S. 535, 549-551 (1972); Dandridge v. Williams, 397 U.S. 471, 487 (1970). The significant question here is whether the requirement of tuition from illegal aliens who attend the public schools — as well as from residents of other States, for example — is a rational and reasonable means of furthering the State's legitimate fiscal ends.

Without laboring what will undoubtedly seem obvious to many, it simply is not "irrational" for a State to conclude that it does not have the same responsibility to provide benefits for persons whose very presence in the State and this country is illegal as it does to provide for persons lawfully present. By definition, illegal aliens have no right whatever to be here, and the State may reasonably, and constitutionally, elect not to provide them with government services at the expense of those who are lawfully in the State. In DeCanas v. Bica, 424 U.S. 351, 357 (1976), we held that a State may protect its "fiscal interests and lawfully resident labor force from the deleterious effects on its economy resulting from the employment of illegal aliens."* And only recently this Court made clear that a State has a legitimate interest in protecting and preserving the quality of its schools and "the right of its own *bona fide residents* to attend such institutions on a preferential tuition basis." Vlandis v. Kline, 412 U.S. 441, 452-453 (1973) (emphasis added).... The Court has failed to offer even a plausible explanation why illegality of residence in this country is not a factor that may legitimately

---

*Justice Brennan's majority opinion had distinguished *De Canas* by stating that there "the State's program reflected Congress' intention to bar from employment all aliens except those possessing a grant of permission to work in this country," whereas here "there is no indication that the disability imposed ... corresponds to any identifiable congressional policy."

bear upon the bona fides of state residence and entitlement to the benefits of lawful residence. . . .

[After disputing the majority's disparagement of the notion that financial savings resulting from §21.031 could result in the improvement of the quality of public education in Texas, Burger concluded:]

In the absence of a constitutional imperative to provide for the education of illegal aliens, the State may "rationally" choose to take advantage of whatever savings will accrue from limiting access to the tuition-free public schools to its own lawful residents, excluding even citizens of neighboring States.

Denying a free education to illegal alien children is not a choice I would make were I a legislator. Apart from compassionate considerations, the long-range costs of excluding any children from the public schools may well outweigh the costs of educating them. But that is not the issue; the fact that there are sound *policy* arguments against the Texas legislature's choice does not render that choice an unconstitutional one.

[The Chief Justice completed his dissent by asserting that the Court was usurping the political processes by providing a remedy for its perceived failings in the instant cases, to him "yet another example of unwarranted judicial action which in the long run tends to contribute to the weakening" of other branches of government. Congress, not the Court, has the "primary responsibility for addressing the problems occasioned by the millions of illegal aliens flooding across our southern border," he stated. By "compensating for congressional inaction" the Court "encourages the political branches to pass their problems to the judiciary," he concluded.]

Page 1070. At the end of Note 2 add:

On June 30, 1982, the time specified by Congress for ratification of the Equal Rights Amendment, as extended, expired without the requisite 38 state legislatures having acted affirmatively. Thus, the so-called ERA failed to become part of the Constitution, falling three states short of obtaining approval from three-quarters of the states.

Page 1073. At the end of Note 2 add:

In 1978 Congress effectively overturned the holding in Geduldig v. Aiello, Casebook p.1071, at least with respect to female employees covered by Title VII of the Civil Rights Act of 1964 (cf. General Electric Co. v. Gilbert, Casebook p.1148), by amending Section 701 of the Act, adding a new subsection (k) that broadens "[t]he terms 'because of sex' or 'on the basis of sex' [to] include . . . because of or on the basis of pregnancy, childbirth, or related medical conditions." Women, so affected, "shall be treated the same for all employment-related purposes" and benefit programs as other persons not so affected. The new subsection "shall not require an employer to pay for health insurance benefits for abortion, except where the life of the mother [may] be endangered ... or except where medical complications have arisen from the abortion." The amendment expressly does not preclude bargaining for abortion benefits.

Page 1074. Add as a new Note 5:

5. In North Haven Board of Education v. Bell, — U.S. — , 102 S. Ct. 1912, — L. Ed. 2d — (1982), the Court construed the language of Section 901(a) of Title IX of the Education Amendments of 1972, which "proscribes gender discrimination in education programs as activities receiving federal financial assistance," as including employees as well as students. Challenging the Department of Health, Education, and Welfare's threat of enforcement proceedings and curtailment of federal funds for alleged sex-based discrimination practices, two Connecticut school systems petitioned the Court to find §901(a) inapplicable to school board employees. The Court stated that Title IX, which was patterned after Title VI of the Civil Rights Act of 1964 and contains the phrase "no person" in describing those covered, prohibited federally funded education programs from discriminating on the basis of gender with respect to employees.

Page 1078. Add as new Note 4:

4. Mississippi University for Women v. Hogan, — U.S. — , 102 S. Ct. — , — L. Ed. 2d — (1982), involved the question whether a state-supported university's policy of limiting its enrollment to women denied equal protection to otherwise qualified males seeking admission to its nursing program. Applying the intermediate standard first enunciated in Reed, the Court, speaking through Justice O'Connor, concluded that the gender-based classification involved had not been shown to serve "important governmental objectives" utilizing means "substantially related to the achievement of those objectives," quoting from Wengler v. Druggists Medical Insurance Co., 446 U.S. 142 (1980), supra in this Supplement, addition to Casebook p.1078. That the restriction "discriminates against males rather than against females does not exempt it from scrutiny or reduce the standard of review." Here, as in other sex-based discrimination cases, an "exceedingly persuasive justification" was required for the classification, quoting from Kirchberg v. Feenstra, 450 U.S. 455 (1981), supra in this Supplement, addition to Casebook p.1073. In addition, "[c]are must be taken in ascertaining whether the statutory objective itself reflects archaic and stereotypic notions ... concerning the roles and abilities of males and females," in which case "the objective itself is illegitimate."

Turning to Mississippi's asserted justification for its "single-sex admissions policy" — that "it compensates for discrimination against women and, therefore, constitutes educational affirmative action" — Justice O'Connor characterized "the state's argument [as] unpersuasive." The "same searching analysis" mandated by Reed and its progeny was applicable where the governmental objective was ostensibly "compensatory," the Court stated. Distinguishing Califano v. Webster, Casebook p.1077, and Schlesinger v. Ballard, Casebook p.1076, O'Connor asserted that Mississippi had made no showing that women had lacked opportunities for training as nurses or to obtain positions of leadership in the nursing profession. Indeed, "[r]ather than compensat[ing] for discriminatory barriers faced by women [in nursing, the] policy of excluding males from admission to [MUW] tends to perpetuate the stereotyped view of nursing as an exclusively woman's job," making "the assumption that nursing is a field for women a self-fulfilling prophecy." Mississippi thus failed to establish the necessary "link between objective and classification." Finally, the Court discarded Mississippi's attempt to justify the exclusion of men on the ground that Title IX of the Education Amendments of 1972 (20 U.S.C. 1681 et seq.). The statutory language does not clearly exempt MUW from any constitutional obligation. And, if it did, it would presumably exceed Congress's power under §5 of the Fourteenth Amendment, for "neither Congress nor a State can validate a law that denies the rights guaranteed by" that constitutional provision.

Chief Justice Burger and Justices Blackmun, Powell, and Rehnquist dissented, maintaining that the equal protection clause does not require all-encompassing coeducation in a state's university system. Some "sexual segregation" of students serves a valid governmental and individual interest in diversity, they stated. Earlier cases were inapposite, the dissenters said, and a state does not discriminate invidiously by allowing freedom to choose a single-sex institution.

Page 1084. At the end of the footnote add:

For another case giving a similarly narrow reading to a federal statute — the Education for All Handicapped Children Act of 1975 — designed to assist handicapped persons, see Hendrick Hudson District Board of Education v. Rowley, — U.S. — , 102 S. Ct. — , — L. Ed. 2d — (1982). Justices White, Brennan, and Marshall dissented.

Page 1091. At the end of Note 4 add:

In Zobel v. Williams, — U.S. — , 102 S. Ct. — , — L. Ed. 2d — (1982), the Court held that Alaska's mineral income distribution program violated the equal protection clause of the Fourteenth Amendment. Alaska's program involved the distribution of dividends, derived from earnings on its windfall oil revenues, to each adult state resident. Duration of residency since 1959, the year of Alaska's statehood, determined the amount of dividend received. The Court described Alaska's program as creating "fixed permanent distinctions between an ever-increasing number of classes of bona fide residents" based on how long they had lived in the state. The Court said that when a state distributes benefits unequally or treats persons dissimilarly, the treatment is subject to equal protection scrutiny, generally under the rational basis test. Speaking for the Court, Chief Justice Burger rejected, as not "rationally related" to the distinctions Alaska made between its residents, the asserted purposes of creating a financial incentive for individuals to establish residency and of encouraging prudent financial and resource management. In firmly rejecting Alaska's stated objective to reward its citizens for past contributions, Burger stated that the objective "was not a legitimate state purpose," citing Shapiro v. Thompson, Casebook p.1085, as involving a similar "past contributions argument made and rejected." Identifying Alaska's reasoning as fostering state apportionment of other rights, benefits, and services according to duration of residency, Burger concluded saying that "the apportionment of state services and the retrospective nature of the program violate the guarantees of the Equal Protection Clause of the Fourteenth Amendment."

Justice Brennan's concurring opinion emphasized that "the pervasive discrimination embodied in Alaska's distribution scheme gives rise to constitutional concerns of somewhat larger proportions." He suggested that a right to travel or "more precisely the federal interest in free interstate migration" provided an independent basis to hold Alaska's law unconstitutional.

Justice O'Connor based her concurring opinion on the privileges and immunities clause of Article IV as the source of "the right to travel," which, in her judgment, Alaska's law infringed. She disclaimed reliance on the majority's equal protection rationale.

Justicer Rehnquist's sole dissent characterized Alaska's scheme as "a state effort to apportion unique economic benefits among its citizens." Since the distribution scheme is in the nature of economic regulation, he reminded the Court that state economic regulations have long been held as "presumptively valid." Rehnquist concluded his dissent by stating the Court had ignored "the principle that the Fourteenth Amendment gives federal courts no power to impose upon the States [its] view of what constitutes wise economic or social policy."

Page 1093. At the end of Note 5 add:

See Schweiker v. Hogan, — U.S. — , 102 S. Ct. — , — L. Ed. 2d — (1982), for a case where a unanimous Court rejected an equal protection challenge to the Social Security Act's Medicaid program as implemented in Massachusetts, in particular as it differentiates between "medically needy" and "categorically needy." Citing Harris v. McRae, infra in this Supplement, addition to Casebook p.1591, the Court said that "the Medicaid program was established for the purpose of providing federal financial assistance to states that choose to reimburse certain costs of medical treatment for needy persons." Citing Blum v. Bacon, supra in this Supplement, addition to Casebook p.470, the Court reiterated its policy that "the interpretation of an agency charged with the administration of a statute is entitled to substantial deference." After surveying Medicaid's legislative history and the agency's analysis of the statutory provisions, the Court concluded that "the discrimination challenged in this case is required by the Social Security Act." The optional character of the congressional scheme, whereby participating states must provide Medicaid benefits to the categorically needy but may elect not to provide any benefits at all to the medically needy, does not itself violate constitutional requirement of equality. The Court stated: "[I]t is rational to define need on the basis of income" and the defined eligibility level is not "unrelated to [the] ability to provide for medical needs."

Page 1114. At the end of Note 5 add:

In June 1982 President Reagan signed into law a congressionally enacted measure further extending the principal provisions of the Voting Rights Act, as amended, for an additional period of 25 years — until 2007.

Page 1125. At the end of Note 1 add:

See Hathorn v. Lovorn, — U.S. — , 102 S. Ct. — , — L. Ed. 2d — (1982), for a case dealing with the power of a state to make an initial determination of whether a proposed election law change is subject to preclearance under §5 of the Voting Rights Act of 1965.

Page 1146. At the end of Note 1 add:

See General Building Contractors Assn., Inc. v. Pennsylvania, — U.S. — , 102 S. Ct. — , — L. Ed. 2d — (1982), where the Court ruled that liability may not be imposed under 42 U.S.C. 1981 absent proof of intentional discrimination. After reviewing the legislative history of §1981, and briefly discussing the equal protection concept as well, the Court reaffirmed that §1981 encompasses both private and governmental actions; nevertheless, there is no implication that the statute reaches more than intentional discrimination, whether public or private. Concluding, the Court said, "§1981, like the Equal Protection Clause, can be violated only by purposeful discrimination."

Justices Marshall and Brennan dissented.

Page 1148. At the end of the carryover paragraph add:

For a Title VII case dealing with the question of whether an individual who has been denied promotion is the proper "class representative" for the purpose of maintaining a class action under Rule 23 of the Federal Rules of Civil Procedure on grounds of discriminatory hiring and promotion practices, see General Telephone Co. of the Southwest v. Falcon, — U.S. — , 102 S. Ct. — , — L. Ed. 2d — (1982).

In Ford Motor Co. v. EEOC, — U.S. — , 102 S. Ct. — , — L. Ed. 2d — (1982), the Court held that an employer charged with discrimination in hiring under Title VII can toll the continuing accrual of potential backpay liability under §706(g) by unintentionally offering the claimant the job previously denied, without also offering seniority retroactive to the date of the alleged discrimination.

For a Title VII case holding that an employer's nondiscriminatory "bottom line" promotion results neither preclude the establishment of a *prima facie* case of employment discrimination by means of a written promotion examination nor provide a defense to such a case, see Connecticut v. Teal, – U.S. – , 102 S. Ct. – , – L. Ed. 2d – (1982).

Page 1148. At the end of the first full paragraph add:

In Kremer v. Chemical Construction Corp., – U.S. – , 102 S. Ct. 1883, – L. Ed. 2d – (1982), the Court held that Title VII did not create an exception to 28 U.S.C. 1738, requiring federal courts to afford full faith and credit to state court judgments. Speaking for the majority, Justice White concluded that there is no "affirmative showing" of a "clear and manifest" legislative purpose in Title VII to deny res judicata or collateral estoppel to a court judgment affirming that a claim of employment discrimination is unproven. Since the petitioner had been accorded "all the process that was constitutionally required," including both administrative and judicial review, he was precluded from litigating in federal court a Title VII claim that was already subject to res judicata in state court. Four justices dissented.

Page 1149. At the end of the carryover paragraph add:

See Sumitomo Shoji America, Inc. v Avagliano, – U.S. – , 102 S. Ct. – , – L. Ed. 2d – (1982), where a unanimous Court held that the Friendship, Commerce, and Navigation Treaty between the United States and Japan was not a defense to a Title VII employment discrimination suit against a wholly-owned U.S. subsidiary of a Japanese company.

Page 1246. At the end of Note 2 add:

Cf. Board of Education, Island Trees Union Free School District No. 26 v. Pico, – U.S. – , 102 S. Ct. – , – L. Ed. 2d – (1982), infra in this Supplement, addition to Casebook p.1429, dealing with First Amendment limitations on the discretion of school boards to remove books from high school and junior high school libraries.

Page 1333. At the end of Note 4 add:

In Globe Newspaper Co. v. Superior Court for the County of Norfolk, – U.S. – , 102 S. Ct. – , – L. Ed. 2d – (1982), a Massachusetts statute required trial judges to exclude the press and general public from the courtroom during the victim's testimony in trials for specified sexual offenses involving a minor victim. This restriction was held unconstitutional by the Court in violation of the First Amendment as applied to the states through the Fourteenth Amendment. Speaking for the majority, Justice Brennan referenced Richmond Newspapers, Inc. v. Virginia, supra in this Supplement, addition to Casebook p.1333, as "firmly [establishing] for the first time that the press and general public have a constitutional right to access to criminal trials." He said that even though this right of access to criminal trials is not explicitly enumerated in the First Amendment, "[t]he First Amendment is broad enough to encompass those rights that, while not unambiguously enumerated in the very terms of the Amendment, are nonetheless necessary to the enjoyment of other First Amendment rights." By affording this protection, "the First Amendment serves to ensure that the individual citizen can effectively participate in ... our republican system of self-government." Brennan identified two features of the criminal justice system, emphasized in *Richmond Newspapers,* which together serve to explain why a "right to access to criminal trails" in particular is protected by the First Amendment. "First, the criminal trial historically has been open to the press and general public, [and] [s]second, the right to access to criminal trials plays a particularly significant role in the functioning of the judicial process and the government as a whole. Public scrutiny of a criminal trial enhances the quality and safeguards the integrity of the factfinding process, with benefits to both the defendant and to society as a whole. Moreover, public access to the criminal trial fosters an appearance of fairness thereby heightening public respect for the judicial process. And in the broadest terms, public access to criminal trials permits the public to participate in and serve as a check upon the judicial process — an essential component in our structure of self-government. In sum, the institutional value of the open criminal trial is recognized in both logic and experience."

Justice Brennan conceded that although "the right of access to criminal trials is of constitutional stature, it is not absolute." However, he said, "the circumstances under which the press and public can be barred from a criminal trial are limited; the state's justification in denying access must be a weighty one. Where, as in the present case, the state attempts to deny the right of access in order to inhibit the disclosure of sensitive information, it must be shown that the denial is necessitated by a compelling governmental interest, and is narrowly tailored to serve that interest." In point of fact, the Court agreed that Massachusetts' interest in safeguarding the physical and psychological well-being of a minor is a compelling one. Still, Brennan continued, "as compelling as that interest is, it does not justify a mandatory-closure rule, for it is clear that circumstances of the particular case may affect the significance of the interest. A trial court can determine on a case-by-case basis whether closure is necessary to protect the welfare of a minor victim." Brennan concluded that the Massachusetts exclusion statute cannot be viewed as a narrowly tailored means of accommodating the state's asserted interest; therefore, the exclusion statute cannot prevent the press from gathering or publicizing the substance of a minor victim's testimony, as well as his or her identity. He viewed the "state's argument ... [as running] contrary to the very foundation of a right of access recognized in *Richmond Newspapers:* namely, 'that a presumption of openness inheres in the very nature of a criminal trial under our system of justice.' "

Chief Justice Burger and Justices Rehnquist and Stevens dissented.

Page 1378. At the end of Note 2 add:

Cf. Board of Education, Island Trees Union Free School District No. 26 v. Pico, — U.S. — , 102 S. Ct. — , — L. Ed. 2d — (1982), infra in this Supplement, addition to Casebook p.1429, relating to removal by school boards of books from high school and junior high school libraries as presenting First Amendment concerns.

Page 1399. After the end of Note 6 add as new Note 7:

7. At issue in New York v. Ferber, — U.S. — , 102 S. Ct. — , — L. Ed. 2d — (1982), was the constitutionality of a New York statute prohibiting persons from knowingly promoting a sexual performance by a child under the age of 16 by distributing material depicting such a performance. Respondent was a bookstore proprietor who was convicted under the statute of selling films depicting young boys masturbating, a form of "sexual conduct" whose depiction was proscribed by the statute's definitional terms. The New York Court of Appeals had overruled the lower state courts and held the statute violative of the First Amendment, as being both underinclusive and overbroad and as failing to include an acceptable obscenity standard. With Justice White writing for a unanimous Court, the statute was upheld as sufficiently comporting with the strictures of the First Amendment as applied to the states through the Fourteenth. White initially stated that "[i]n recent years, the exploitive use of children in the production of pornography has become a serious national problem. The federal government and forty-seven States have sought to combat the problem with statutes specifically directed at the production of child pornography. At least half of such statutes do not require that the materials produced be legally obscene. Thirty-five States and the United States have also passed legislation prohibiting the distribution of such materials; twenty States prohibit the distribution of material depicting children engaged in sexual conduct without requiring that the material be legally obscene." After noting that New York is such a state, White discussed the New York statute at length and then described the factual background of the instant case, including the approach taken by the Court of Appeals. Distinguishing earlier obscenity cases, White pointed out that "[t]his case ... constitutes our first examination of a statute directed at

and limited to depiction of sexual activity involving children, [and] our inquiry should [thus] begin with the question of whether a State has somewhat more freedom in proscribing works which portray sexual acts or lewd exhibitions of genitalia by children."

Tracing the Court's treatment of obscenity regulation from the *Chaplinsky* dictum through the definitional approach of *Roth* as modified and restated in *Miller*, the Court alluded to *Ginsberg* as allowing a more restrictive attitude where minors are involved. For a variety of reasons, including the state's recognized interest in the well-being of children, judicial deference to legislative judgment, the harm inherent in the sexual abuse of children incident to the production and distribution of child pornography, the economic motives that underlie the activity, and the *de minimis* First Amendment values served thereby, the Court concluded that "the States are entitled to greater leeway in the regulation of pornographic depictions of children." In point of fact, the Court elaborated, "recognizing and classifying child pornography as a category of material outside the protection of the First Amendment is not incompatible with our earlier decisions," citing, e.g., Young v. American Mini Theatres and FCC v. Pacifica Foundation. "When a definable class of material, such as that covered by [the New York statute], bears so heavily and pervasively on the welfare of children engaged in its production, ... the balance of competing interests is clearly struck [by considering] these materials as without the protection of the First Amendment," White stated. He noted that there are limits on the category of child pornography unprotected by the First Amendment, indicating that the matter in question involves visual depiction of sexual conduct by children below a specified age and that the conduct to be prohibited must be adequately defined by applicable state law. He continued: "The test for child pornography is separate from the obscenity standard enunciated in *Miller*, but may be compared to it for purpose of clarity. The *Miller* formulation is adjusted in the following respects: A trier of fact need not find that the material appeals to the prurient interest of the average person; it is not required that sexual conduct portrayed be done so in a patently offensive manner; and the material at issue need not be considered as a whole. We note that the distribution of descriptions or other depictions of sexual conduct, not otherwise obscene, which do not involve live performance or photographic or other visual reproduction of live performances, retains First Amendment protection. As with obscenity laws, criminal responsibility may not be imposed without some element of scienter on the part of the defendant. Smith v. California, 361 U.S. 147 (1959). . . . The New York statute "incorporates a definition of sexual conduct that comports with [these] principles," White stated, and thus the Court concluded that the law in question "sufficiently describes a category of material the production and distribution of which is not entitled to First Amendment protection." The statute is neither underinclusive nor, under the "substantial overbreadth" notion of Broadrick v.

Oklahoma, Casebook p.1193, is it unconstitutionally overbroad, for its "legitimate reach dwarfs its arguably impermissible applications."

Justice O'Connor wrote a short concurring opinion. Justices Brennan and Marshall concurred in the judgment, but wrote separately to indicate their view that statutes such as New York's were consistent with the First Amendment only because they seek narrowly to reflect a specific interest in protecting minors, suggesting that depictions of children that "do have serious literary, artistic, scientific or medical value" are protected by the First Amendment. Justice Stevens also concurred separately, disassociating himself from the Court's overbreadth analysis.

Page 1429. At the end of Note 6 add:

For an interesting but inconclusive decision dealing with the extent to which the First Amendment imposes limitations upon the discretion of a local school board to order the removal of certain books characterized as "anti-American, anti-Christian, anti-Semitic, and just plain filthy" from high school and junior high school libraries, see Board of Education, Island Trees Union Free School District No. 26 v. Pico, — U.S. — , 102 S. Ct. — , — L. Ed. 2d — (1982). The district court had granted summary judgment for the school board, and the court of appeals reversed and remanded for a trial on the merits. An acutely divided Supreme Court affirmed, with Justice White's narrowly written concurring opinion being decisive. White disdained consideration of the constitutional questions and instead endorsed only a remand for a trial that would focus on the "unresolved factual issue" as to "the reason or reasons underlying the school board's removal of the books."

Justice Brennan's plurality opinion maintained that public school students have First Amendment rights that must be balanced against the admitted discretion of school boards to manage matters relating to the institutions they operate. Such discretion is absolute with respect to curriculum questions, but not as to libraries. While school boards have significant discretion to determine the content of school libraries, that discretion may not be exercised in a narrowly partisan or political manner. More specifically, Brennan asserted, school boards cannot, consistent with the First Amendment, remove books from school libraries simply because they dislike the ideas contained in them. A different issue would be presented, however, if the books were shown to be "pervasively vulgar" or if the removal decision was based solely on their "educational suitability." Brennan cited and relied upon a variety of cases, including Meyer v. Nebraska, Epperson v. Arkansas, Tinker v. Des Moines School District, West Virginia v. Barnette, Stanley v. Georgia, and Keyishian v. Board of Regents. The right to receive ideas exists in the public school setting, Brennan stated, and may be unconstitutionally impaired by a school board's removal of certain books from school libraries because of their content. The prescribing of curricula, the designation of textbooks for required reading, and even the acquisition (in contrast to removal) of library books all posed distinct questions, he maintained. He concluded that "the special characteristics of the school *library* make that environment especially appropriate for the recognition of the First Amendment rights of students."

Justice Blackmun wrote a separate concurring opinion, asserting that even in the context of public school libraries "the State may not suppress exposure to ideas — for the sole *purpose* of suppressing exposure to those ideas — absent sufficiently compelling reasons."

Chief Justice Burger, joined by Justices Powell, Rehnquist, and O'Connor, wrote a stinging dissent. "In an attempt to deal with a problem in an area traditionally left to the states," he wrote, "a plurality of the Court, in a lavish expansion going beyond any prior holding under the First Amendment, expresses its view that a school board's decision concerning what books are to be in the school library is subject to federal court review." Students have constitutional rights, he conceded, but this did not include entitlement to have access to particular books in a school library. The cases relied on by the Brennan plurality opinion are either distinguishable or inapposite, Burger maintained. Schools cannot be made into a "slavish courier" of any and all ideas, he stated. Concluding, he wrote: "Through use of bits and pieces of prior opinions unrelated to the issue of this case, the plurality demeans our function of constitutional adjudication. Today the plurality suggests that the *Constitution* distinguishes between school libraries and school classrooms, between *removing* unwanted books and *acquiring* books. Even more extreme, the plurality concludes that the Constitution *requires* school boards to justify to its teenage pupils the decision to remove a particular book from a school library. I categorically reject this notion that the Constitution dictates that judges, rather than parents, teachers, and local school boards, must determine how the standards of morality and vulgarity are to be treated in the classroom."

Justice Powell's dissent stressed the importance of leaving the determination of "educational policy" questions to "the States and locally elected school boards." The Brennan plurality opinion asserts a "standless standard" and its reasoning "is marked by contradiction," he stated. He concluded: "In different contexts and in different times, the destruction of written materials has been the symbol of despotism and intolerance. But the removal of nine vulgar or racist books from a high school library by a concerned local school board does not raise this specter. For me, today's decision symbolizes a debilitating encroachment upon the institutions of a free people." Powell included an appendix containing excerpts from the books in question.

Justice Rehnquist also wrote a separate dissent, indicating that he agreed entirely with Chief Justice Burger but emphasizing as well the procedural posture of the case. Justice O'Connor also wrote a short dissenting opinion.

Page 1596. At the end of the third full paragraph add:

See Justice O'Connor's concurring opinion in Zobel v. Williams, — U.S. — , 102 S. Ct. — , — L. Ed. 2d — (1982), supra in this Supplement, addition to Casebook p.871, for an extensive discussion of the interstate privileges and immunities clause as the primary source of the constitutionally guaranteed right to travel.